ARIS & PHILLIPS HISPANIC CLASSICS

# *Christians and Moors*
# *in Spain*

## VOLUME I: AD 711–1150

T0313521

## Colin Smith

Aris & Phillips is an imprint of Oxbow Books

Published in the United Kingdom by
OXBOW BOOKS
10 Hythe Bridge Street, Oxford OX1 2EW

and in the United States by
OXBOW BOOKS
908 Darby Road, Havertown, PA 19083

Paperback Edition: ISBN 978-0-856684-11-1

First published 1988
Paperback reprinted 2014

A CIP record for this book is available from the British Library

For a complete list of Aris & Phillips titles, please contact:

UNITED KINGDOM
Oxbow Books
Telephone (01865) 241249
Fax (01865) 794449
Email: oxbow@oxbowbooks.com
www.oxbowbooks.com

UNITED STATES OF AMERICA
Oxbow Books
Telephone (800) 791-9354
Fax (610) 853-9146
Email: queries@casemateacademic.com
www.casemateacademic.com/oxbow

Oxbow Books is part of the Casemate Group

Printed and bound by CPI Group (UK) Ltd, Croydon, CR0 4YY

# CONTENTS

Introduction                                                                    v

Booklist                                                                        x

Maps                                                                            xi

Texts
1.   Origins of Islam (7th century)                                             2
2.   The prophecy of the fall of Spain (711)                                    8
3.   The invasion of Spain (711)                                               10
4.   The invasion of Spain: another view (711)                                 14
5.   Lament for the destruction of Spain (711)                                 18
6.   The occupation and the first resistance (711−22)                          24
7.   Charlemagne in Spain (778)                                                30
8.   Charlemagne converts the infidels (late 8th century)                      32
9.   The Franks take Gerona (786)                                              38
10.  The martyrdom of Isaac de Tábanos (851)                                   42
11.  A prophecy of reconquest (883)                                            48
12.  Advance and settlement under Alfonso III (late 9th century)               50
13.  Miraculous aid in battle (934)                                            54
14.  Otto I's embassy to the Caliph (956)                                      62
15.  Two miracles concerning al−Mansur (997)                                   76
16.  St James announces the capture of Coimbra (1064)                          80
17.  The capture of Barbastro (1064)                                           84
18.  The mosque of Toledo (1085)                                               88
19.  St Dominic of Silos frees a captive (1087)                                92
20.  Campaigns and politics in and around Valencia (1088)                      98
21.  A romantic interlude (1091 or 1092)                                      104
22.  Lament for the loss of Valencia (1094)                                   108
23.  The Cid's speech to the Moors of Valencia (1094)                         114
24.  Moorish honour, Christian treachery (about 1098)                         120
25.  The Cid takes Murviedro (1098)                                           124
26.  The Cid endows the Cathedral of Valencia (1098)                          130
27.  St James frees a captive (1100)                                          134
28.  Alvar Fáñez's defence of Toledo (1109)                                   138
29.  The Pisans attack the Balearics (1114−15)                                144
30.  St James cures a Muslim ambassador (1121)                                148
31.  Alfonso VII's first Andalusian campaign (1133)                           154
32.  A sense of chivalry? (1139)                                              160
33.  Spain as crusading territory (about 1140)                                162
34.  Peter the Venerable has the Koran translated (1142)                      166
35.  Preparations for the Almería campaign (1147)                             168
36.  The Genoese expedition to Almería (1147)                                 172

# INTRODUCTION

A few years ago this book might have been titled 'Texts of the Reconquest of Spain', and it is true that this term, and 'Reconquista', are still widely used and are incapable of being misapplied. The emphasis of a whole school of historical writing in recent decades has, however, been less on military aspects of the relations between Christian and Moor in medieval Spain, and more on *convivencia*, 'coexistence' and 'living—together', and on peaceable aspects of contact and mutual influence. In military terms too the concept of 'eight centuries of Reconquest' (still more, 'of Crusade') hardly holds good. Whereas the Islamic conquest of Iberia took at most three years (711—14) and evidently obeyed a conscious policy, it took until 1492 for the land to be brought again under Christian rule. At times there was indeed a coherent belief in this objective, sometimes aided by biblical parallel, prophecy (our text 11), and the spirit of crusade (text 7 and several others), that is, in elements of a divine plan according to which God was aiding His chosen people. At other times, indeed over long periods, the aim of the Christians was simple survival, or an extension of territory towards the warmer and richer lands of the south and east, or the acquisition of booty and captives who would work or bring in a ransom. As one recent writer puts it: "Luego vinieron los moros y empezó esa extraña danza de la muerte que conocemos con el disparatado nombre de *reconquista*. ¿Reconquista por quién y de qué? ¡Una empresa política maquinada ocho siglos antes de su terminación! Por supuesto no hubo tal, sino simple obra de marquetería en cuya trama mil veces se compuso y recompuso la esgrima plurivalente de las Españas. Ningún fenómeno tan proclive a la mixtificación como esta larga fiesta de moros y cristianos cuyas recíprocas y fecundas imitaciones suenan más alto que el entrechocar de los aceros' (F. Sánchez Dragó, *Gárgoris y Habidis* (Barcelona, 1985, 2 vols), I, 25). The writer is not a professional historian, but then history on a broad scale — the record and interpretation of human experience — is after all too important to be left to the historians; and if the remarks quoted are intended to be provocative, it is because the concept which he attacks deserves to be challenged.

Texts are gathered here from the Christian side only, of, or relating to, the early medieval centuries. A second volume will contain those from the later centuries, and a third will present those written in Arabic. Texts are ordered — after some doubt about which might be the better method — according to the date to which they refer, not in order of their composition.

The present texts illustrate hatred and hostility more than tolerance and peaceful contact, but it is this latter aspect, together with 'recíprocas y fecundas imitaciones' which has, as mentioned above, captured great interest

since the publication in 1948 of Américo Castro's *España en su historia*, in a way a continuation of the debate initiated half a century before by Ganivet and Unamuno and the intellectuals of the 'Generation of 1898' about the origins and nature of Spanish society. The emphasis of this study of cultural history is firmly upon the coexistence and interaction of Christians, Moors, and of course Jews (the last—named being, except for occasional mentions, excluded from this selection of texts, but amply deserving of another). The data upon which Castro based his work are mostly not of the sort which could be reproduced in a book of the present kind, of extensive extracts, but are obviously complementary. It is unfortunate, for example, that it is not possible to find contemporary texts about the immensely important products of the schools of translators who in Toledo in the 12th century and again from about 1240 in Toledo, Seville, and elsewhere, brought the learning of classical Greece and of the contemporary Muslim world out of Arabic into Latin for circulation to the learned centres of France and other countries, and, also, in the second period, into Castilian. Our texts do not allow us even to glimpse the wealth of ways in which the arts and craft products of al—Andalus influenced so much in Christian lands, from building to the use of soap. No Christian text has left an impression of the copying and reading of the Koran, the relatively high rate of literacy in al—Andalus which was related to this, or the enormous library possessed by the Cordovese Caliphs at the height of their splendour. To quote the amazement of Peter the Venerable, Abbot of Cluny, on seeing paper (probably from the factory at Játiva in Muslim lands) in use among Christians when he was making his tour of inspection of monasteries in Spain in 1142 would take only a few words. No contemporary text comments on the fact (to tell us whether it was unexceptional), revealed only by modern investigation when tombs were opened, that Queen Berenguela of Castile—León and her sister Queen Leonor of Aragón, who died in 1246 and 1244 respectively, were buried at Las Huelgas in Burgos with their heads resting on cushions covered with Koranic invocations. No Christian text of the early period records impressions of Muslims at home or at work, walking the streets, collecting taxes, curing the sick, adorning their persons, bathing, or making love. Our texts are by men who, however much they may have observed and known such things, disdained them, or rather to whom, concerned as they were with the struggle of faiths and campaigns on a large scale, it would never have occurred to write them down. Writing was a rare art, a valued privilege, and parchment was expensive.

Even so, some of our texts do show the peoples on terms other than those of enmity. In 14 and 30, diplomatic missions are involved. In 24, the Cid is on terms not merely of alliance but also of warm esteem with the Moor Avengalvón (in a work of poetic fiction, but not one divorced from reality). In 10 we learn something of the conditions of Christians living under Muslim rule. In 15 and 30, St James gives miraculous aid to

a Muslim, no less.   In 20, an extraordinarily complex tale of diplomacy and pressures by men of all three religions in and around Valencia is told.   In 21, some Christian writer saw his chance and forged a splendid romance on the basis of a slender historical fact, creating a love–story which bridged the religious divide.   In 22, another Christian writer was sufficiently moved by Ibn Alqama's lament for the loss of Muslim Valencia to allow this noble literary creation to remain among the more purely historical materials he was translating, and others then gave it space in the *Primera crónica general*: perhaps by then — in the 14th century — the enemy was so much less of a threat that his voice, which was human too, could be given a lengthy hearing.   In 32, relating to 1139 and composed a few years later, the Muslim enemy even in the midst of a siege can be credited (whatever the real facts of the matter) with a modicum at least of finer feelings.

Many of the texts are inevitably military in nature, about battles, sieges, and campaigns: some told in plain style, some (notably 13) in epical manner with full prominence given to divine aid, others in richly rhetorical fashion.   The invasion of 711 is the theme of texts 2 to 6.   The concept of 'reconquest' in its purest form is expressed in 11, and 12 records the first attempt systematically to *poblar* (resettle) newly conquered lands, this at a time of *neogoticismo* when the Kings of Asturias saw themselves as true heirs to the old Visigothic kingdom of Toledo.   Capitulation terms granted to Muslims as they surrendered are mentioned in 18, and the sort of truce which was often normal enough in border regions figures in 19; also the probably exaggerated harshness of the conditions under which Christians lived as captives of Muslims is described in 19 and 27.   Those from outside the Peninsula thought the Spaniards too tolerant of their enemies, especially in the matter of capitulation terms: the inclination of the French (7, 8, 17, 18, 33) was to slaughter all the men who would not convert and to remove the women and children into slavery, and the Genoese probably thought the same (36).   It was also from outside the Peninsula that the whole concept of the Crusade began to affect warfare within it (17).

Even if the concept of Crusade was usually no part of it, warfare in the Peninsula between Christians and Moors was habitually portrayed by our writers as having a religious basis: good fought evil, the true faith fought the false, orthodoxy fought 'heresy' (very curiously, it may be thought: 34). Many of our writers were churchmen whose influence over monarchs and the governing class was paramount and whose preaching must often have echoed their writings.   Biblical parallels are everywhere as the new Israelites fight God's battles and as the moral message stemming from the disaster of 711 is driven home.   To the force of the Old Testment prophecy in 11 is added the practical aid of miracles and the apparition of saints (6, 7, 8, 9, 13, 15, 16, 27, 30), with St James the warrior and Patron of Spain often active.   Far from the frontier or the battle–lines, Isaac and others in an extremity of faith sought martyrdom (10).

Finally,   whatever   Christians   may   have   learned   from   Muslims   and

however much their craft and intellectual products may have been used and admired, and however much the author of the *Poema de mio Cid* may have seen to admire in Avengalvón (perhaps with a practical exemplary intention as he wrote in about 1207), the typical view which the writers expressed of the Muslims who inhabited the Peninsula was probably also that of the man−in−the−field or street or army, having percolated down to him. An amalgam of our texts numbered 1, 13, and 15 would express it all: Muhammad was a liar and false prophet who promised his followers a paradise of indecent delights; the Moors are 'black' (5, 13); they are fearsome in battle, and in any circumstances cruel (19, 27); they are learned, yes, but only as a result of their black arts, expertise in astrology, and association with daemons (13). There can be no doubt that Castro, Sánchez Dragó, and many others who have written in the same vein are right at least in part, but to prove it requires an immense effort to 'deconstruct' the virtually unanimous written record of the times.

## The texts

These are reproduced as found except for the correction of a few misprints and occasional adjustment of punctuation. I am most grateful to those who have kindly allowed their copyright materials to be used. The source is stated in the introduction to each extract.

## The translations

These are entirely mine. They are not quite fully literal, but are nearly enough so. I remain responsible for possible errors (particularly with what is sometimes rather obscure Latin). A few explanations of use to the modern reader of English are incorporated in the translations in square brackets, in order to avoid the use of footnotes. I have not attempted any running commentary: for many historical, geographical, and other details, the reader should consult general works of reference.

## A note on proper names

My practice has been to translate some personal names when they are translatable, e.g. King Roderick, but to leave others in the original, e.g. Rodrigo Díaz; this may produce anomalies within some texts. Arab names are mostly in accord with forms used by Derek Lomax (see the Booklist). A few notes on other usages may be helpful.

In the original texts, terms equivalent to 'Muslim, Mohammetan' (or 'Islam') do not appear. Pejoratively, *barbarus, paganus*, and similar are all too frequent. *Maurus* is found occasionally in Latin, and in Spanish *moro* is of course standard. *Arabes* may appear for 'Muslims in general'. *Sarraceni, sarracenos* is the most commonly used term as it was in Europe in general; the Saracens were originally nomadic tribes of the Arabian and Syrian deserts, early known as peoples who attacked the borders of the Roman Empire. Another very general term is *Ismaelitae, ismaelitas*. The

Ishmaelites of Old Testament times were a desert people descended from Ishmael, Abraham's son by Hagar; he was 'a wild man; his hand will be against every man, and every man's hand against him' (Genesis 16.12), and in Genesis 21.10−21 Hagar and her son are cast out. Muhammad was said to be descended from Ishmael (our text 1). Other names of O.T. peoples hostile to the Israelites might be applied to the Muslims: Assyrians, Chaldeans. When the Almoravids of N. Africa began to appear in the Peninsula from 1086 a name was needed to distinguish them, generally *Moabitae, moabitas* (of the kingdom of Moab east of the Dead Sea in the O.T.), a name which seems to have been adopted because of its similarity to Arabic *(al−)Mo(r)abit*. The old−established Spanish Muslims then appear as *Agareni, agarenos*, descendants of (H)Agar the Egyptian bondswoman mentioned above; the contrast or opposition between *Moabitae* and *Agareni* is specifically mentioned in texts 28 and 31. Old Testament 'Babylon' also figures, as the seat of the Caliph (that is, Damascus at the time text 6 was written). The purpose of all this persistent echoing of biblical names is naturally to insist that the Spanish Christians are the modern Israelites who are fighting God's battles, with all the glory but also all the awesome responsibility which that implies.

There is nothing to remark about the nomenclature of Christian peoples, except to note that in text 35 (stanza 4), the *Francigenae* 'Frankish peoples' are mentioned because the poet is about to make comparisons involving Charlemagne, Emperor of the Franks. Their descendants the French did not take part in the Almería campaign of 1147, but the Catalans, regularly called *francos* by other Spaniards, with their S. French allies, did, and the reference is specifically to them.

Among geographical names, it should be noted that for some centuries *Spania* might designate 'al−Andalus' (as in text 12) rather than 'all Iberia'. In text 6, it is confusingly used in both senses, which have been distinguished in the translation.

## A note on coinage

For centuries after 711 the Christian states had no coinage of their own, but used Frankish and later especially Muslim coins. The tribute, *parias*, paid by the *taifa* kings and others in the 11th and 12th centuries, was in the form of gold *dinar* coins of al−Andalus. This was imitated by Alfonso VIII of Castile in 1175 when he coined gold *maravedís* (*morabetinos*, from Arabic *murabitî* 'of the Almoravids') 'with a quaint Arabic inscription alluding to the Pope as *imam* of the Catholics' (Glick, p. 128), this being the unit much mentioned in our texts.

## A note on dates

Christian Spain except Catalonia reckoned years from a date corresponding to 38 BC, the origin of this not being fully clear; the word derives from Late Latin *aera* 'number, quantity', based on earlier *aes, aeris*

'bronze (coin), money, quantity'. In 1383 Spain changed to the European AD system.

## BOOKLIST

Isidro de las Cagigas, *Los mozárabes* (Madrid, 1948, 2 vols).

Américo Castro, *The Structure of Spanish History* (Princeton, 1954) (a revised and translated version of *España en su historia*, 1948).

Roger Collins, *Early Medieval Spain* (London & Basingstoke, 1983).

Norman Daniel, *The Arabs and Medieval Europe* (London, 1975).

Marcelin Defourneaux, *Les Français en Espagne aux XIᵉ et XIIᵉ siècles* (Paris, 1949).

Thomas F. Glick, *Islamic and Christian Spain in the early Middle Ages: Comparative Perspectives on Social and Cultural Formation* (Princeton, 1979).

Juan Goytisolo, *Crónicas sarracinas* (Madrid, 1980).

J. N. Hillgarth, *The Spanish Kingdoms, 1250-1516* (Oxford, 1976-78, 2 vols).

A. Huici Miranda, *Las grandes batallas de la Reconquista durante las invasiones africanas* (Madrid, 1956).

B. Z. Kedar, *Crusade and Mission: European Approaches toward the Muslims* (Princeton, 1984)

Derek W. Lomax, *The Reconquest of Spain* (London & New York, 1978).

Angus Mackay, *Spain in the Middle Ages* (London, 1977).

J. F. O'Callaghan, *A History of Medieval Spain* (Ithaca, 1975).

C. Sánchez-Albornoz, *La España musulmana según los autores islamitas y cristianos medievales* (Barcelona, 1960, 2 vols)

F. Simonet, *Historia de los mozárabes de España* (Madrid, 1903).

R.W. Southern, *Western Views of Islam in the Middle Ages* (Cambridge, Mass., 1962).

Luis Suárez Fernández, *Historia de España, I: La Edad Media* (Madrid, 1970).

Luis Vázquez de Parga, *Textos históricos en latin medieval* (Madrid, 1952).

W. Montgomery Watt, *A History of Islamic Spain* (Edinburgh, 1965).

The Peninsula in about 1130

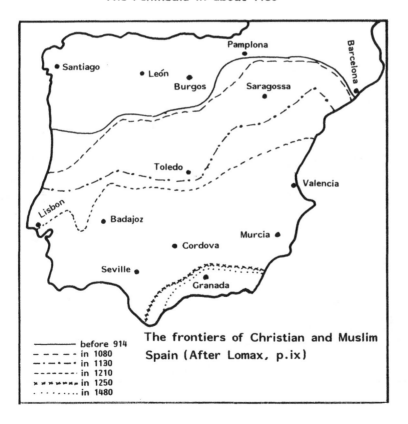

The frontiers of Christian and Muslim Spain (After Lomax, p.ix)

| | |
|---|---|
| ————— | before 914 |
| – – – – | in 1080 |
| –·—·—· | in 1130 |
| ———— | in 1210 |
| ×××××× | in 1250 |
| ·········· | in 1480 |

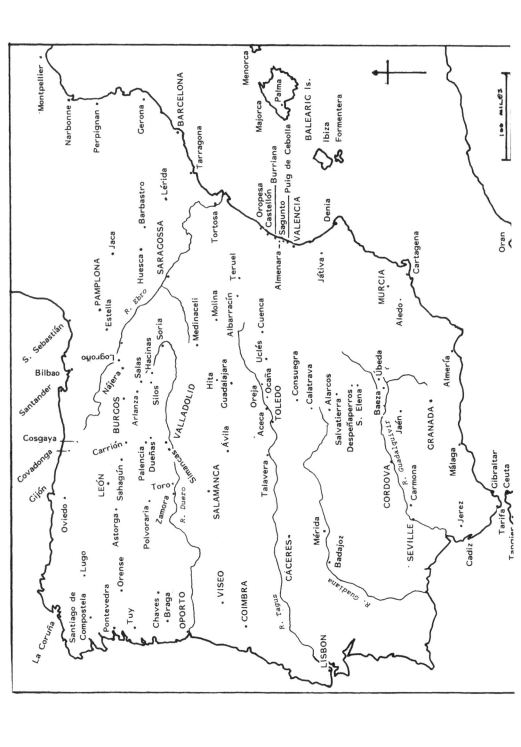

# CHRISTIANS AND MOORS IN SPAIN I

2

## 1. Origins of Islam (7th century)

*The* Estoria de España *or* Primera crónica general *produced under the direction of King Alfonso X 'el Sabio' of Castile—León (1252—84) was intended to be the definitive history of Spain from mythical prehistoric origins up to the death of Alfonso's father, Fernando III, in 1252. Work on it began in 1270 but proceeded only sporadically after 1274, when the King's scholarly team turned to other enterprises; a further effort ended in 1289, and the later parts (from the Cid in Valencia, 1094, onward) were put together not very satisfactorily on the basis of Alfonso's drafts at some date well on in the 14th century.*

*The chronicle has 14 chapters on the origins and early extension of Islam, between chapters 466 to 494, entered at intervals into the chronology of Visigothic Spain. These are authentic Alphonsine work. As in all else that he did, the King's aim was to present to his people in their own language what had hitherto been available only to the learned in Latin or in that equally learned language of the Middle Ages, Arabic. The consequences for the development of Castilian were great. For the*

En aquel quinzeno anno en que el rey Recaredo murio, era ya Mahomat de edad de ueynticinco annos, et tomo por muger una que auie nombre Hadiga. Este Mahomat era omne fermoso et rezio et muy sabidor en las artes a que llaman magicas, e en aqueste tiempo era el ya uno de los mas sabios de Arauia et de Affrica. Este Mahomat otrossi uinie del linage de Ysmael, fijo de Abraham, assi como lo auemos ya contado ante desto en esta estoria, e començo de seer mercador, ca era omne pobre et lazrado, e yua muy amenudo con sus camellos a tierra de Egipto et de Palestina; et moraua alla con los judios et los cristianos que y auie una sazon dell anno, e mayormientre con un monge natural de Anthiochia, que auie nombre Johan, que tenie el por su amigo et era herege; e daquel monge malo aprendio el muchas cosas tan bien de la nueua ley como de la uieia pora deffender se contra los iudios et los cristianos quando con ellos departiesse, ca todo lo que aquel monge le demostraua, todo era contra Dios et contra la ley, et todo a manera de heregia. Ell andando con sus camellos, assi commo dexiemos, de la una part a la otra cargados de especias et dotras cosas pora ganar y su cabdal et su logro, auinol assi una uez que ouo de entrar en la prouincia que dizien Corrozante. Desta prouincia era sennora una duenna que auie nombre Cadiga; esta Cadiga quandol uio mançebo tan grand et tan aguisado et fremoso et bien fablant, fue toda enamorada dell; e por auer razon de allegarse a ell et de fablar con el, fazie enfinta que cataua et ueye aquellas cosas que traye. Mahomat, quando aquello uio, començo de coytar la mucho et de costrennir la por sus coniuraçiones et sus espiramientos que se el sabie, de guisa que lo non entendiesse ella, diziendol con tod esto que ell era Messias, el que los judios atendien que auie de uenir. Los judios ~~ando oyron et supieron aquello

*chapter on Islam Alfonso naturally followed respected authorities when informing his people about the basis of the faith which was their permanent enemy: the* Chronica Albeldensis *(883), the* Chronographia *of Sigebert of Gembloux (about 1105); and the* Historia Arabum *of Rodrigo Jiménez de Rada (composed soon after 1243). For the extract here chosen the chief source was Lucas de Tuy's* Chronicon mundi *of 1236.*

*The chapter is 478 of the* Estoria de España, *from the edition of R. Menéndez Pidal,* Primera crónica general de España *(Madrid, 1955, 2 vols).*

*The two women mentioned in the passage as wives of Muhammad were in good Islamic tradition one only: Khadija. Lucas de Tuy mentions only one, Cadiga, and calls her Queen. But Jiménez de Rada by some error made two of her, Hadiga and Hadeya, and Alfonso's team followed him. That Muhammad preached in Cordova is said by Lucas de Tuy, and since this is found in no earlier source, was presumably his invention. The motive would have been to bring the revered St Isidore (whose remains were removed from Seville to León in 1063 and whose cult became very important) into early action against Muhammad: they were indeed contemporaries, Muhammad dying in 632 and Isidore in 636.*

When King Recared died in the fifteenth year of his reign, Muhammad was already twenty—five, and took as his wife a lady named Khadija. Muhammad was handsome and strong, and was already very learned in the magical arts, being already by then one of the most learned men in Arabia and Africa. Muhammad was of the lineage of Ishmael, son of Abraham, as we explained earlier. He was a poor man when he began life as a merchant, travelling frequently to Egypt and Palestine with his camels. He stayed part of the year there with Jews and Christians, particularly with a monk of Antioch named John, a heretic, who was a close friend; from that monk Muhammad learned many things both of the New Law and of the Old, and used these things to defend himself against the Jews and Christians when he had discussions with them, for everything which the monk explained to him was a sort of heresy against God and the Faith. As Muhammad travelled from one region to another with his camels, loaded with spices and other goods with which he hoped to make a profit, he happened to enter the province of Khurasan. This was ruled by a lady named [Khadija]. She, when she met such a tall and well—mannered young man, and one so handsome and eloquent, fell deeply in love with him; and, in order to approach him and be able to speak with him, she pretended that she wanted to see the goods he was carrying. When Muhammad realized this he began, by means of charms and spells which he knew, to press and persuade her, telling her that he was the Messiah, he whom the Jews were awaiting. The Jews, when they heard of this, came to him in

que el dizie, uinien pora ell a compannas de cada logar, et aguardauan lo et creyen le de quanto les el dizie; otrossi los ysmaelitas et los alaraues uinien se pora ell, et acompannauan le et aguardauan le, ca tenien por marauilla lo quell oyen dezir et fazer. E el començaua les de predigar et de fazer enfintosamientre nueuas leys, e traye los en aquellas malas et descomulgadas leys otoridades de la uieia ley et de la nueua, e destruye el por esta guisa la ley de Nuestro Sennor Dios, assi que muchas uezes auien razon los cristianos et los iudios de desputar con los moros. E dio aquel Mahomat tal ley et tal mandamiento a aquellos que creyen lo que les dizie: que tod aquel que otra cosa predicasse nin dixiesse, si non aquello que el dizie, que luego le descabeçassen. A estos mandamientos descomulgados llaman oy en dia los moros por su arauigo *zoharas*, que quiere dezir 'leys de Dios', e dizen et creen ellos por çierto que fue Mahomat mandadero de Dios, et que ge le enuio el pora demostrar les aquella su ley.

Quando la reyna Cadiga uio que assil onrrauan yl aguardauan todos, cuedo ella en su coraçon que yazie en el ascondido el poder de Dios, e por quel auie muy grand amor cassosse con ell et tomol por marido; e dalli adelant fue Mahomat rico et poderoso et rey et sennor de tierra.

Este Mahomat era mal dolient duna emfermedad a que dizien *caduco morbo* et de epilesia, e acaesçio assi un dia quel tomo aquella emfermedad et quel derribo en tierra. La reyna Cadiga quando lo uio ouo ende muy grand pesar; e pues que uio la emfermedad partida del, preguntol que dolençia era aquella tan mala et tan lixosa; e dixol Mahomat: 'Amiga, non es emfermedad, mas el angel sant Gabriel es que uien a mi et fabla comigo demientre que yago en tierra; e por que nol puedo catar en derecho nin puedo sofrir su uista, tanto es claro et fremoso, por que so omne carnal, fallesçe me ell spirito et cayo assi como ueedes por muerto en tierra.' Luego que estol ouo dicho trabaiosse por sus encantamientos et sus artes magicas, et con la ayuda del diablo por quien se el guiaua, de fazer antella assi como sennales et miraglos, e por que a las uezes se torna el diablo assi como diz la Escriptura en figura de angel de lux, entraua el diablo en ell a las uezes et faziel dezir algunas cosas daquellas que auien de uenir, e por esta manera le auien de creer todas las yentes de lo que les dizie.

Despues desto passo ell a Espanna et fuesse pora Cordoua, et predigo y aquella su mala secta; e dizie les en su predicaçion que Nuestro Sennor Ihesu Cristo que nasçiera de uirgen por obra dell Spiritu Sancto, mas non que fuesse el Dios. Quando esto sopo el buen padre sant Esidro, que llegara estonçes de la corte de Roma, enuio luego sus omnes a Cordoua quel prisiessen et ge le leuassen; mas el diablo apparesçio a Mahomat, et dixol que se partiesse daquel logar; ell estonçes saliosse de Cordoua et fuxo et passo allend mar, e predigo en Arauia et en Affrica, et enganno y et coffondio muchos pueblos ademas, assi como oy en dia ueedes, et tornolos a su creençia por que les prouaua et les affirmaua aquello que les dizie por la ley de los iudios et de los cristianos. E aun dizie les, et fazie ge lo creer, que tod aquel que mata a su enemigo et aun aquell a que matan sus

groups from many places, and waited upon him and believed everything that he told them; and the Ishmaelites and Arabs came to him and did the same, being amazed at what they heard him say and saw him do. He began to preach to them and deceitfully make new laws for them, citing as his authorities portions of the New Law and the Old; in this way he destroyed the Law of our Lord God, causing Christians and Jews to dispute frequently with the Moors. The law and the commandment which Muhammad gave to those who believed what he said was as follows: that anyone who preached or said anything other than what he, Muhammad, taught, should immediately have his head cut off. These extraordinary commandments are known today by the Moors in Arabic as *Zoharas* [suras?] which means 'laws of God', and the Moors believe that Muhammad was truly a messenger of God, and that God sent him in order to teach people his law.

When Queen [Khadija] saw that everyone honoured and respected Muhammad, she thought that the power of God lay hidden in him; and, being much in love with him, she married him. Thenceforth Muhammad was rich and powerful, and was king and lord of the land.

Muhammad suffered greatly from a disease known as *morbus caducus* and epilepsy, and it happened that one day he was overcome by that complaint and fell to the ground. Queen [Khadija] was greatly grieved when she saw this, and as soon as the fit had passed, she asked him the nature of this dangerous and foul complaint. Muhammad replied: 'My lady, it is not a disease. The Archangel Gabriel comes and speaks to me while I am lying on the ground. Since I am a fleshly man and he is so bright and handsome, I am unable to look at him, and my mind reels and I fall to the ground as if dead, as you see.' After this Muhammad strove by charms and by his skill in magic, and also with the aid of the devil by whom he was guided, to produce portents and miracles in her presence; and since, as Holy Writ tells us, the devil can turn himself into an angel of light, the devil entered into his body and made him prophesy things which lay in the future, so that everyone began to believe what he told them.

After this he crossed into Spain and went to Cordova, where he preached his evil doctrine, saying that Our Lord Jesus Christ was indeed born of a virgin by the act of the Holy Spirit, but that he was not God. When the good father St Isidore heard of this, having just arrived from the Pope's court at Rome, he sent his men to Cordova in order to arrest Muhammad. However, the devil appeared to Muhammad, and told him to leave the place, which he did, crossing the sea and preaching then in Arabia and Africa. There he deceived and confounded many more peoples, as you can see is the case today, justifying his new faith with much reference to the Law of the Jews and to the Law of the Christians. He even told them, and made them believe, that the man who kills his enemy, and he who is killed by his enemies, goes straight to paradise; and that

enemigos, que luego se ua derechamientre a parayso; e dizie les que el parayso era logar muy sabroso et muy delectoso de comer et de beuer, et que corrien por y tres rios: vno de uino, otro de miel, e otro de leche; e que auran los que y fueren mugeres escosas, non destas que son agora en este mundo mas dotras que uernan despues, e auran otrossi complidamientre todas las cosas que cobdiçiaren en sus coraçones. [...]

paradise was a delightful place where one ate and drank well, having three rivers, one of wine, one of honey, and one of milk; also that men in paradise would have virgin women, not of the kind that inhabit this world, but others of kinds here unknown; and that men would have to the full all those things they covet in their hearts. [...]

## 2.  The prophecy of the fall of Spain (711)

*We do not know precisely what happened when the Gothic kingdom of Spain fell with startling ease to Islamic invaders from North Africa in 711 and the following years.  There is no surviving contemporary account of the political and military events in any language.  There are naturally numerous later narrations, those on the Christian side being inevitably coloured by the need to explain and palliate the disaster or to sermonize about it or to urge on the reconquest of Islamized lands by the Christians of the north and from beyond the Pyrenees.  This extract should be taken in conjunction with the three following.  For a sober historical account see Lomax, chapter 1.  For the literary and legendary aspects of the theme, still of major importance in the 15th and 16th centuries (for example, the*

Hortante autem et adiuvante senatu, et adhuc Vitiza vivente, coepit conregnare Rodericus ultimus Rex Gothorum, anno Ulit quarto, Arabum vero XCI, Aera DCCXLIX, anno septimo Vitizae: et tantum tribus annis regnavit, uno per se, duobus etiam cum Vitiza.  Erat autem Rodericus durus in bellis, et ad negotia expeditus, sed in moribus non dissimilis Vitizae, nam et circa initium regni sui Vitizae filios Sisibertum et Ebam probris et iniuriis lacessitos a patria propulsavit, qui, relicta patria, ad Recilam Comitem Tingitaniae ob patris amicitiam transfretarunt.  Erat autem tunc temporis Toleti palatium a multorum Regum temporibus semper clausum, et seris pluribus obseratum.  Hoc fecit Rex Rodericus contra voluntatem omnium aperiri, ut sciret quid interius haberetur, putebat enim thesauros maximos invenire; sed cum aperuit, praeter unam arcam repositam nil invenit.  Qua aperta, reperiit quemdam pannum, in quo latinis litteris erat scriptum: 'Quod cum contigeret seras frangi, arcam atque palatium aperiri, et videri quae inibi habebantur, gentes eius effigiei quae in eo panno erant depictae, Hispanias invaderent, et suo dominio subiugarent.'  Quod Rex videns, doluit aperuisse, et, ut erat prius, fecit arcam et palatium inserari.  Erant autem in panno depictae facies, ut vultus, dispositio, et habitus Arabum adhuc monstrat, qui sua capita tegunt vittis, sedentes in equis, habentes vestes diversis coloribus variegatas, tenentes gladios, et ballistas, et vexilla in altum tensa: qua pictura Rex et proceres timuerunt.

*fine ballads numbered 27—30 in Roger Wright's collection), see R. Menéndez Pidal,* El rey Rodrigo en la literatura española *(Madrid, 1924), and* Floresta de leyendas heroicas españolas. Rodrigo, el último godo *(Madrid, 1925—27, 3 vols).*

*The extract is from* De rebus Hispaniae *(III.18), the general history of Spain completed by Rodrigo Jiménez de Rada in 1243. He was Archbishop of Toledo and Primate of Spain, and the leading churchman, latinist, and scholar of his time. His work was to be a principal source for Alfonso X's* Estoria de España *and many later writers. The edition used is that of 1793* (Roderici Toletani Antistitis Opera), *reproduced at Valencia in 1968.*

With the encouragement and support of the nobles, Witiza being still alive, Roderick, the last King of the Goths, began to reign jointly. This was in the 4th year of al—Walid [Caliph of Damascus], the 91st year of the Arabs, Era 749 [= AD 711], and the 7th year of Witiza's reign. Roderick ruled for only three years, two jointly with Witiza, one alone. Roderick was a great warrior and efficient in conducting business, but in his morals was not unlike Witiza, for early in his reign he banished Sisibert and Eba, the sons of Witiza, from his realm, after harassing them with accusations and reproaches; and they, leaving Spain, crossed the Strait to join Recila, Count of Tingitania [part of the former Roman province of Mauretania, with its capital at Tangier], because of the friendship of this man for their father. At that time there was a palace in Toledo which had remained closed during the reigns of many monarchs, firmly barred to all. This, against the advice of everybody else, Roderick caused to be opened, so that he could find out what was concealed within, and because he thought he might find great treasures; but when it was opened, he found nothing except one chest. When this was opened, he found a cloth on which was written, in Latin letters: 'Should it happen that the bars are broken, and the palace and the chest opened, and the contents of the latter revealed, it should be known that the people whose pictures are drawn on the cloth will invade Spain and subject the country to their rule.' When the King saw this he was sorry he had opened the palace, and he had the chest and the palace sealed again just as they had been before. What was depicted on the cloth was the faces, persons, and dress of Arabs, with their heads covered in cloths, seated on horses, wearing dress of varied colours, holding swords and bows and banners on high. The king and his chief nobles were terrified by these pictures.

### 3. The invasion of Spain (711)

*This extract consists of four sections from the chronicle designated in modern times* Continuatio Isidoriana Hispana ad annum 754. *As a work completed in or soon after that year, it is much the earliest Christian account. It is noticeable that, although King Roderick is said to have 'violently usurped the crown' and although the Gothic realm was weakened at the time by 'internal dissent', there is as yet no Gothic ruler of an area of N. Africa to act as collaborator (that role is filled, however, by Oppa after the invasion), and there is no suggestion yet of the sexual sin by a Gothic monarch which was to be such a substantial motif later.*

*The chronicle is the work of a priest who knew Cordova and Toledo under Muslim rule. Since section 70 in part repeats the start of 68 and has materials which properly precede those of 68, it may be that the writer ws uniting — not very intelligently — two diverse sources. Section 72 foreshadows the much greater rhetorical development of the same theme in the* Estoria de España *(text 5): modern historians seem to agree that the invasion was not specially cruel or destructive, and it is certain that Muslims — already familiar with both religions in the Middle East — were taught to respect Christians and Jews as 'peoples of the Book'; moreover, a large Christian population lived on for centuries in al—Andalus, with legal*

(68) Huius temporibus, in era DCCXLVIIII, anno imperii eius quarto, Arabum LXLII, Ulit sceptra regni quinto per anno retinente, Rudericus tumultuose regnum ortante senatu invadit. Regnat anno uno. Nam adgregata copia exercitus adversus Arabes una cum Mauros a Muze missos, id est Taric Abuzara et ceteros diu sibi provinciam creditam incursantibus simulque et plerasque civitates devastantibus, anno imperii Iustiniani quinto, Arabum nonagesimo tertio, Ulit sexto, in era DCCL Transductos promontoriis sese cum eis confligendo recepit eoque prelio fugatum omnem Gothorum exercitum, qui cum eo emulanter fraudulenterque ob ambitionem regni advenerant, cecidit. Sicque regnum simulque cum patriam male cum emulorum internicione amisit, peragente Ulit anno sexto. [...]

(70) Huius temporibus in era DCCXLVIIII, anno imperii eius quarto, Arabum LXLII, Ulit quinto, dum supra nominatos missos Spania vastaretur et nimium non solum hostili, verum etiam intestino furore confligeretur, Muze et ipse ut miserrimam adiens per Gaditanum fretum columnas Herculis pertendentes, et quasi tomi indicio porti aditum demonstrantes, vel clabes in

*rights and relative freedom of worship (text 14).*
The text is taken from Monumenta Germaniae Historica, Auct. Antiq.,
*II (Chronica minora, 2), pp. 352—53. It is also in Vázquez de Parga, pp.
14—16.*
Transductos *partly preserves the Roman name* Julia Traducta, *with
reference to the crossing to N. Africa.*
The great statue at Cádiz was of, or imitated another statue of,
Hercules. *Among many contemporary mentions of it is one in chapter 4
of the* Historia Turpini *(see text 8), where in a prejudiced way it is taken
to be a representation of Muhammad. The figure was broken up in 1145
by the Muslim ruler of the area when in need of funds, but what had
been taken to be of gold turned out to consist of gilded bronze. Chapter
5 of* Alfonso X's Estoria de España *attributes the building to Hercules
himself: '... fizo y una torre muy grand, e puso ensomo una ymagen de
cobre bien fecha que cataua contra orient e tenie en la mano diestra una
grand llaue en semeiante cuemo que querie abrir puerta, e la mano
siniestra alçada e tenduda contra orient e auie escripto en la palma "Estos
son los moiones de Hercules".' The principal manuscript of the* Estoria
*has, among the few miniatures in it completed, a depiction of the famous
statue.*

(68) In Era 749 [= AD 711], which was the fourth year of the rule of
Justinian II [of Byzantium] and year 92 of the Arabs, and when al—Walid I
[705—15] was in the fifth year of his rule as Caliph, Roderick violently
usurped the crown with the support of leading members of the nobility. He
reigned for one year. He gathered the full strength of his army to face the
Arabs together with the Moors sent by Musa [Musa ibn Nusayr, governor of
the Maghrib], that is Tariq ibn Ziyad [governor of Tangier] and the others
who had for long been raiding the province assigned to him and despoiling
many cities. That was in the fifth year of Justinian II's rule, year 93 of
the Arabs, the sixth of al—Walid, and Era 750 [= AD 712]. Roderick met
and joined battle with them on the hills behind Tarifa, and was killed in
the fight together with the whole Gothic army as it fled, those who had
supported him when he treacherously sought to win the crown. In this way
Roderick lost both the crown and his realm in the general destruction caused
by wicked rivalries, al—Walid being the agent of it in the sixth year of his
reign.
(69) [Sindered, Metropolitan of Toledo, took fright at the invasion, and
fled to Constantinople].
(70) In Era 749 [= AD 711], the fourth year of the rule of Justinian
II and year 92 of the Arabs, and the fifth year of al—Walid's rule, while
Spain was being laid waste by the aforementioned invaders and was being
devastated by the fury not only of the enemy but also of internal dissent,
Musa himself crossed the Strait marked by the pillars of Hercules. The
statue of Hercules seems to point the way to the harbour with its sign of a

manu transitum Spanie presagantes vel reserantes iam olim male direptam et omnino impie adgressam perditans penetrat atque Toleto urbem regiam usque inrumpendo, adiacentes regiones pace fraudifica male diverberans nonnullos seniores nobiles viros, qui utqumque remanserant, per Oppam filium Egiche regis a Toleto fugam arripientem gladio patibuli iugulat et per eius occasionem cunctos ense detruncat. Sicque non solum ulteriorem Spaniam, sed etiam et citeriorem usque ultra Cesaragustam antiquissimam ac florentissimam civitatem dudum iam iudicio Dei patenter apertam gladio, fame et captivitate depopulat, civitates decoras igne concremando precipitat, seniores et potentes seculi cruci adiudicat, iubenes atque lactantes pugionibus trucidat.

(71) Sicque dum tali terrore cunctos stimulat, pacem nonnulle civitates, que residue erant, iam coacte proclamitant adque suadendo et inridendo astu quoddam, nec more, petita condonant. Sed ubi inpetrata territi metu recalcitrant, ad montana temti iterum effugientes fame et diversa morte periclitant adque in eandem infelicem Spaniam Cordoba in sede dudum Patricia, que semper extitit pre ceteras adiacentes civitates opulentissima et regno Wisegothorum primitibas inferebat delicias, regnum efferum conlocant.

(72) Quis enim narrare queat tanta pericula? Quis dinumerare tam inportuna naufragia? Nam si omnia menbra verterentur in linguam, omnino nequaquam Spanie ruinas vel eius tot tantaque mala dicere poterit humana natura. Sed ut in brebi cuncta legenti renotem pagella, relictis seculi inumerabilibus ab Adam usque nunc cladibus, quas per infinitas regionibus et civitatibus crudelis intulit mundus iste inmundus, quidquid historialiter capta Troia pertulit, quidquit Iherosolima predicta per prophetarum eloquia baiulabit, quidquid Babilonia per scripturarum eloquia substulit, quidquid postremo Roma apostolorum novilitate decorata martirialiter confecit, omnia et tot ut Spania condam deliciosa et nunc misera effecta tam in honore quam etiam in dedecore experibit.

piece of papyrus, or the keys in its hand foreshadow the free passage of invaders into Spain or the unlocking of what was now no longer a barrier. Altogether pitiless, destroying everything as he went, Musa reached the royal city of Toledo. He separated off the areas around it by offering deceitful peace, and beheaded certain noblemen who had for some reason stayed, through the agency of Oppa, son of King Egica [687—701], when they tried to escape from Toledo. Thus by famine and by leading people into captivity Musa depopulated not only the further parts of Spain, but also the nearer parts as far as Saragossa, a most ancient and splendid city for long up till now, by the judgement of God laid open to the sword. He speedily burned fair cities, sentenced noble and leading men of the time to be tortured, and had children and nursing mothers beaten to death.

(71) While he filled everyone with such terror, some cities which remained soon sued for peace, and the Muslims, with blandishments and mockery and guile, granted these wishes. But in cases where the Muslims refused their requests, the terrified inhabitants fled again into the hills to risk hunger and other kinds of death. The Muslims established their barbarous capital in unhappy Cordova, for long titled 'Patricia' ['Cordoba colonia Patricia cognomine', Pliny, III.10], always outstanding as the wealthiest among neighbouring cities and which had earlier furnished delights for the kingdom of the Visigoths.

(72) Who can bear to tell such disasters? Who can count such terrible calamities? If all our limbs could be turned into tongues, human intelligence could never describe the ruin of Spain and so many evils. But in order that I can sum up all these things in brief form for the reader, setting aside the innumerable slaughters which history records from Adam to the present, which this cruel and wicked world has inflicted upon so many regions and cities, I say: whatever Troy suffered when it was captured, whatever Jerusalem endured following the utterances of the prophets, whatever Babylon underwent as a result of the words of the Scriptures, and finally whatever Rome lived through when adorned by the noble martyrdom of the Apostles, I shall preserve a memory both in honour and in shame of just as many things which Spain — once delightful, now wretched — experienced.

## 4. The invasion of Spain: another view (711)

*In about the year 1000 a priest of Toledo composed a brief general history of Spain, beginning with a description of the Peninsula and the line of Noah as it continued down to the Gothic monarchs, then Rome and her empire, and finally the Muslim invasion. Among sources for the early materials are St Jerome, St Isidore, and for later periods the* Continuatio *from which our text 3 is taken. The sources for the sections on the invasion are not known, but may well have included Arabic texts and legends. Indeed, it has recently been proposed by P. Gautier Dalché in* Anuario de Estudios Medievales, *14 (1984), 13−32, that the text originated in Catalonia in the second half of the 12th century, and was in part*

(18) [...] Post regnavit Toleti Geticus XXVII annis, bene morigeratus et bone indolis, qui omnes quos pater suus in carcere et compedibus afflixerat, eripuit. Erga populum suum bonus et temperatus extitit et in omni consilio suo episcopos et proceres regni convocavit.

(19) Interim in regia curia Ispalensi inter alia ceperunt loqui de pulcritudine mulierum. Inter quos quidam in hec verba erupit dicens, quod nulla pulcrior filia Iuliani esset in tota terra. Hoc audito Geticus cum quodam duce ab aliis semotus locutus est, quomodo ad illam caute nuntium mitteret; qui illam quantocius exiberet. Cui ille: 'Mitte', inquid, 'pro Iuliano ut veniat. Et esto cum eo per aliquot dies in potacione et alacritate cibi et potus.' Interim cum Iulianus esset in convivio, Geticus scripsit literas sub nomine Iuliani, quas eius sigillo munitas direxit comitisse illius uxori, ut filiam suam Olibam sibi velocius Ispalim adduceret. Iuliano in illa delectacione potacionis et comestione occupato Gethicus eam per dies plurimos habuit et stupravit. Adhuc Iulianus comessationi deditus quadam die respexit et vidit armigerum suum, quem Tingitane reliquerat, vocavitque eum ad se et ait: 'Quomodo hic venisti?' Qui respondit: 'Tu misisti pro uxore tua et filia et in comitatu eorum veni.' 'Vade', inquit Iulianus armigero, 'ad uxorem meam, ut cito ad me veniat.' Quae veniens nunciavit ei, quomodo Geticus eam et filiam suam ad se sub dolo fecit adduci. 'Vade', inquit Iulianus, 'et collige omnes res tuas et ad ripam usque fluminis propera ibique navim ascendentes repatriabimus dimissa filia.' Qui navim ascendentes recto et veloci cursu Leptam venerunt. Qui congregans omnem pecuniam in auro et argento et vestimentis ad Alcala usque properavit ad Tarech regem dixitque ei: 'Vis ingredi Ispaniam? Ego te ducam, quia claves maris et terre habeo et bene te dirigere possum.' 'Que fiducia', inquit Tarech, 'erit mihi in te, cum tu sis Christianus et ego Maurus?' 'In hoc bene confidere poteris in me, quia dimittam tibi uxorem meam et filios

*translated from Arabic. It is in the present work that the motif of sexual sin by the Gothic monarch, and the accompanying motif of Count Julian's vengeance and treachery, are first documented; but the sinner is here Witiza, later to be replaced by Roderick. Ceuta on the Moroccan coast had been a bastion of the Visigoths since about 542. The sons of Witiza here have different names from those given in our text 2, and in neither case do these names correspond to any of those borne by the three sons of Witiza as given by modern historians (e.g. by Lomax: Akhila, Ardabast, Olmund).*

*The text bears the modern title* Historia pseudo—Isidoriana. *The extract is taken from the same source as the preceding, pp. 387—88. It is also in Vázquez de Parga, pp. 17—19.*

(18) [...] After that Witiza ruled at Toledo for 27 years. He was a kindly man of good character, who freed from prison all those whom his father had mistreated, so that he showed himself to be good and well—disposed to his people; and for every council he called together the bishops and chief men of the kingdom.

(19) Meanwhile in the royal court in Seville they began to talk, among other things, about the beauty of women. One of those present intervened to say that no woman in the whole world was more lovely than the daughter of Count Julian. On hearing this Witiza drew one of his chief men aside, asking him how he might secretly send a messenger to her so that he might see her. This man advised: 'Send for Julian to come here, and spend some days with him eating and drinking.' While Julian was banqueting in this way, Witiza wrote a letter in Julian's name, and this, accompanied by Julian's seal, was sent to the Countess his wife. It told her to bring her daughter Oliva to Seville as soon as possible. While Julian was occupied in the delights of feasting and drinking, Witiza illicitly had intercourse with the girl over several days. One day Julian, abandoned to the pleasures of the table, looked around and saw his squire, whom he had left in Morocco. He called the man over and said to him: "How did you get here?' The man replied: 'You sent for your wife and daughter, and I came accompanying them.' Julian said to the squire: 'Go to my wife and tell her to come here at once.' When she arrived she told Julian how Witiza had had her and her daughter brought to him by fraudulent means. Julian said to her: 'Go and assemble all your belongings and go quickly down to the riverside. We will leave our daughter behind and board our ship to go home.' This they did, and quickly reached Ceuta. Julian gathered together all his money in gold and silver and clothing and hastened to Alcala. There he said to King Tariq: 'Do you want to invade Spain? I will lead you, for I possess the keys to land and sea and can well guide you.' Tariq asked: 'What trust can I have in you, since you are a Christian and I am a Muslim?' Julian answered: 'You may have full confidence in me, since I will hand over to you both my wife and children

infinitamque peccuniam.' Tunc securitate accepta Tarech maximam militum multitudinem collegit et ad insulam Tarif cum Iuliano veniens inter Malacam et Leptam ascendit in montem, qui usque hodie mons Tarech dicitur, inde cum exercitu suo Tarech Yspalim usque veniens expugnavit eam et cepit.

(20) Interim Gethicus mortuus est duosque filios dimisit Sebastinum et Euo. Et quoniam essent pueri, habitatores terre noluerunt eos regnare super se, sed elegerunt sibi regem nomine Rodericum. Qui infinitum congregans exercitum contra Tarec processit. Filii vero Gethici miserunt ad Tarec dicentes: 'Nos praecedemus cum maxima exercitus multitudine fingentes nos quasi contra te pugnaturos. Qui cito terga dabimus et tu persequere nos 'dabiturque tibi de hoste tropheum.' Tarec vero non immemor utilitatis sue persecutus eos et multi corruerunt, quin et Rodericus mortuus est. Fecitque èis privilegium, ut omni tempore vite sue manerent ingenui Sebastinus et Euo. Numerus villarum quas habebant tria millia LX.

and a vast amount of money.' On this surety, Tariq assembled all his forces and, coming to the island of Tarifa with Julian, he climbed a hill between Malaga and Ceuta, a hill which to this day is called 'hill of Tariq' [Jebel−al−Tariq, Gibraltar]; thence with his army he attacked and took Seville.

(20) When Witiza died he left two sons, Sebastinus and Evo. Since they were only boys the people were unwilling to have these to reign over them, and chose as king a man by the name of Roderick, who gathered a large army and set out against Tariq. The sons of Witiza sent a message to Tariq to say: 'We shall come with a large army pretending to do battle against you. But when the battle starts we will withdraw from it; you will pursue the others and will be granted victory over your enemy.' Tariq was fully aware how useful this was to him. Many Christians fled and Tariq chased them, killing Roderick himself. Tariq granted Sebastinus and Evo a special privilege: they should remain free for the rest of their lives, the number of their estates amounting to 3,060.

## 5. Lament for the destruction of Spain (711)

*The following text is chapter 559 of the* Estoria de España *or* Primera crónica general *of Alfonso X (see text 1).* *The previous chapter, 558, is the famous 'Loor de España' (praise of Spain): the promised land of the Goths, rich in all things, has been taken from them as punishment for the sins of its rulers.* *Chapter 559 continues the moral message and describes in rhetorical fashion — the whole section being a remarkable triumph of medieval Latin rhetoric applied to a vernacular — the horrors of the invasion and its aftermath.* *British readers may find a comparison with* Gildas, De excidio, *about the Saxon invasion of Romano—Celtic Britain, illustrative.*

*The principal model for chapters 558 and 559 was Rodrigo Jiménez de Rada,* De rebus Hispaniae *(see text 2), with much expansion.*

*Among the details to be noted is the belief that there had always been 'Espanna' and 'espannoles', from the time of Hercules: a God—given unity of land and people repeatedly wounded by invaders, among whom Romans*

Pues que la batalla fue acabada desauenturadamientre et fueron todos muertos los unos et los otros — ca en uerdad non fincara ninguno de los cristianos en la tierra que a la batalla non uiniesse, que dell un cabo que dell otro, dellos en ayuda del rey Rodrigo, dellos del cuende Julian — finco toda la tierra uazia del pueblo, lena de sangre, bannada de lagrimas, conplida de appellidos, huespeda de los estrannos, enagenada de los uezinos, desamparada de los moradores, bibda et dessolada de sus fijos, coffonduda de los barbaros, esmedrida por la llaga, ffallida de fortaleza, fflaca de fuerça, menguada de conort, et desolada de solaz de los suyos. Alli se renouaron las mortandades del tiempo de Hercules, alli se refrescaron et podresçieron las llagas del tiempo de los vuandalos, de los alanos et de los sueuos que començaran ya a sanar. Espanna que en ell otro tiempo fuera llagada por la espada de los romanos, pues que guaresçiera et cobrara por la melezina et la bondad de los godos, estonçes era crebantada, pues que eran muertos et aterrados quantos ella criara. Oblidados le son los sus cantares, et el su lenguage ya tornado es en ageno et en palabra estranna. Los moros de la hueste todos uestidos del sirgo et de los pannos de color que ganaran, las riendas de los sus cauallos tales eran como de fuego, las sus caras dellos negras como la pez, el mas fremoso dellos era negro como la olla, assi luzien sus oios como candelas; el su cauallo dellos ligero e. no leopardo, e el su cauallero mucho mas cruel et mas dannoso que es el lobo en la grey de las oueias en la noche. La uil yente de los affricanos que se non solie preçiar de fuerça nin de bondad, et todos sus fechos fazie con art et a enganno, et non se solien amparar si non pechando grandes riquezas et grand auer, essora era exaltada, ca crebanto en una ora mas ayna la nobleza de los godos que lo non podrie omne dezir por lengua. ¡Espanna mezquina! tanto fue la su muert coytada que solamientre non finco y

*who held sway for six centuries are on a level with the Vandals and other marauding Germanic tribes who were in the Peninsula for a few years early in the 5th century, and the Suevi who for long maintained a kingdom in the north—west.* 'Spain' awaited the Goths as her rescuer according to the divine plan, and of course like his predecessors Alfonso X claimed descent from the better element among the Gothic monarchs. That the Moors had 'faces ... black as pitch' — an obvious untruth, one would have thought, for Alfonso's readers, well acquainted with mudéjares in their own cities and countryside, and with Moors on the borders of the Kingdom of Granada — shows that this particular prejudice did not begin in the 16th century against the Moor Othello ('an old black ram', I.i.88); in any case, Spanish moreno 'dark, swarthy, black' derived from Latin maurus.*

On the connotations of this important section of the chronicle (relating to the Fall and Redemption), see A. Deyermond, 'The death and rebirth of Visigothic Spain in the Estoria de España', Revista Canadiense de Estudios Hispánicos, 9 (1984—85), 345—67.

After the battle was over so disastrously and all our people on both sides were killed — for indeed there had not been any Christian fighting—man in the land, from one end of it to the other, who did not go to the battle, some to the aid of King Roderick, some to that of Count Julian — the whole realm was empty of inhabitants, full of blood, bathed in tears, and loud with war—cries; a host to foreigners, alienated from its natives, abandoned by its inhabitants, widowed, and bereft of its children, plunged into confusion by the barbarians, weakened by wounds, lacking all sinew and strength, comfortless and without the support of its own people. Then there were renewed the slaughters of the time of Hercules, and the wounds of the time of the Vandals, the Alans, and the Suevi — which had begun to heal — were reopened and festered anew. Spain, which in an earlier time had been wounded by the sword of the Romans, but had been healed and helped to recover by the medicine and goodness of the Goths, was then again shattered, for all her sons were dead. Her songs are forgotten, and her language is changed into foreign and strange words. The Moors of the host wore silks and colourful cloths which they had taken as booty, their horses' reins were like fire, their faces were black as pitch, the handsomest among them was black as a cooking—pot, and their eyes blazed like fire; their horses as swift as leopards, their horsemen more cruel and hurtful than the wolf that comes at night to the flock of sheep. The vile African people who were not wont to boast of their strength nor their goodness, and who achieved everything by stealth and deceit, and who were not accustomed to help each other except by paying over great quantities of wealth, was at that moment raised on high, for in a short time they speedily shattered the greatness of the Goths in a way that man has no words to express. Wretched Spain! So grievous was her destruction that

ninguno qui la llante; laman la dolorida, ya mas muerta que uiua, et suena
su uoz assi como dell otro sieglo, e sal la su palabra assi como de so
tierra, e diz con la grande cueta: 'vos, omnes, que passades por la carrera,
parad mientes et veed si a cueta nin dolor que se semeie con el mio.'
Doloroso es el llanto, llorosos los alaridos, ca Espanna llora los sus fijos et
non se puede conortar porque ya non son. Las sus casas et las sus
moradas todas fincaron yermas et despobladas; la su onrra et el su prez
tornado es en confusion, ca los sus fijos et los sus criados todos moriron a
espada, los nobles et fijos dalgo cayeron en catiuo, los prínçipes et los altos
omnes ydos son en fonta et en denosto, e los buenos conbatientes perdieron
se en estremo. Los que antes estauan libres, estonçes eran tornados en
sieruos; los que se preçiauan de caualleria, coruos andauan a labrar con
reias et açadas; los uiçiosos del comer non se abondauan de uil maniar; los
que fueran criados en pannos de seda, non auien de que se crobir nin de
tan uil uestidura en que ante non pornien ellos sus pies. Tan assoora fue
la su cueta et el su destroymiento que non a toruellinno nin lluuia nin
tempestad de mar a que lo omne pudiesse asmar. ¿Qual mal o qual
tempestad non passo Espanna? Con los ninnos chicos de teta dieron a las
paredes, a los moços mayores desfizieron con feridas, a los mançebos
grandes metieronlos a espada, los ançianos et uieios de dias moriron en las
batallas, et fueron todos acabados por guerra; los que eran ya pora onrrar
et en cabo de sus dias echolos a mala fonta la crueleza de los moros; a las
mezquinas de las mugieres guardauan las pora desonrrar las, e la su
fermosura dellas era guardada pora su denosto. [...] Aqui se remato la
santidad et la religion de los obispos et de los saçerdotes; aqui quedo et
minguo ell abondamiento de los clerigos que siruien las eglesias; aqui
peresçio ell entendimiento de los prelados et de los omnes de orden; aqui
fallesçio ell ensennamiento de la ley et de la sancta fe. Los padres et los
sennores todos peresçieron en uno; los santuarios fueron destroydos, las
eglesias crebantadas; los logares que loauan a Dios con alegria, essora le
denostauan yl maltrayen; las cruzes et los altares echaron de las eglesias; la
crisma et los libros et las cosas que eran pora onrra de la cristiandat todo
fue esparzudo et echado a mala part; las fiestas et las sollempnias, todas
fueron oblidadas; la onrra de los santos et la beldad de la eglesia toda fue
tornada en laydeza et en uiltança; las eglesias et las torres o solien loar a
Dios, essora confessauan en ellas et llamauan a Mahomat; las uestimentas et
los calzes et los otros uasos de los santuarios eran tornados en uso de mal,
et enlixados de los descreydos. Toda la tierra desgastaron los enemigos, las
casas hermaron, los omnes mataron, las çibdades quemaron, los arbores, las
uinnas et quanto fallaron uerde cortaron. Tanto puio esta pestilençia et esta
cueta que non finco en toda Espanna buena uilla nin çibdad o obispo
ouiesse que non fuesse o quemada o derribada o retenida de moros; ca las
çibdades que los alaraues non pudieron conquerir, engannaron las et
conquiriron las por falsas pleytesias. Oppa, fijo del rey Egica, arçobispo
que fue de Seuilla andaua predigando a los cristianos que se tornassen con

none was left to weep for her; men call her the wounded one, already more dead than alive; her voice sounds as if it came from the other world, and is heard as if it came from beneath the earth, saying in her great suffering: 'You men who pass along the road, think if there can be any grief or pain to equal mine.' The weeping is most pitiful and the wails most tearful, for Spain mourns her sons and cannot console herself for the fact that they are no more. Her houses and dwellings were left abandoned and empty; her honour and great name are cast down, for her sons and those she nourished all died by the sword, the nobles and knights were all captured, the princes and chief men were put to shame, and good fighters were lost. Those who before were free were enslaved; those who were proud of their military caste now go bent down to till with ploughshares and hoes; those who ate richly were left with a little poor food; those who were brought up in silken clothes were left with nothing to cover themselves, not even with such covering as that in which formerly they would not even have shod their feet. So overwhelming was their suffering and destruction that there is no whirlwind or storm of rain or tempest at sea with which one could compare them. What kind of evil or storm was there that Spain did not suffer? The Moors dashed babies at the breast against the walls, killed the older boys with wounds, put the grown young men to the sword; the old men died in the battles, and all were destroyed by war; the cruelty of the Moors put to shame those who were to be honoured at the end of their days. They put the wretched women aside to dishonour them later, and their beauty was reserved to be their downfall. [...] Then was destroyed the holiness and religion of the bishops and the priests, and the number of the clergy who served the churches was reduced. The learning of the prelates and monks perished, and the teachings of the law and of holy faith ceased. Fathers and lords perished together; sanctuaries were destroyed and churches shattered; in those places where God had been praised with joy, He was cursed and insulted. The Moors cast the crosses and altars out of the churches; the holy oils and the books and those things that were the honour of Christendom were all scattered and wasted. Church feasts and solemnities were all forgotten; the honour of the saints and the beauty of the Church were all turned into ugliness and vileness. The churches and towers in which people were wont to praise God became places in which they confessed to and called upon Muhammad. The vestments and chalices and other vessels of the sanctuaries were put to evil uses, and were fouled by the unbelievers. Our enemies wasted the whole land, razed dwellings, killed people, burned cities, and cut down trees and vineyards and everything else they found. So widely did this pestilence and destruction spread that there did not remain in all Spain a single episcopal city that was not burned or razed or occupied by the Moors; for the cities which the Arabs were not able to capture, they deceived and took over by false terms of capitulation. Oppa, son of King Egica, Archbishop of Seville, went about preaching to the Christians that they should go over to the Moors and

los moros et uisquiessen so ellos et les diessen tributo; e si por uentura ouiesse Dios dellos merçed et acorriesse a la tierra, que darien ellos ayuda a los que acorriessen. Et por tal encubierta fueron los omnes engannados, e dieron los castiellos et las fortalezas de las uillas; et fincaron los cristianos mezclados con los alaraues, et aquellos ouieron nombre dalli adelante moçaraues por que uiuien de buelta con ellos, e este nombre et el linnage dura oy en dia entre los toledanos. Los moros por este enganno prisieron toda la tierra; et pues que la ouieron en su poder, crebantaron toda la pleytesia et robaron las eglesias et los omnes, et leuaron todos los tesoros dellos et tod ell auer de la tierra, que non finco y nada sinon los obispos que fuxieron con las reliquias et se acogieron a las Asturias. Quanto mal sufrio aquella grand Babilonna, que fue la primera et la mayoral en todos los regnos del mundo, quanto fue destroyda del rey Çiro et del rey Dario, si non tanto que el destroymiento de Babilonna dura por siempre et non moran y sinon bestias brauas et sierpes; e quanto mal sufrio Roma, que era sennora de todas las tierras, quando la priso et la destruxo Alarigo et despues Adaulpho reys de los godos, desi Genserico rey de los vuandalos; e quanto mal sufrio Iherusalem que segund la propheçia de Nuestro Sennor Ihesu Cristo fue derribada et quemada que non finco en ella piedra sobre piedra; e quanto mal sufrio aquella noble Cartago quando la priso et la quemo Scipion consul de Roma, dos tanto mal et mas que aquesta sufrio la mezquina de Espanna, ca en ella se ayuntaron todas estas cuitas et estas tribulaçiones et aun mas desto, en guisa que non finco y ninguno que della ouiesse duelo. [...]

E digamos agora onde le uino esta cueta et este mal et por qual razon: Todos los omnes del mundo se forman et se assemeian a manera de su rey, e por ende los que fueron en tiempo del rey Vitiza et del rey Rodrigo, que fue el postrimero rey de los godos, et de los otros reys que fueron ante dellos et de quales algunos fueron alçados reys por aleue, algunos por trayçion de muerte de sus hermanos o de sus parientes, non guardando la uerdad nin el derecho que deuieran y guardar por quexa de ganar el sennorio mal et tortiçieramientre como non deuien, por ende los otros omnes que fueron otrossi en sus tiempos dellos formaron se con ellos et semeiaron les en los peccados; e por esta razon auiuose la yra de Dios sobrellos, et desamparoles la tierra que les mantouiera et guardara fasta alli, et tollio dellos la su graçia. E pero que Dios les sofrira en la heregia arriana desdel tiempo dell emperador Valent fastal tiempo del rey Recaredo, como dixiemos ya ante desto en la estoria, essora fue ya yrado por las nemigas de Vitiza et por las auolezas de los otros reys, et non les quiso mas sofrir nin los quiso mantener.

live under their rule and pay them tribute, saying that if perchance God should take pity on them and come to the aid of the kingdom, then they would help those coming to their aid. By this trick men were deceived, and handed over the castles and the fortified positions inside the towns. The Christians mingled with the Arabs, and thenceforth acquired the name of Mozarabs because they lived among them; this name and this race survive to this day among the Toledans. By this ruse the Moors took the whole kingdom; but once they had it in their power, they broke the agreement and robbed churches and people, and carried off all the treasures and wealth of the country, so that nothing was left in it, except that the bishops were able to flee with their relics and take refuge in Asturias. How much harm did great Babylon suffer, she being the first and greatest of all the kingdoms of the earth, when she was destroyed by King Cyrus and King Darius, to the extent that the destruction of Babylon has lasted for ever and nothing dwells there except wild beasts and serpents. And how much harm did Rome suffer, she who was mistress of all lands, when she was taken and destroyed by Alaric and then Ataulfo, kings of the Goths, and then by Genseric, king of the Vandals. And how much harm did Jerusalem suffer, when, as was prophesied by our Lord Jesus Christ, she was cast down and burned and left with no stone standing upon another. And how much harm was suffered by noble Carthage when Scipio, the Roman consul, took and burned her. Twice as much and more did wretched Spain suffer, for in her all these troubles and sufferings came together, and worse, to the extent that there was none left to grieve for her. [...]

Let us now show whence and for what reason all this trouble and this evil came upon her. All the people in the world are formed and shaped in the likeness of their kings. In the time of King Witiza and King Roderick, who was the last king of the Goths, and in the time of the other kings who came before them, there were some who were raised to the throne by treachery, and others by the treacherous murder of their brothers or other relatives, observing neither the truth nor the right of succession which should have applied (they being urged on in evil and twisted fashion to win the crown for themselves). Hence the other men who lived in those times formed themselves on those models and resembled them in their sins; and for this reason the wrath of God was stirred up against them, and He abandoned the land which He had maintained and protected for them up to that point, and took away His grace from them. And even though God had tolerated them in their Arrian heresy from the time of Emperor Valens up to the time of King Recared, as we have mentioned earlier in this history, He was later angered by the crimes of Witiza and the treacheries of the other kings, and He would no longer tolerate them nor protect them.

## 6. The occupation and the first resistance (711–22)

*These extracts are taken from the Chronicle of Alfonso III of Asturias (866–910), composed or finished in 883, and probably the work of the King himself; the monarch is described in a contemporary text as 'scientia clarus', 'famous in learning'. The chronicle survives in two redactions, the earlier and better now being considered to be the 'Rotense' (of Roda), from which the extracts are taken according to the edition by Juan Gil Fernández and others, Crónicas asturianas (Oviedo, 1985); see also Vázquez de Parga, pp. 21–27.*

*This chronicle is firm in attributing the disaster of 711 to the sins of the Goths and the treachery of the sons of Witiza: God punished the people accordingly. The text then concentrates upon Pelayo as the first resistance leader. In this account he is simply a prominent nobleman of the entourage of the dead King Roderick, and is eventually elected King of Asturias and, by implication, successor to Roderick on the throne of the Goths: a reasonable and probably accurate account, since the former Gothic monarchy had in principle been elective, even though later texts show desperate efforts being made to prove that Pelayo was of the blood–royal. An Arabic text explains Pelayo's presence in Cordova: he was of Asturian*

(7) Postquam Uitiza fuit defunctus, Rudericus in regno est perhunctus. Cuius tempore adhuc in peiori nequitia creuit Spania. Anno regni illius tertio ob causam fraudis filiorum Uitizani Sarrazeni ingressi sunt Spaniam. Quumque rex ingressum eorum cognouisset, statim cum exercitu egressus est eis ad uellum. Sed suorum peccatorum classe oppressi et filiorum Uitizani fraude detecti in fuga sunt uersi. Quo exercitus fugatus usque ad internicionem eo pene est deletus. Et quia derelinquerunt Dominum ne seruirent ei in iustitia et ueritatem, derelicti sunt a Domino ne auitarent terram desiderauilem. De Ruderico uero rege, cuius iam mentionem fecimus, non certum cognouimus interitum eius. Rudis namque nostris temporibus quum ciuitas Uiseo et suburbis eius iussum nostrum esset populatus, in quadam ibi baselica monumentus inuentus est, ubi desuper epitafion huiusmodi est conscriptus: 'Hic requiescit Rudericus ultimus rex Gotorum'. Sed redeamus ad illum tempus quo Sarrazeni Spaniam sunt adgressi.

(8) III Idus Nouembris era DCCLII Araues tamen regionem simul et regno opresso plures gladio interfecerunt, relicos uero pacis federe blandiendo siui subiugauerunt. Urbs quoque Toletana, cunctarum gentium uictris, Ismaeliticis triumfis uicta subcubuit et eis subiugata deseruit. Per omnes prouincias Spanie prefectos posuerunt et pluribus annis Bauilonico regi tributa persolberunt quousque sibi regem elegerunt, et Cordoba urbem patriciam regnum sibi firmaberunt. Per idem ferre tempus in hac regione Asturiensium prefectus erat in ciuitate Ieione nomine Munnuza conpar Tarec. Ipso quoque prefecturam agente, Pelagius quidam, spatarius Uitizani et

*origin (probably, it has been suggested, dux or governor of that province at the time of the Muslim invasion), and was taken to Cordova as a hostage for the good behaviour of the people of the region.*

*Although it has been thought that Covadonga was the theme of an early vernacular epic, adapted here in the chronicle account, it is clear that the text is solidly ecclesiastical in inspiration and sense. Some of the phrasing is from Augustine, Gregory of Tours, etc., but the essential models are biblical: Oppa addresses Pelayo in terms of I Samuel 3.4, etc., Pelayo directly quotes Matthew 13.31, and so on. The miracle of the missiles turned back on those who fired them repeats the miracle of the arrows in the legend of Saints Cosme and Damian, present in the 'Mozarabic' liturgical cycle, and the final sentence of this extract shows that Asturians were encouraged to think of themselves as modern Israelites fighting battles under God's special protection.*

*Covadonga has long been a national shrine. The 'window' in the cave presumably shows that a building already existed in the mouth of the cave in the 9th century. The episode, with all its legendary and spiritual accretions, is absolutely fundamental in the history or story of what was to become the Spanish people.*

(7) After Witiza died, Roderick was anointed King. In his time Spain plunged deeper into iniquity. In the third year of his reign, by the treachery of the sons of Witiza, the Saracens invaded Spain. When the King learned of the invasion he went out at once with his army to do battle with them; but, oppressed with the burden of their sins and betrayed by the treachery of the sons of Witiza, they turned in flight, and the army was nearly exterminated in the rout. Because they had abandoned the Lord and had not served Him in righteousness and truth, they were abandoned by the Lord and were not allowed to dwell in the promised land. As for King Roderick, whom we mentioned earlier, we never learned anything definite about his death. In our own uncultivated times, when the city of Viseo and its outlying areas were settled by our order, there was found a tombstone in a certain church, with an epitaph upon it as follows: 'Here lies Roderick, last King of the Goths'. But let us return to the time when the Saracens entered Spain.

(8) On 11 November 714 the Arabs, having dominated the land together with the kingdom, killed many and brought the rest under their control, winning them over with a peace treaty. Even the city of Toledo, victorious over all peoples, fell in defeat to the triumphs of the Ishmaelites and was subjugated to them. They placed governors in all the provinces of Spain and for some years paid tribute to the King of Babylon, until they chose a ruler for themselves, and established his realm in the noble city of Cordova. At about the same time a man named Munnuza, a colleague of Tariq's, was governor of Gijón in this region of Asturias. During his governorship a certain Pelayo, sword—bearer of Kings Witiza and Roderick,

Ruderici regum, dicione Ismaelitarum oppressus cum propria sorore Asturias est ingressus. Qui supra nominatus Munnuza prefatum Pelagium ob occassionem sororis eius legationis causa Cordoua misit; sed antequam rediret, per quodam ingenium sororem illius sibi in coniungio sociauit. Quo ille dum reuertit, nulatenus consentit, set quod iam cogitauerat de salbationem eclesie cum omni animositate agere festinauit. Tunc nefandus Tarec ad prefatum Munnuza milites direxit, qui Pelagium conprehenderent et Cordoua usque ferrum uinctum perducerent. Qui dum Asturias peruenissent uolentes eum fraudulenter conprendere, in uico cui nomen erat Brece per quendam amicum Pelagium manifestum est consilio Caldeorum. Sed quia Sarrazeni plures erant, uidens se non posse eis resistere de inter illis paulatim exiens cursum arripuit et ad ripam flubii Pianonie peruenit. Que foris litus plenum inuenit, sed natandi adminiculum super equum quod sedebat ad aliam ripam se transtulit et montem ascendit. Quem Sarrazeni persequere cessaberunt. Ille quidem montana petens, quantoscumque ad concilium properantes inuenit, secum adiuncxit adque ad montem magnum, cui nomen est Aseuua, ascendit et in latere montis antrum quod sciebat tutissimum se contulit; ex qua spelunca magna flubius egreditur nomine Enna. Qui per omnes Astores mandatum dirigens, in unum colecti sunt et sibi Pelagium principem elegerunt. Quo audito, milites qui eum conprehendere uenerant Cordoua reuersi regi suo omnia retulerunt. Pelagium, de quo Munnuza suggessionem fecerat, manifestum esse reuellem. Quo ut rex audiuit, uessanie ira commotus hoste innumerauilem ex omni Spania exire precepit et Alcamanem sibi socium super exercitum posuit; Oppanem quendam, Toletane sedis episcopum, filium Uitizani regis ob cuius fraudem Goti perierunt, eum cum Alkamanem in exercitum Asturias adire precepit. Qui Alkama sic a consorte suo consilio aceperat ut, si episcopo Pelagius consentire noluisset, fortitudine prelii captus Cordoua usque fuisset adductus. Uenientesque cum omni exercitu CLXXXVII ferre milia armatorum Asturias sunt ingressi.

(9) Pelagius uero in montem erat Asseuua cum sociis suis. Exercitus uero ad eum perrexit et ante ostium cobe innumera fixerunt temptoria. Predictus uero Oppa episcopus in tumulo ascendens ante coba dominica Pelagium sic adloquitur, dicens: 'Pelagi, Pelagi, ubi es?' Qui ex fenestra respondens ait: 'Adsum.' Cui episcopo: 'Puto te non latere, confrater et fili, qualiter omnis Spania dudum in uno ordine sub regimine Gotorum esset ordinata et pre ceteris terris doctrina atque scientia rutilaret. Et quum, ut supra dixi, omnis exercitus Gotorum esset congregatus, Ismaelitarum non ualuit sustinere impetum; quamto magis tu in isto montis cacumine defendere te poteris, quod mici difficile uidetur. Immo audi consilium meum at ab hac uolumtate animum reuoca, ut multis uonis utaris et consortia Caldeorum fruaris.' Ad hec Pelagius respondit: 'Non legisti in scripturis diuinis quia eclesia Domini ad granum sinapis deuenitur et inde rursus per Domini misericordia in magis erigitur?' Episcopus respondit: 'Uere scriptum sic est.'

worn down by the rule of the Ishmaelites, took refuge in Asturias with his sister. The aforementioned Munnuza sent Pelayo on a pretended mission to Cordova, [his true motive] concerning Pelayo's sister; but before he got back, Munnuza by some ruse married the sister. When Pelayo returned, he in no way approved of this, but with great resolution hastened to put into effect what he had already planned for the salvation of the Church. Then the villainous Tariq sent soldiers to Munnuza with orders to arrest Pelayo and take him in fetters to Cordova. When they reached Asturias intending to arrest him by trickery, in a village called Brece, Pelayo was told of the Chaldeans' plan by a friend. Since the Saracens were many, he realized that he could not hold out against them, but managed to slip away from them, rode off and reached the bank of the River Piloña. He found this in spate, but by swimming beside his horse he reached the opposite bank and climbed the mountain beyond. Then the Saracens gave up their pursuit. Pelayo went deeper into the mountains, and bringing together all those he found on their way to a council meeting, he climbed a high mountain named Aseuva, and took refuge in a cave on the hillside which he knew to be safe. From this cave there flows a considerable stream, by name Enna. Then he sent his orders to all the Asturians, who gathered and chose Pelayo as their leader. On hearing this, the soldiers who had come to capture him went back to Cordova and reported it all to their King: that Pelayo, about whom Munnuza had sent a request, was in open rebellion. When the King heard this he was greatly angered, and ordered a large army to be formed from all al−Andalus, placing his colleague al−Qama in command of it; and he ordered Oppa, Bishop of the see of Toledo, the son of Witiza by whose treachery the Goths had perished, to go to Asturias with al−Qama and the army. Al−Qama had received from his colleague the advice that, if Pelayo should refuse to obey the bishop, he should be taken in battle and brought to Cordova. They entered Asturias with an army of about 185,000 soldiers.

(9) Pelayo stayed on Aseuva mountain with his comrades. The enemy army arrived there and pitched a huge number of tents before the mouth of the cave. Then the aforementioned bishop Oppa climbed on to a hillock in front of the Covadonga cave and addressed Pelayo, saying: 'Pelayo, Pelayo, where are you?' Pelayo answered him from a window: 'Here I am.' The bishop then said: 'My son, I think you are not unaware that all Spain was formerly governed as one realm under the rule of the Goths, and outshone all other lands in wisdom and learning. Also, as I said before, that the whole army of the Goths when gathered together was not strong enough to withstand the onrush of the Ishmaelites. How will you therefore be able to defend yourself on the peak of this mountain, which seems impossible to me! Listen to my advice and banish this intention from your mind, in order to enjoy many good things and the friendship of the Chaldeans.' To this Pelayo replied: 'Have you not read in Holy Scripture that the Church of God can become as small as a grain of mustard and can then, by God's grace, be made to grow again much larger?' The bishop answered: 'Indeed

Pelagius dixit: 'Spes nostra Xps est quod per istum modicum monticulum quem conspicis sit Spanie salus et Gotorum gentis exercitus reparatus. Confido enim quod promissio Domini impleatur in nobis quod dictum est per David: "Uisitauo in uirga iniquitates eorum et in flagellis peccata eorum; misericordia autem meam non abertam ab eis." Et nunc ex oc fidens in misericordia Ihesu Xpi hanc multitudinem despicio et minime pertimesco. Prelium ergo quam tu minas nobis, habemus aduocatum aput Patrem Dominum Ihesum Xpm, qui ab istis paucis potens est liuerare nos.' Et conuersus episcopus ad exercitum dixit: 'Properate et pugnate. Uos enim audistis qualiter mici respondit. Ut uolumtatem eius preuideo, nisi per gladii uindicta non habetis cum eo pacis federe.'

(10) Iam nunc uero prefatus Alkama iubet comitti prelium. Arma adsumunt, eriguntur fundiuali, abtantur funde, migantur enses, crispantur aste hac incessanter emittuntur sagitte. Sed in hoc non defuisse Domini magnalia, nam quum lapides egresse essent a fundiualis et ad domum sancte uirginis Marie peruenissent, qui intus est in coba, super mittentes reuertebant et Caldeos fortiter trucidabant. Et quia Dominus non dinumerat astas, set cui uult porrigit palmas, egressisque de coba ad pugnam, Caldei conuersi sunt in fugam et in duabus diuisi sunt turmas. Ubique statim Oppa episcopus est conprehensus et Alkama interfectus. In eodem namque loco CXXIIII milia ex Caldeis sunt interfecti, sexaginta uero et tria milia qui remanserunt in uertize montis Aseuua ascenderunt atque per locum Amossa ad Liuianam descenderunt. Set nec ipsi Domini euaserunt uindictam. Quumque per uerticem montis pergerent, qui est super ripam fluminis cui nomen est Deua, iuxta uillam qui dicitur Causegaudia, sin iudicio Domini hactum est, ut mons ipse a fundamentis se rebolbens LX$^a$ tria milia uirorum in flumine proiecit et ibi eos omnes mons ipse opressit, ubi nunc ipse flumen, dum limite suo requirit, ex eis multa signa euidentia ostendit. Non istut inannem aut fabulosum putetis, sed recordamini quia, qui Rubri Maris fluenta ad transitum filiorum Israhel aperuit, ipse hos Arabes persequentes eclesiam Domini immenso montis mole oppressit.

it is so written.' Pelayo said: 'Christ is our hope, that by this tiny hillock which you see, Spain may be saved and the army of the Gothic people restored. I trust therefore that the promise of the Lord may be fulfilled in us as it was announced through David: "With the rod I will punish their iniquities, and with whips their sins; but I will not take my pity away from them." Now I, trusting in the pity of Jesus Christ, scorn this host and fear it hardly at all. In the battle with which you are threatening us, we have our Lord Jesus Christ as our advocate before the Father, and He is powerful enough to save us few from them.' Turning to his army the bishop said: 'Move forward and fight. You have heard how he answered me. As I judge their intentions, you will get no peace agreement from him except by force of arms.'

(10) Then al—Qama orders battle to be joined. They take up arms, catapults are aimed, slings are made ready, swords flash, spears are brandished and arrows are repeatedly loosed. 'Yet in this the greatness of the Lord was not lacking': for as the stones left the catapults and were about to strike the shrine of St Mary the Virgin, which is inside the cave, they turned back on those who had fired them and wrought great loss of life upon the Chaldeans. And since the Lord makes no count of spears, but holds out palms to whomsoever He will, when the Christians emerged from the cave to fight, the Chaldeans turned to flee and divided into two groups. There Oppa the bishop was at once captured and al—Qama was killed. In that same place 124,000 of the Chaldeans were killed, and the remaining 63,000 climbed to the peak of Mount Aseuva and by way of Amuesa went down to Liébana. But not even these escaped the vengeance of the Lord. As they were proceeding along the ridge of the mountain, which hangs over the bank of the River Deva, near Cosgaya village, the judgement of God brought it about that the mountain, turning upon its foundations, cast 63,000 men into the river, and then the mountain itself fell upon all of them; and there the river, when it returns to its bed, now reveals many obvious signs of them. Do not think this vain or fabulous, for remember that He who opened the waters of the Red Sea to allow the passage of the children of Israel, buried these Arabs who were persecuting the Church of God under the immense mass of the mountain.

## 7. Charlemagne in Spain (778)

*The* Chanson de Roland. *whose materials had evolved over the centuries in monkish texts and popular legend and possibly verse of various kinds, survives for us in seven versions or fragments of versions (among the dozens or scores that may have existed). The earliest and most impressive of these is the version by 'Turoldus' in the MS now at Oxford. Its date of composition is debated, but it makes obvious sense to put this date at about 1100 and to relate the composition to the First Crusade: the story of Charlemagne's high endeavour against the infidels of Spain in 778 is gloriously evoked in order to inspire the crusaders in the Holy Land. This is a text which echoed like a trumpet—call all over Europe in its original language, in translations and adaptations, and the call to arms is nowhere clearer than in the first laisse of the poem, here reproduced.*

*The Charlemagne myth had many ramifications. The tragically unsuccessful expedition of 778 with its strictly limited objectives in Navarre, so muted and palliated by the Carolingian court chroniclers, was on one level transformed in vernacular verse into an epic martyrdom (Roland taken up into heaven) and a divinely—aided vengeance (Charlemagne's final defeat of Baligant). Spaniards had no objection to adopting this in their* Roncesvalles *poem — early 14th century? — and in their ballad literature; although on this level also they produced a nationalistic counterblast by creating their epic of* Bernardo del Carpio *whose existence is first recorded in a text of 1236. What was said by chroniclers and monks in authoritative Latin prose had to be taken more seriously. In 1028 Adhémar de Chabannes held that Charlemagne had conquered all Spain. About 1140, the* Historia Turpini *(on which see text*

Carles li reis, nostre emperere magnes,
Set anz tuz pleins ad estét en Espaigne.
Tresqu'en la mer cunquist la tere altaigne.
N'i ad castel ki devant lui remaigne,
Mur ne citét n'i est remés a fraindre,
Fors Sarraguce, ki est en une muntaigne;
Li reis Marsilie la tient ki Deu nen aimet,
Mahumet sert e Apollin recleimet;
Ne·s poet guarder que mals ne l'i ateignet.     AOI

*said that Charlemagne had a vision of St James in which the Apostle revealed to the Emperor that he was buried in Santiago de Compostela, urging him to free the land from infidels; this Charlemagne did, becoming the first pilgrim to this great shrine. This was acceptable enough in Santiago, whose clergy had collaborated with French monks in the production of the* Liber Sancti Jacobi *(including the* Historia Turpini*), but elsewhere in Spain feelings were aroused, in the interests of national pride rather than of historical accuracy. In the mid—12th century the author of the* Historia Seminensis *(a monk writing probably in the city of León) remarked severely that Charlemagne 'Inde cum Cesaraugustam ciuitatem accessisset, more Francorum auro corruptus, absque vilo sudore pro eripienda a barbarorum dominatione santa ecclesia, ad propria reuertitur' ('Then, when he reached Saragossa, he was bought off with gold as is the way with the Franks, and without sweating uncomfortably to rescue the Church from the rule of the infidels, he went home'), adding for good measure that 'Anelebat etenim Carolus in termis illis citius lauari, quos Grani ad hoc opus delitiose construxerat' ('Charles badly wanted to wash himself as soon as possible in the ·baths which he had luxuriously built at Aix—la—Chapelle for this purpose'). In Catalonia, conquered as far as Barcelona by Charlemagne's son in 800—801, efforts were made at the same time to reject much larger claims about the extent of the Emperor's conquests (see text 9).*

*A substantial selection of Old French epic texts concerning action against the Moors in Spain could readily be made, but it would illustrate nothing much beyond a set of tediously repeated commonplaces having little to do with reality. See Norman Daniel,* Heroes and Saracens: an interpretation of the Chansons de Geste *(Edinburgh, 1984).*

Charles the king, our great emperor,
has been in Spain seven long years:
he has conquered the proud land as far as the sea.
There is no castle that can stand before him,
no wall or city remaining to be broken down,
except Saragossa, which stands on a mountain.
King Marsilie, who loves not God, is master of it;
he serves Muhammad and calls upon Apollo;
he cannot save himself from harm which must befall him.

### 8.  Charlemagne converts the infidels (late 8th century)

*The* Liber Sancti Jacobi *(also known as the* Codex Calixtinus, *from a prime MS of Compostela) was one of the most influential works of the Middle Ages.  It was composed, or perhaps its parts were assembled and revised, in about 1140, and the revision at least may have been done by that Aymeri Picaud whose name is the only one associated with the production.  The tendency at one time was to associate the composition with the great Burgundian abbey of Cluny, but more recently a connection with the abbey of Saint—Denis at Paris is suggested.  The aim of the work was chiefly to propagate the cult of St James and especially the pilgrimage to what was claimed to be his tomb at Compostela: thus Book I consists of 31 sermons on Jacobean themes, Book 2 has 22 miracles of St James, Book 3 has four diverse Jacobean items, and Book 5 is the famous Pilgrims' Guide for those crossing France and N. Spain, which is followed by hymns, epistles, further miracles, etc.*

*Book 4 of the* Liber *is the* Historia Turpini: *the spurious memoir of Turpin, Archbishop of Rheims, who in the* Chanson de Roland *tradition dies with the Peers and the rest of the rearguard at Roncevaux, but who here survives (after recovering from wounds) to write his true account, in authoritative Latin prose as befits a high churchman, of what Charlemagne really achieved in Spain.  The account is naturally military in part — of a very simple—minded kind — and in part geographical too, since chapter 3 is a detailed survey of Spain, but this is handled in such a fashion that one can assert its author had probably never been there.  But the chief purpose seems to have been to assert Charlemagne's reputation as a great Christian patriarch who wanted to conquer lands for Christianity, defeat the infidel and if possible convert him.  This is the theme of chapter 12, here reproduced.  It is not the only theological exposition in the text, for in chapter 17, Roland explains to the docile Muslim giant Ferracutus the*

Itaque datis inter se trebis, egressus est Aigolandus cum suis exercitibus ab urbe, et dimissis illis iuxta urbem uenit cum sexaginta e maioribus suis ante Karoli tribunal, qui cum suis exercitibus uno miliario ab urbe distabat. Et erat tunc exercitus Aigolandi et exercitus Karoli in quodam plano loco et obtimo qui est iuxta urbem, habens in longitudine et latitudine sex miliaria. Uia Iacobitana diuidebat utrumque exercitum.  Tunc dixit Karolus Aigolando: 'Tu es Aigolandus qui terram meam fraudulenter a me abstulisti.  Tellurem Hispanicam et Gasconicam brachio inuincibili potentie Dei adquisiui, Christianis legibus subiugaui, omnesque eius reges meo imperio euerti.  Tu autem Dei Christianos, me ad Galliam remeante, peremisti, meas urbes et castella deuastasti, totamque terram igne et gladio combusisti, unde multum conqueror in presenti'.  Mox ut Aigolandus agnouit loquelam suam

*essential beliefs of Christianity: the Trinity, the Virgin Birth, the Resurrection.*
*Already in the 12th century, the* Historia Turpini *was being copied separately from the rest of the* Liber, *and was enormously influential in European historiography well into the 15th century. Over 100 MSS survive, together with vernacular translations, including a Galician one of the 14th century in a collection entitled* Miragres de Santiago. *The objective of encouraging the pilgrimage was certainly achieved, for millions from all over Europe made the journey, and the see of Compostela for a time rivalled Toledo in dignity and wealth.*
*Aigolandus appears first in chapter 6: '... quidam paganus rex Affricanus nomine Aigolandus cum suis exercitibus terram Yspanorum sibi adquisivit.' In chapter 9 he gathers a vast army from all parts. Chapter 12 is headed 'De disputacione Karoli et Aigolandi'. The discussion is only made possible by the Emperor's knowledge of Arabic, as explained in our text: this shows that the writer was acquainted with the legend, and perhaps already the poem, of* Mainet, *in which the youthful Charles lives for a time in Moorish Toledo and wins the love of Princess Galiana, daughter of its ruler. The origin of both elements may lie in Spain itself, in that Alfonso VI of León spent some months in exile in Moorish Toledo in 1072 after defeat in battle by his brother Sancho of Castile, and later received as concubine the Sevillian Princess Sa'ida (on whom see text 21).*
*Chapter 12 of the* Historia Turpini *is taken from* Liber Sancti Jacobi *(Codex Calixtinus), ed. by W.M. Whitehill (Santiago de Compostela, 1944, 3 vols). A useful text with good notes is that of C. Meredith Jones (Paris, 1936), and more recently there is the study and edition by A. Hämel and A. de Mandach in the* Sitzungsberichte *of the Bayerische Akademie der Wissenschaften, Heft 1 of the 1965 volume; these are of the* Historia Turpini *alone.*

A truce being agreed, Aigolandus left the city with his forces, and, leaving them just outside the place, went forward with sixty of his chief men to the dais where Charles was seated, surrounded by his men, about a mile from the city. Both armies were thus stationed on a goodly plain close to the town, measuring about six miles in each direction. The Pilgrims' Way ran between the two armies. Then Charles said to Aigolandus: 'You are Aigolandus who deceitfully stole my lands from me. I took the lands of Spain and Gascony aided by the invincible strength of the power of God, and brought it all under Christian rule, and asserted my dominion over all their kings. But while I was in Gaul you destroyed God's Christian peoples, and ravaged my cities and castles, and wasted all the land with fire and sword, all of which now gives me great cause for complaint.' Aigolandus at once understood Charles's Arabic speech, and was amazed and overjoyed to hear it (Charles had learned the language in Toledo, where he had lived for some time in his youth). Then Aigolandus

Arabicam, quam Karolus loquebatur, miratus est multum et gauisus est. Didicerat enim Karolus linguam Sarracenicam apud urbem Toletam, in qua cum esset iuuenis per aliquot tempus commoratus est. Tunc Aigolandus Karolo: 'Obsecro', inquit, 'ut michi tantum dicas cur terram que iure hereditario tibi non contingit, aut pater tuus, aut auus, aut abauus, aut atauus non possedit, a nostra gente abstulisti?' 'Ideo', inquit Karolus, 'quod dominus noster Ihesus Christus, creator celi et terre, gentem nostram, scilicet Christianam, pre omnibus gentibus elegit et super omnes gentes totius mundi eam dominari instituit, tuam gentem Sarracenicam legi nostre in quantum potui conuerti.' 'Ualde indignum est', inquit Aigolandus, 'ut gens nostra tue genti subiaceat, cum lex nostra magis quam uestra ualeat. Nos habemus Mahummet qui Dei nuncius fuit nobis a Deo missus, cuius precepta tenemus; immo deos omnipotentes habemus qui iussu Mahummet nobis futura manifestant, quos colimus, per quos uiuimus et regnamus.' 'Aigolande', inquit Karolus, 'in hoc erras, quia nos Dei mandata tenemus; uos uani hominis precepta uana tenetis; nos Deum Patrem et Filium et Spiritum Sanctum credimus et adoramus; uos diabolum in simulachris uestris et creditis et adoratis. Anime nostre per fidem quam tenemus post mortem ad paradisum et ad uitam perhennem tendunt; uestre anime ad Orcum profiscuntur. Unde patet quia magis ualet lex nostra quam uestra. Quapropter aut babtismum accipe tu et gens tua et uiue, aut ueni in bello erga me et necem pessimam accipe.' 'Absit a me', inquit Aigolandus, 'ut babtismum accipiam, et Mahummet deum meum omnipotentem abnegem, sed pugnabo ego et gens mea contra te et gentem tuam tali pacto quod si lex nostra magis Deo est placita quam uestra ut nos conuincamus uos, et si lex uestra magis ualeat quam nostra ut uos conuincatis nos. Et sit usque in ultimo die uictis opprobrium, inuictis autem laus et exultatio in sempiternum. Insuper, si gens mea conuincitur, ego babtismum accipiam si uiuere possum.'

Quod ex utraque parte conceditur. Statim eliguntur uiginti milites Christiani contra uiginti ex Sarracenis in campo belli, et tali pacto ceperunt debellari. Quid plura? Ilico interfecti sunt omnes Sarraceni. Inde mittuntur quadraginta contra quadraginta, et perimuntur Sarraceni. Postea mittuntur centum contra centum et statim fugientes retro Christiani interficiuntur, ideo quod mori timentes fugerunt. Hii uero tipum gerunt certantium fidelium Christi, quia, qui pro Dei fide uolunt pugnare, nullo modo debent retro abire. Et sic illi ideo occiduntur quia retro fugerunt; sic Christi fideles, qui debent fortiter contra uicia pugnare, si retro reuersi fuerint, in uiciis turpiter moriuntur. Sed qui bene contra uicia pugnant, ni inimicos, id est demones qui uicia administrant, leuiter occidunt. Non coronabitur quis, inquit apostolus, nisi qui legitime certauerit.

Inde mittuntur ducenti contra ducentos, et interficiuntur omnes Sarraceni. Denique mittuntur mille contra mille, et occiduntur ilico omnes Sarraceni. Tunc, data ex utraque parte treba, uenit Aigolandus ad loquendum ad Karolum, affirmans legem Christianorum meliorem esse quam

said to Charles: 'I ask you to tell me why you took from our people lands which by no hereditary right had ever belonged to you, or your father, or grandfather, or great−grandfather, or great−great−grandfather.' 'I did it because Our Lord Jesus Christ, creator of heaven and earth, chose our people − that is the Christians − over all others, and ordered them to rule over all the peoples of the world, and as far as possible to convert your Saracen people to our law.' 'But' − said Aigolandus − 'it is shameful that our people should live under yours, for our law is better than yours. We have Muhammad, who was God's messenger to us, sent by God, and we obey his commands. More concretely, we have other all−powerful gods who, by Muhammad's order, show us what is to be done; these we worship, and through them we live and reign.' 'Aigolandus' − said Charles − 'you are wrong in this; for we keep God's commandments, while you follow the empty precepts of a useless man; we worship and believe in God the Father, God the Son, and God the Holy Ghost, whereas you believe in the devil and worship him at your shrines. Our souls, by the faith which we hold, go after death to paradise and to life everlasting; your souls go to the underworld. So it is plain that our religion is better than yours. Now: either you and your people accept baptism, and live, or meet me in battle and go to a grievous death.' 'Far be it from me' − said Aigolandus − 'to accept baptism and to renounce my almighty God Muhammad, but I and my people will fight against you and yours, on the understanding that if our law is more pleasing to God we shall prove you wrong, and if your law prevails against ours you shall prove us wrong. Let shame lie upon the vanquished till the last day, and for the victors let there be praise and joy everlastingly. Furthermore: if my people are shown to be in the wrong, I will accept baptism if I am alive to do so.'

This was agreed by both sides. Immediately twenty Christian knights were chosen to fight against twenty Saracens, and they began to do battle under the terms of the agreement. What next? All the Saracens were killed at once. Then forty were sent against forty, and all the Saracens perished. Then a hundred were sent against a hundred, and all the Moors died. Again a hundred were sent against a hundred, and this time the Christians, turning in flight in fear of death, were killed. These latter bore no more than the semblance of Christ's faithful followers, for those who wish to fight for the faith in no wise should turn their backs. Thus it is that those who turn to flee are killed; and Christ's faithful, who should battle strongly against vices, if they turn their backs, die in foul vices. But those who battle well against vices, find it easy to kill their enemies, that is the devils who propagate vices. No−one shall be crowned in heaven, says the Apostle, except those who struggle manfully.

Then two hundred were sent against two hundred, and all the Saracens were killed. Then a thousand against a thousand, with the same result. Finally, a truce being agreed on both sides, Aigolandus came to speak to Charles, confessing that the Christian religion was superior to that of the

Sarracenorum. Et pollicitus est Karolo quod die crastina babtismum ipse et gens sua acciperet. Itaque rediit ad gentem suam et dixit regibus et maioribus suis se uelle babtismum accipere. Et precepit cunctis gentibus suis ut babtizarentur omnes. Quod alii concesserunt, alii renuerunt.

Saracens. And he promised that the following day he and his men would be baptized. Then he returned to his people and told the leaders and chief men that he wished to accept baptism, ordering all his people to be baptized also. Some agreed, others did not.

## 9. The Franks take Gerona (786)

*In 785 or soon after the important town of Gerona, in Catalonia on the main route from what is now the French border to Barcelona (which was to be taken by the Franks later) passed into Frankish control. The circumstances are not known, but it is certain that Charlemagne himself was not present, since at the time he was campaigning against the Saxons. At no very great remove of time the belief (hardened into historical 'fact') grew up that Charlemagne, in miraculous circumstances, had liberated the city from the Moors. In the 10th century the Latin* Fragment of the Hague *concerns the siege of a Muslim city which was probably Gerona, and the personage Ernaut de Girone mentioned in it held the city and its region as his fief. He and his fief figure in several French* chansons de geste *later. Many other Latin texts produced in France and elsewhere in the 11th and 12th centuries credit this conquest, together with many others in Spain, to the Emperor. This piece of pseudohistory, doubtless of learned clerical origin, was adopted by the inhabitants of the city and embroidered in all kinds of ways, to the extent that in quite recent times inhabitants can point to local toponymy, spots related to military actions, etc., all associated with Charlemagne.*

*The Church eventually placed the massive stamp of its authority on all this. Charlemagne was canonized in 1165 by an anti—Pope, his feast being on 28 January. In 1345 one of nine chapels in the Cathedral of Gerona was set aside for him, and a statue of him was placed on its altar. There was composed a special liturgy for St Charlemagne, liberator of Gerona, consisting of a prayer and nine lessons, to be read at vespers and lauds on the feast—day in the Cathedral and in all churches of the*

[...]

**Lectio I.** Cupiens Sanctus Karolus Magnus Beati Jacobi apostoli monitis obedire disposuit ire versus Ispaniam et eam catholice fidei subjugare. Capta vero civitate Narbona et munita in qua Ispania inchoatur, perveniens ad terram Rossilionis que est principium Cathaloniae Christi auxilium et Beate Virginis humiliter imploravit.

**Lectio II.** Oratione vero completa intendens in coelum vidit Beatam Mariam Christum ejus filium defferentem. Vidit etiam Beatos Jacobum et Andream manentes unum a dextris et alium a sinistris. Quos cum inspiceret Sanctus Karolus stupens in splendoribus percepit Beatam Virginem sic loquentem: 'Ne paveas, Christi miles, Karole, braccium et deffensor Ecclesiae, quoniam nos tecum in bello erimus et liberabimus te cum victoria et salute.'

**Lectio III.** 'Sed cum montes transieris Pirineos obsidebis civitatem Gerundae et eam licet cum laboribus obtinebis. In qua ad mei honorem et

*diocese, and this was maintained until Sixtus IV (1471—84) prohibited it, presumably because of doubts about the validity of Charlemagne's canonization.   Later the text of the abandoned liturgy was expanded into a* Tractatus de captione Gerunde *composed to justify the tradition.   For centuries a panegyric of the Emperor continued to be recited in the Cathedral.   In 1883 the Bishop had the statue of Charlemagne removed from the altar.*

*Whereas (see text 7) serious historians in Castile and León in the 12th and 13th centuries took violent objection to claims from beyond the Pyrenees about Charlemagne's conquests in Spain, correctly limiting these to his activities in Navarre in 778 and to the capture of Barcelona by the Franks led by his son in 800—801, at extremes of the Peninsula — Compostela and Gerona — church authorities and local people clearly favoured the entirely fictitious association with Charlemagne as liberator. In such a context, a few anachronisms hardly matter: in this extract, Roland and Turpin evidently survived the slaughter at Roncevaux a few years earlier.   The chief concern of the person who composed the liturgy was, beyond Charlemagne's role, to emphasize divine aid and to give churches of the diocese a respectable antiquity and heroic founders.*

*There is a full study of the texts and the tradition by J. Coulet,* Etude sur l'office de Girone en l'honneur de Saint Charlemagne *(Montpellier, 1907), with the text of the Office (from which the extract is taken) on pp. 57—59, and of the* Tractatus *on pp. 77—82.   I have put the date '786' because it is under this year that the event figures in the* Chronicon Rivipullense *(= of Ripoll).   The response to each* lectio *is omitted.*

[...]

**Lesson I** Eager to obey the instructions of the Blessed Apostle, James [as explained at the start of the *Historia Turpini*: the Emperor was to liberate Spain and especially to free the route to the Apostle's tomb], St Charlemagne prepared to journey towards Spain and bring the country to the Catholic faith.   Having taken and fortified the city of Narbonne, where Spain begins, on reaching the Roussillon region which is the border of Catalonia he humbly prayed for the help of Christ and the Blessed Virgin.

**Lesson II** On ending his prayer he looked up to heaven and there beheld the Blessed Mary bearing the Christ—child.   He also saw the Blessed James and Andrew at her right hand and at her left.   When he saw them St Charlemagne was amazed at their brightness, and heard the Blessed Virgin say to him: 'Have no fear, Charles, soldier of Christ, arm and defender of the Church, for we shall be with you in war and will bring you to victory and safety.'

**Lesson III** 'When you have passed through the Pyrenees you will besiege the city of Gerona, and after much effort you will take it.   There in my honour you will build a cathedral.   I give you my blessing and will guide

reverentiam edificabis ecclesiam cathedralem. Benedicam tibi et dirigam te super omnes milites hujus mundi et habebis Sanctum Jacobum nepotem meum directorem et tocius Ispaniae protectorem.' Quibus dictis, disparuit visio premonstrata.

**Lectio IV.** Tunc Sanctus Karolus confortatus suum exercitum animavit et cum in fervore spiritus exercitum infidelium invasisset, ceperunt terga vertere et totis viribus fugere, non valentes resistere Christianis. Finaliter obtenta victoria in campo qui dicitur Milet edificavit ecclesiam sub invocatione Beati Andreae apostoli, in qua nunc religiosorum monasterium est constructum. Captis insuper castris et villis Vallispirii et cum ad locum qui dicitur Sa Clusa Sanctus Karolus devenisset, scivit regem Marcilium iterum fuisse inclusum. Ideoque ex tunc Sa Clusa vocatur qui Mons Acutus antea vocabatur.

**Lectio V.** Infidelibus tandem inde fugatis pervenit ad montis verticem qui vocatur Albarras (postea nominatus est Malpartus) ubi invenit resistentiam ne transiret. Tunc Sanctus Karolus aciem divisit per partes; unam per Collum de Panissas ubi ad honorem Sancti Martini ecclesiam fabricavit, aliam vero partem per abrupta montium destinavit. Sarraceni vero divisam aciem intuentes ceperunt fugere versus civitatem Gerundam timentes ne capti in medio remanerent inclusi.

**Lectio VI.** Quod audiens, Sanctus Karolus destruxit omnia fortalicia de quibus Christianis transeuntibus periculum imminebat. Qui persequendo impios versus Gerundam arripuit viam suam et perveniens ad locum de Ramis in honorem Sancti Juliani ecclesiam edificavit. Rotulandus etiam capellam Sanctae Teclae Virginis in eisdem terminis ordinavit. Beatus vero Turpinus Remensis archiepiscopus altare Sancti Vincentii ibidem exaltavit. [...]

**Lectio IX.** Recedens inde Sanctus Karolus rediit ad montem de Barufa qui est juxta vallem tenebrosam et obsedit civitatem Gerundae quam nequivit tunc capere licet eam multis vicibus debellasset. Contigit tamen, divina operante virtute, constat enim quadam die Veneris, hora completorii, coeli facie clarescente, crucem magnam et rubeam lumine undique adornatam super mesquitam civitatis Gerundae ubi nunc edificata est ecclesia cathedralis, per quatuor horas cunctis videntibus permansisse, guttas etiam sanguinis cecidisse.

you above all the soldiers of this world, and you will have St James, my nephew, as your general and as the protector of all Spain.' With these words, the vision faded.

**Lesson IV**  Then St Charlemagne, greatly encouraged, kindled enthusiasm in his men, and as they began to attack the infidel army with great fervour, the enemy began to turn their backs and flee as fast as they could, being powerless to resist the Christians.  After his victory, Charles built a church at Milet and dedicated it to the Blessed Apostle Andrew, where there is now a monastery.  When he had also taken the forts and villages of Vallis Spirii and had reached Sa Clusa, St Charlemagne learned that King Marsilie had shut himself up inside it.  That is why from that time onward it is called Sa Clusa, having earlier been called Montagut.

**Lesson V**  The infidels having fled from that, Charlemagne reached the hilltop of Albarras (later known as Malpartus [a mistaken form of Es Pertus]), where he found the enemy resisting his passage.  Then St Charlemagne divided his forces into two: he ordered one to go through the Coll de Panissas, where he built a church dedicated to St Martin, while he sent the other through a trackless area of the mountains.  The Saracens, realizing he had divided his forces and fearing they might be caught in a pincer movement, began to withdraw towards the city of Gerona.

**Lesson VI**  On learning this, St Charlemagne destroyed all the fortresses which might threaten danger to the Christians as they passed through. Then, pursuing the infidels towards Gerona, he reached Ramos, and built a church there in honour of St Julian.  In addition, Roland ordered a chapel to be built in the same place to St Tecla the Virgin; and Turpin, Archbishop of Rheims, raised an altar there to St Vincent.

[...]

**Lesson IX**  Moving on from there, St Charlemagne made his way to Barufa mountain, close by the dark valley [the Latin form may conceal a now lost place—name], from where he directed the siege of Gerona, being unable to capture it even though he attacked it constantly.  However, it happened that one Friday, by divine aid, at the hour of compline, the sky being full of brightness, there appeared over the mosque of Gerona (where the Cathedral now stands) a huge cross fringed on all sides by a red glow.  It remained there for four hours and was observed by everybody, drops of blood being seen to fall at the same time.

## 10. The martyrdom of Isaac de Tábanos (851)

*In the mid—9th century an extraordinary wave of fervour swept through the Christian community of Cordova and its region: priests, monks, and lay people sought a self—imposed martyrdom by publicly insulting Islam and reviling the name of Muhammad. The penalty automatically imposed for this was death, but the authorities seem to have given the offenders a chance to listen to reason and retract before ordering their execution (as in the present extract, when Isaac is offered the suggestion that he should plead he was drunk or temporarily deranged at the time of the offence). The first case was that of Perfecto in 850, and he was rapidly followed by others down to at least 857. A full record was made by (St) Eulogius of Cordova, himself eventually martyred on 11 March 859, in his Memoriale sanctorum, and also by Alvaro de Córdoba, friend and biographer of Eulogius, in his Indiculum luminosum composed in 854. Both these works were contributions to the passionate debate which raged among the Christians of al—Andalus about the legitimacy of this kind of martyrdom by self—immolation. Such voluntary seeking of death could not, it was said by some, allow Christians to count as martyrs and saints of the honoured kind which filled the Church's calendars. Eulogius himself recognized that a majority of clergy and laymen were opposed to such acts. What degree of pressure or persecution by the authorities, or what kind of passionate preaching contributed to the Christian fervour is unsure. The moderate party could assert: 'Is not the freedom of Christian worship guaranteed by the laws, and are we not indeed free to practise our*

Ego quidem volumen hoc Memoriale Sanctorum appellans, illis tantummodo ascysteriis commentaueram, e quibus prior ille monachorum globus ad resistendum mendacissimo vati processerat. Sed postquam ex urbibus, viculis, oppidiculis, et castellis certatim proruere ad hoc certamen viros ac mulieres cognoui, neque quenquam vereri praesidis tribunal comperi, sed omnes pro testamento et legibus Dei nostri mortem incunctanter elegisse conspexi, uniuersis illud ecclesiis supra solidissimam petram fundatis dicaui, ut tantum haberent cuncti de triumpho eorum suae consolationis et gloriae exemplum et gaudium, quantum fuit illos ex diuersis locis venisse, et in exemplum totius Ecclesiae discrimina passionum subiisse. Sed reor, quod inter ipsos haud dubie principatum obtinet sanctus Isaac monachus.

Qui prior e Tabanensi coenobio in forum descendens, iudicem adiit, atque his verbis eum aggreditur: 'Vellum', inquit, 'iudex, cultor fidei strenuus fieri, si modo tu non differres ordinem, rationemque eius mihi exponere.' Cui cum libenter, quasi iam tyrunculo fidei suae, credituro iuueni inflatis buccis, turgenti gutture, crepitantia infra caua palati verba institutionis lingua

*holy religion?' Eventually Abd—al—Rahman II, using powers he possessed as ruler, called a Council of the Church to try to resolve the problem. Recafredo, Metropolitan of Seville, presided, and the spokesman of the moderates was Gómez, a learned layman who held a post in the administration. The Council did not quite venture to resolve that those already put to death were not martyrs and saints in the full sense, but it did resolve to discourage a continuation of such acts by the Christian faithful: it was obviously unwise to provoke the Muslim authorities into action which might disturb the conditions of relative liberty and tolerance which Christians, although a subject people, enjoyed under the law. The eloquent and passionate pleading of Eulogius and Alvaro should be read as noble documents of the extremes of faith; it is uncritically adopted by Simonet in his very full account, chapters 13—17, and excerpts are translated by Sánchez—Albornoz, pp. 191—201. For a balanced account, see E.P. Colbert,* The Martyrs of Cordoba, 850—859 *(Washington, 1962), and, most recently, with full bibliography, K.B. Wolf,* Christian Martyrs in Muslim Spain *(Cambridge, 1988).*

*Tábanos is in the hills a few miles to the north of Cordova. Isaac was born in 824, of good Cordovese family.*

*The text is taken from Andreas Schott (ed.),* Hispania illustrata, *IV (Frankfurt, 1608), pp. 237—38. It is also in Vázquez de Parga, pp. 59—62. The complete text of Eulogius and texts of other Mozarabic writers are published by J. Gil,* Corpus Scriptorum Muzarabicorum *(Madrid, 1973, 2 vols).*

When entitling this volume A Record of the Saints, I had in mind only those monasteries from which the first body of monks had emerged to combat the lying prophet [i.e., Muhammad]. But when I heard that men and women were eagerly rushing from cities, hamlets, villages, and towns, to join in this struggle, and that none of them feared to face an accusation in the high court, and when I saw that all unhesitatingly chose to die as witnesses for the faith, I resolved to publish it in all our churches (founded on most solid rock), so that all might learn from and rejoice in their victory, since they had come from various places, and so that the variety of their sufferings should be an example for the whole Church. I think, however, that beyond doubt St Isaac the monk was the most notable of all of them.

When Isaac first went down into the public square [of Cordova] from his monastery at Tábanos [a few miles to the north of Cordova], he approached the judge and addressed him as follows: 'Your Honour, I wish to become an active supporter of the faith [i.e., Islam]: I beg you not to delay the order that I should be instructed therein.' The judge then spoke freely to him with his lying tongue, as though he were addressing a neophyte of his faith: with cheeks puffed out, and throat muscles working vigorously, and with crackling noises up in the roof of his mouth, he said

fallax proferret, sectae huius auctorem Mahomad fore praedixit; qui angeli Gabrielis magisterio illustratus, verbum prophetismi ab Altissimo nationibus relaturus accepit: legem instituit, paradisum disseruit, regnumque coelorum plenum epulis et fluxibus foeminarum edocuit. Sed et alia plura, quae hic disponi perlongum est, ex ritu pro vano arbitrio prosequente, protinus ephebus ille venerabilis monachus, ut erat apprime literis arabicis imbutus, arabice dans illi responsum: 'Mentitus', ait, 'est vobis, ita maledictionibus tabescat diuinis, qui tanto scelere implicatus, tantorum agmina perditorum inuasit, secumque inferorum barathro mancipauit. Ille etenim daemonio plenus, daemonicis favens praestigiis, lethale morbidis propinans poculum, aeternae perditionis luet interitum. Quare vos scientia praediti a talibus non abdicatis periculis? Quare non renuntiantes ulcus pestiferi dogmatis, perennem fidei christiane euangelicam sospitatem optatis?' Hec, et his similia ore pudico, summis reuerentiae ausibus viribusque lingua peracuta beato disserente Isaac, stupore nimio iudex turbatus, ac veluti amens effectus, ubertim lachrymasse perhibetur: et quadam mentis hebetudine occupatus vix potuisse fertur, exprobranti se monacho respondere: sicque manu extensa faciem eius verberanti, confestim monachus dixit: 'Consimilem imagini Dei vultum audes ferire? vide qualem propter hoc redditurus sis rationem.' Iccirco, a consedentibus secum sapientibus deprehensus, arguitur quod grauitatis censoris oblitus leuiter per semetipsum ad caedendum martyrem egerit: et praesertim, quia secundum legum suarum sententiam, is qui pro crimine dignus est mori, nullius poenae conuitiis lacerari debet. Tunc iudex ad sanctum Isaac conuersus ait: 'Forte madidus vino, aut frenesi captus ad ista, quae profers, non facile potes aduertere. Nam ipsius vatis nostri, quem tu temere conuitiis impetis, sententia manet irrefragabilis, animaduerti debere in eos, qui talia de ipso non verentur profiteri.' Ad quem venerabilis Isaac intrepida responsione ait: 'Ego quidem, iudex, nec vino madidus, nec quolibet morbo saucius sum, sed zelo iustitiae conflagrans, quia vatem vestrum, vosque expertes existere comperi, veritatem vobis exposui: propter quam si mors furibunda occurrerit, libens excipiam, placidus subeam, nec ab eius casibus ceruices meas auertam. Noui enim, Dominum dixisse: 'Beati qui persequutionem patiuntur propter iustitiam, quoniam ipsorum est regnum coelorum.' Tunc index carceri illum tradens, protinus regi causa eius innotuit, qui tante accusationis euentu perterritus, illico ferocioribus animis ferox promit edictum, dicens morti usquequaque fieri debere obnoxium, talem in auctorem fidei suae ferentem conuitium. Hinc Dei seruus ad necem damnatus vertice plectitur: hinc in stipite eleuatus capite deorsum appenditur,

the words of his ritual prayers. He explained that Muhammad was the founder of this sect: Muhammad, inspired by the teaching of the Archangel Gabriel, accepted the task of spreading the message from the Most High to the nations; he instituted a code of laws, discussed paradise, and taught that the kingdom of heaven was full of rich foods and the sensuous movements of women. The judge continued in pompous tones with other matters, too lengthy to be set out here, concerning their religious practices. Then the youthful monk, being well versed in Arabic learning, made this reply in Arabic: 'May he who lies to you in such a way, he who is involved in so much sinfulness, he who has made his way into the ranks of so many accursed souls, and has delivered himself into the abyss of the nether regions, rot under heaven's curse! Such a man is full of the devil, is promoting devilish delusions, is handing out a cup of deadly poison, and will suffer the pains of eternal damnation. Why do you, possessing as you do such learning, not draw back from such dangers? Why do you not choose the everlasting assurance of the Christian faith, putting an end to the running sores of your detestable dogma?' The Blessed Isaac said all this, and more in the same vein, arguing in a very clear voice and with great daring and devotion. The judge was utterly amazed, and like a man bereft of his senses, was seen to weep copiously; and, as though he was suffering some sort of mental confusion, which he could not begin to overcome, he answered the monk with reproaches. He struck the monk with upraised hand, and the monk at once cried: 'Do you dare to strike a face with bears a semblance to the image of God? Think that you will one day have to account for this action to Him.' The knowledgeable persons sitting with the judge at once intervened to remind him that judicial gravity should not lightly be set aside as it had been by his striking the martyr, and especially that, according to the letter of their law, he who deserves death for a crime should not be shamed with any other penalty. Then the judge, turning to St Isaac, said: 'Maybe you are drunk, or a prey to some frenzy, and cannot readily control what you have said. The doctrine of our Prophet, whom you rashly assail with insults, remains unshakeable, and this has to be drawn to the attention of those who openly and disrespectfully say such things about him.' The reverend Isaac boldly answered him: 'I am not drunk, Your Honour, nor am I suffering from any disease, but I am afire with a zeal for justice, in which your prophet and you yourselves are shown to be lacking; and I have declared the truth to you. If I should meet a violent death because of it, I will gladly meet it, and will not draw my neck away from it. I know that the Lord said "Blessed are they who suffer persecution for the sake of justice, for theirs is the kingdom of heaven".' Then the judge cast him into prison, and at once sent a report to the ruler who, alarmed that such a grave charge had been made, immediately issued a decree couched in violent terms, in which it was said that when someone insulted the Islamic faith the crime was under all circumstances punishable by death. So this servant of God bent his head under sentence of death:

atque ultra amnem in spectaculum urbis locatur tertio Nonas Iunias, Feria quarta. Era octingentesima, octuagesima nona. Cuius corpus post aliquot dies cum caeteris, qui eum imitando perempti sunt, igne crematum, et in fauillam conuersum, deinceps in amnem proiectum est.

he was hanged head downwards on the gallows. That took place beyond the river within sight of the city, on Wednesday, 3 June, Era 889 [= AD 851]. His body was cremated (with the bodies of others who were moved to imitate him) after a few days; the ashes were scattered in the river.

## 11.   A prophecy of reconquest (883)

*The brief text known as the* Chronica prophetica *from which the extract is taken was composed in Oviedo, capital of Asturias, perhaps by Dulcidio, a close collaborator of Alfonso III (on whom see text 6), and a priest probably of Toledan origin who went on a royal mission to Cordova in 883.* *The text was copied into a MS of the* Chronica Albeldensis *(of the monastery of Albelda, near Logroño in La Rioja), from which an important MS came, this also having been composed in Oviedo.* *The prophecy stems from Ezekiel, chapters 38 and 39.* *Gog of the Bible had long been taken to refer to the Gothic people: as in Genesis 10, Noah's third son was Japhet, who received Europe; Japhet's second son was Magog, who peopled Scythia, that is Scandinavia, the original home of the Goths (Gothland); and Japhet's fifth son was Tubal, who peopled Spain 140 years after the Flood.* *The Ishmaelites were identified with the*

(2) Quod uero idem profheta ad Smael iterum dicit: 'Quia dereliquisti Dominum et ego derelinquam te et tradam te in manu Gog, et reddet uicem tibi.   Postquam aflixeris eos CLXX tempora, faciet tibi sicut fecisti ei', spes nostra Xps est quod, conpletis proximiori tempore CLXX annis de quod in Spaniam ingressi sunt, inimici ad nicilum redigantur et pax Xpi eclesie sancte reddatur, quia tempora pro annis ponuntur.   Quod prestet omnipotens Deus, ut inimicorum crebro deficiente audacia in melius semper crescat eclesia.   Amen.

(3) Quod etiam ipsi Sarrazeni quosdam prodigiis uel astrorum signis interitum suum adpropinquare predicunt et Gotorum regnum restaurari per hunc nostrum principem dicunt; etiam et multorum Xpianorum reuelationibus atque ostensionibus hic princebs noster gloriosus domnus Adefonsus proximiori tempore in omni Spania predicetur regnaturus.   Sicque protegente diuina clementia inimicorum terminus quoddidie defecit et ecclesia Domini in maius et melius crescit.   Et quantum perficit Xpi nominis dignitas, tantum inimicorum tabescit ludibriosa calamitas.

(4) Remanent usque ad diem sancti Martini III Idus Nouembris m. VII et erunt conpleti anni CLXVIIII et incipieuit annus centesimus septuagesimus. Que dum Sarraceni conplerint, secundum predictum Ezecielis prophete superius adnotatum expectauitur ultio inimicorum aduenire et salus Xpianorum adesse.   Quod prestet omnipotens Deus, ut sicut filii eius Domini nostri Ihesu Xpi cruore uniuersum mundum dignatus est a potestate diaboli redimere, ita proximiori tempore eclesiam suam iubeat ab Ismaelitarum iugo eripere ipse qui uiuit et regnat in secula seculorum.   Amen.

*Muslims.   The predicted date of the fulfilment of the prophecy was 11 November 883, that is 170 years after the Muslim conquest of Spain; and the* Chronica prophetica *is dated by a precise internal reference to 11 April 883.   The prophecy was less unrealistic than we might think: Alfonso III 'el Magno' was a noted warrior—king, and al—Andalus was in turmoil at the time.   However, when it was plain that the prophecy had not been fulfilled, a C was prudently added to the dates (CCLXX years = 270) when the text was copied again in AD 976.   By such means — a prefiguring by an Old Testament prophet, the creation of a sense of being part of the divine plan — were the ambitions of Christian rulers and the fighting spirit of their soldiers kept alive in dark times.*

*The text is taken from the same source as text 6.   On the fundamental belief in Gothic continuity, see Colin Smith, 'History as myth in medieval France and Spain', in R.L. Thomson (ed.),* A Medieval Miscellany in honour of Prof. John Le Patourel *(Leeds, 1982), pp. 54—68.*

(2) As indeed the same prophet says again to Ishmael: 'Since you have abandoned the Lord, I will abandon you and hand you over to Gog, who will give you your deserts.   After you have punished them 170 times, he will do to you as you did to him.'   Christ is our hope that very soon, the 170 years since they entered Spain being completed, our enemies should be made as nothing and peace should be restored to the Holy Church of Christ (for *times* are to be taken as *years*).   May Almighty God grant this, so that, the courage of our enemies being constantly reduced, the Church may grow everlastingly for the better.   Amen.

(3) The Saracens themselves also predict, from certain portents and signs of the stars, that their destruction is approaching, and they say that the kingdom of the Goths is to be restored by this our Prince; and it is predicted also by the revelations and apparitions experienced by many Christians that Don Alfonso, our glorious Prince, will soon reign in all Spain.   And so, with divine clemency protecting us, our enemies' territory is shrinking day by day and the Church of the Lord grows larger and better. And as much as the honour of the name of Christ achieves, by so much does the shameful misfortune [brought upon us by our enemies] decline.

(4) There remain until St Martin's Day, 11 November, seven months, when 169 years will be completed and the 170th year will begin.   When the Saracens reach this point, according to the prediction of the prophet Ezekiel mentioned above, it is expected that the vengeance of their enemies will come and the salvation of the Christians will arrive.   May Almighty God grant this, so that, just as by the blood of His Son Jesus Christ our Lord He deigned to redeem the whole world from the power of the devil, so very soon He, who lives and reigns for evermore, may order that His Church be free from the yoke of the Ishmaelites.   Amen.

## 12. Advance and settlement under Alfonso III (late 9th century)

*This is from the chronicle of Sampiro, Bishop of Astorga (León), who wrote about the year 1000. The work was incorporated into the Historia Seminensis (or Silense) in the 12th century. Sampiro's less than fully classical Latin has been adjusted, not always for the best, by the Seminensis author, and had evidently suffered a good deal of miscopying of proper names. For example, Aucensis is thus in all MSS and in the Albeldensis of 883, but the true reading is Auriensis, that is modern Orense. The phrase 'regis obtutibus est presentatus' is meaningless and corrupt; the Albeldensis puts us on the right track, reading here 'regique nostro in Ouetao perducitur' which is what I have translated. These examples illustrate the defects of many of our medieval texts and the near—idiocy of some copyists, since it seems incredible that one of them could so mistake the name of the capital of Asturias (Ouetao = Oviedo).*

*The interest of the extract is that it shows how a writer about a century after the events looked back to the noble achievements of a great monarch. Sampiro, a few years after the devastating raids of al—Mansur on much of León and parts of Castile, looks back to a time of powerful Christian advance: an enemy commander is captured and a huge ransom obtained for him; three armies are routed, and the infidel is made to sue for peace; notable territorial advances are made. The act of populare, poblar, was more far—reaching than any temporary conquest. The process,*

Eius quoque tempore ecclesia ampliata est: vrbes namque Portugalensis, Bragarensis, Vessensis, Flauensis, Aucensis a christianis populantur, et secundum sentenciam canonicam episcopi ordinantur, et usque ad flumen Tagum populando producitur.

Sub cuius imperio dux quidam Yspanie et proconsul nomine Abofalit bello comprehensus, regis obtutibus est presentatus: qui se precio redimens, C millia solidorum in redemptionem suam dedit.

Per idem fere tempus cordubensis exercitus venit ad ciuitatem Legionensem atque Astoricensem urbem. Et exercitum Toletane urbis atque alium ex aliis Yspanie ciuitatibus post eum venientem, in unum se tunc agregari voluit ad destruendam Dei Ecclesiam. Sed prudentissimus rex per exploratores omnia noscens, magno consilio Dei iuuante instat adiutus. Nam cordubensse agmen post tergum relinquens, sequenti exercitui obuiam properauit. Illi quidem pre multitudine armatorum nil metuentes, Poluorariam tendentes venerunt. Sed gloriossimus rex ex latere silue progressus, irruit super eos in predictum locum Poluorarie, iuxta flumen cui nomen est Urbicum, ubi interempti ad duodecim milia corruerunt. Illa quidem alia azeyfa cordubensis valle de Niora uenit fugiendo. Rege uero persequente, omnes ibidem gladio interempti sunt. Nullus inde euasit preter X inuolutos sanguine inter cadauera mortuorum.

Post hoc arabes ad regem Adefonsum legatos miserunt pro pace. Sed

*which I have translated as 'settle', is a complex one of moving settlers, organizing forts and defensive lines, dividing and assigning lands, providing judicial and governmental frameworks, and — with due emphasis on proper canonical procedures, as in the first paragraph — establishing new bishoprics or revivifying old ones, this being the clearest sign of intended permanence. Alfonso was, indeed, the first to proceed with a true policy of such settlement, on a large scale over whole provinces 'deserted since ancient times', and with permanent success.*

*The dates of the capture and settlement of some of the places is known: Oporto, 868; Braga, 885; Viseo, 880, Chaves, 872; Orense, 872. Alfonso did at one time advance to and beyond the Tagus, reaching Mérida, but any notion of settlement as far as the Tagus at that time is fanciful. Portucale, Portugale applied to what is now Oporto and its region: the independence and monarchy of Portugal were still far distant (1139).*

*It may be noted that one of the conditions set by the King for the truce mentioned towards the end of the extract was that the Cordovese authorities should allow the remains of St Eulogius, martyred in 859 (see text 10), to be transferred to Oviedo.*

*The text is taken from the* Historia Silense, *edited by Dom Justo Pérez de Urbel and Atilano González Ruiz—Zorrilla (Madrid, 1959), pp. 160—61.*

In his time the Church was extended: for the towns of Oporto, Braga, Viseu, Chaves, and Orense were settled by the Christians, bishops being established in accordance with canon law; and Christian settlement was extended as far as the River Tagus.

During Alfonso's reign, a certain commander and governor of al—Andalus, Abofalit, was captured in battle, and taken to the King at Oviedo; he paid 100,000 *solidi* for his ransom.

At about this time the army of Cordova came to the cities of León and Astorga, joining up then with the army of Toledo and with another formed from other cities of al—Andalus which arrived later, in order to destroy the Church of God. However, the King in his great wisdom, informed of all this by scouts, was able to take a stand helped by God's great power. Leaving the Cordovese force at his back, he went forward to meet the army which was following it. They, fearing nothing and confident in their numbers of soldiers, advanced towards Polvorosa. Then our most glorious King, emerging from the side of a wood, burst upon them there at Polvorosa, on the Orbigo river, where up to twelve thousand were killed. The other army from Cordova went down the Niora valley in flight, but the King pursued them, and all were killed. None escaped except ten who ran, covered in blood, over the corpses of the dead.

After this the Arabs sent messengers to King Alfonso to sue for peace. The King, granting them a three—year truce, broke the boldness of his

rex per trienium illis pacem acomodans, fregit audaciam inimicorum. Rex hinc magna exultauit gloria.

Ac trienio peracto, sub era DCCCCXXXVII, vrbes desertas ab antiquitus, populare iussit. Hec sunt Çemora, Septimancas, et Donnas uel omnes Campi Gotorum; Taurum namque dedit ad populandum filio suo Garseano.

enemies and covered himself in glory.

When the truce was over after three years, in Era 937 [= AD 899] the King ordered the following towns, which had been deserted since ancient times, to be settled: Zamora, Simancas, and Dueñas, and all the Campi Gotorum; and he assigned Toro to his son García for settlement.

### 13. Miraculous aid in battle (934)

*The* Poema de Fernán González *was composed soon after 1264 by a monk of San Pedro de Arlanza south of Burgos, in the* cuaderna vía *metre devised a few decades earlier. The poem survives in a single very defective MS of 15th—century date, but only some 750 stanzas of a more extensive text remain; the defects and missing portions can to some extent be made good by reference to the prose version of the poem made for Alfonso X's* Estoria de España. *Arlanza claimed connections with Fernán González and maintained a cult of the man who ruled Castile for a long period in the 10th century until his death in 970, securing for what had been a simple 'county' (a fief governed by a Count) of León a virtual independence and the right of succession by his descendants. Such a founding father is honoured in the legend and literature of any country.*

*Although many believe that the* Poema *is partly based on an early epic* cantar, *there is no real evidence of this, and the materials of the poem can be explained as derived from monastic legend, library texts, and of course the poet's fervent imagination. The section selected here in two extracts concerns the entirely mythical battle of Hacinas, a place situated in the ancient and strongly epical Alfoz de Lara to the south—east of Burgos. The episode occupies a considerable space in the poem from stanza 380 (al—Mansur assembles his army) to 563 (Christian victory, burial of the dead heroes in Arlanza). Although the poem has at times a true epic ring, and much in common with epic texts of France and Spain (for example in descriptions of battles), it is plain that we are in a much more elevated world than that of mere men: the Moors are the devil's agents, the devil has called up the fiery serpent to frighten the Christians, the Count has struck his bargain with divine powers and after his prayer these will appear to fight and secure victory. As at the climactic moments of the* Chanson de Roland *(whose heroes, with those of other French epics, were well known to the Spanish monk: stanza 352, following mention of Alexander, David, and Judas Maccabeus) we are in the midst of a great battle between the forces of light and darkness.*

*The poet commits several anachronisms (although the term probably meant nothing to the medieval mind with its very different perception of the past). In stanza 467, the soldiers could not be 'crusaders' in the early 10th century. In 549, al—Mansur (as often elsewhere) is the perpetual infidel enemy of any Christian leader. The historical al—Mansur was not 'king' (as in 560), but virtual dictator of al—Andalus from 977 till his death in 1002, and the scourge of the Christian states. The* carbonientos *or 'dark ones' (literally, 'coal—faced') of 478 are presumably the devils and the Moors equally, perpetuating the prejudice already noted in text 5; I note here that the great Caliph Abd—al—Rahman III, contemporary of*

(467) Çenaron e folgaron    essa gente cruzada,

*Fernán González, not surprisingly in view of the amount of the blood of nordic princesses in his veins, was fair—haired and blue—eyed, and so conscious of his pale complexion that he used a cosmetic to darken it.*
 *Both sides can call upon other—worldly powers. The serpent of 468 has many possible models, including several in the Apocalypse, but the poet may have spent many hours staring at one. The chapter—house of Arlanza had two panels set high on one wall. One represented a lion. The other had a serpent or dragon, with a bird—like head bearing horns, wings, and bird's feet, the most notable aspect being the creature's swirling movement which filled the panel with menace. These date from about 1220. Copies of the frescos on canvas are in the Cloisters Museum, New York. In 476 and following stanzas we find the common prejudice against the Moors and their learning in the black arts and in devilish contrivances. The sages of al—Andalus had, by the time of the poem, an immense reputation as astronomers/astrologers (hardly differentiated in the Middle Ages in Christian or Muslim lands). It was normal for Christian authorities to condemn astrology and its implications, while often being learned in it themselves. Much important material both scientific and pseudo—scientific was translated from Arabic into Latin, and later from Arabic into Castilian, in the 12th and 13th centuries at Toledo, Seville, etc.; at first under Church patronage, later under the royal aegis.*
 *In 551, the modern mind may find the basis of the Count's plea very strange. In the Middle Ages, the relationship of a ruler with God or with a saint is often envisaged in these terms, which echo (and share the mentality of) the feudal bargain struck between vassal and lord. The reference here is quite specific. Earlier in the episode, the Count went to Arlanza and, while keeping vigil at the altar and praying for divine aid in the coming battle, fell into a sleep during which he had a vision of (San) Pelayo, the hermit who had become the first abbot of the monastery, and who had died a week before. Pelayo promised the Count that victory would be assured by the appearance of Santiago (St James) and a host of angels in white armour bearing crusading emblems. Here, therefore, the Count is calling upon God to fulfil his side of the 'bargain'. Santiago, the Apostle St James (557), had long been the accepted patron saint of the Christians. He was Santiago 'Matamoros', the Moor—slayer, and his name was shouted as a battle—cry, as first recorded in the* Poem of the Cid.
 *Textual difficulties are illustrated by the first half of the second line of stanza 547. I give it as it is in all the editions, but it makes no sense; the prose version of the* Estoria de España *has 'si Dios non acorriese', which I have adapted in the translation.*
 *The extracts are taken from the edition of Juan Victorio (Madrid, 1981).*

(467) The crusading army supped and rested.

todos a Dios rogaron   con voluntad pagada
que y les ayudasse   la su virtud sagrada,
et fuessen venturosos   d'aver la lid rancada.

(468) Vieron aquella noche   una muy fiera cosa:
venia por el aire   una sierpe rabiosa,
dando muy fuertes gritos   la fantasma astrosa,
toda venie sangrienta,   bermeja commo rosa.

(469) Fazia ella senblante   que ferida venia,
semejava en los gritos   que el çielo partia,
alunbrava las uestes   el fuego que vertia,
todos ovieron miedo   que quemar los queria.

(470) Non ovo ende ninguno   que fues' tan esforçado
que grand miedo non ovo   e fuesse espantado;
cayo y mucho omne   en tierra deserrado,
ovieron muy grand miedo   todo el pueblo cruzado.

(471) Despertaron al conde,   que era ya dormido;
ante que el veniesse   el culuebro era ido,
fallo todo el su pueblo   commo muy desmaido,
demando del culuebro   commo fuera venido.

(472) Dixeron gelo todo   de qual guisa veniera,
commo cosa ferida   que grandes gritos diera,
vuelta venia en sangre   aquella bestia fiera;
la tierra s' maravillan   commo non la ençendiera.

(473) Quando gelo contaron   assi como lo vieron,
entendio bien el conde   que grand miedo ovieron,
que esta atal figura   diablos la fizieron,
e a los pueblos cruzados   revolverlos quisieron.

(474) A los moros tenian   que los venie ayudar
ca coidavan sin duda   cristianos espantar;
por tal que los cristianos   se ovieran a tornar,
quisieran en la ueste   algun fuego echar.

(475) Mando a sus varones   el buen conde llamar,
quando fueron juntados   mando los escuchar:
el derie que queria   la serpient demostrar;
luego de estrelleros   començo de fablar.

(476) 'Los moros, bien sabedes,   se guian por estrellas,
non se guian por Dios,   que se guian por ellas;
otro Criador nuevo   han fecho ellos d'ellas,
diz que por ellas veen   muchas de maravellas.

(477) Ha y otros que saben   muchos encantamientos,
fazen muy malos gestos   con sus espiramientos,
de revolver las nuves   e revolver los vientos
muestra les el diablo   estos entendimientos.

(478) Ayuntan los diablos   con sus conjuramentos,
aliegan se con ellos   e fazen sus conventos,

God that His holy power should help them in the enterprise and give them good fortune to win the battle.

(468) That night they witnessed a terrifying thing: a raging serpent flew through the air; the terrifying apparition was screaming loudly and came all bloodied, as red as the rose.

(469) She seemed to be wounded and was howling enough to shatter heaven; the fire that she poured forth lit up the armies, and all feared that she intended to burn them up.

(470) There was none present so brave that he did not feel immense fear and terror; many a man there fell senseless to the ground, and the whole crusading army was in great dread.

(471) They awoke the Count, who had already gone to sleep. Before he arrived the serpent had already gone. He found all his people in a faint, and began to ask how the serpent had made its appearance.

(472) They told him all about how it had come, like a wounded beast giving great howls, and streaming blood; and how they had marvelled that it did not burn up the land.

(473) When they told him what they had seen, the Count readily understood how frightened they had been; he thought that the beast was the work of devils, who had hoped to sow dismay in the crusading army.

(474) They thought it had come to help the Moors, for they [the Moors] doubtless believed they could frighten the Christians, and that the Christians would be forced to retreat; they also hoped to spread fire in the Christian army.

(475) The good Count ordered his men to be called together. When they had gathered he ordered them to listen: he would tell them what the serpent signified. Then he began to speak of astrologers.

(476) 'The Moors, you realize, are guided by the stars; they do not take God as a guide, but the stars; they have made of them [the stars] a new Creator, and hold that in them they perceive many marvels.

(477) 'There are others among them who know many charms, and can create very evil simulations with their spells; the devil teaches them how to stir up the clouds and the winds.

(478) 'They associate the devils with their spells, and join up with them to form their covens; they reveal all the errors of people now dead,

dizen de los passados    todos sus fallimientos,
todos fazen conçejo    los falsos carbonientos.
(479) Algun moro astroso    que sabe encantar
fizo aquel diablo    en sierpe figurar
por amor que podiesse    a vos mal espantar,
con este tal engaño    cuidaron nos torvar.
(480) Commo sodes sesudos,    bien podedes saber
que non ha el poder    de mal a nos fazer,
ca tollo le don Cristus    el su fuerte poder,
veades que son locos    los que l' quieren creer.'
[...]
(547) Era en fuerte cuita    el conde don Fernando,
iva, si se l' fiziesse,    su muerte aguisando;
alço al çielo los ojos    al Criador rogando,
com' si fuesse con el,    assi le esta llamando:
(548) 'Pues non so venturoso    d'esta lid arrancar,
quier que escapar pudiesse,    yo non quiero escapar,
nin nunca vere yo    mas coita nin pesar,
meter me he en logar    do me hayan de matar.
(549) Castiella, quebrantada,    quedara sin señor,
ire con esta rabia,    mesquino pecador;
sera en cautiverio    del moro Almançor;
por non ver aquel dia,    la muerte es mejor.
(550) Señor, ¿por que nos tienes    a todos fuerte saña?
por los nuestros pecados,    non estruyas a España;
perder se ella por nos    semejarie fazaña,
que de buenos cristianos    non avria calaña.
(551) Padre, Señor del mundo,    e vero Jesucriste:
de lo que me dixeron,    nada non me toviste:
que me acorrerias    comigo lo posiste;
yo non te fallesçiendo,    tu ¿por que me falleçiste?
(552) Señor, pues es el conde    de ti desanparado,
que por alguna cosa    eres d'el despagado,
resçibe tu, Señor,    en comienda el condado;
si non, sera aina    por suelo astragado.
(553) Pero yo non morre    assi desanparado;
antes avran de mi    los moros mal mercado;
tal cosa fara antes    este cuerpo lazrado,
que, quanto el mundo dure,    sienpre sera contado.
(554) Si atanta de graçia    me quesiesses tu dar
que yo a Almançor    me pudiesse allegar,
non creo yo que a vida    me pudiesse escapar:
yo mismo cuidaria    la mi muerte vengar.
(555) Todos los mis vassallos    que aqui son finados
serien por su señor    este dia vengados,

and the treacherous dark ones hold council together.

(479) 'Some evil Moor who knows how to cast a spell made that devil take the shape of a serpent, in order to give you all a bad fright; they thought they could dismay us by such a deceit.

(480) 'Since you are sensible men, you fully realize that he has no power to do us harm, for Christ took away his great power; you can see that anyone who believes in him [the devil] is mad.'

[...]

(547) Count Fernando was in dire trouble; he was going to his own death unless something was done to help. He raised his eyes to heaven and prayed to God as though he were with Him, calling upon Him as follows:

(548) 'Since I am not so fortunate as to win this battle — and even though I might escape, I have no wish to do so — and since I shall never see greater trouble or sadness, I shall put myself in a place where they will kill me.

(549) 'Castile will be shattered and lordless, and I — wretched sinner that I am — will depart this life with this maddening thought. Castile will be al—Mansur's captive, and in order not to see that day, I prefer to die.

(550) 'O Lord, why are you so angry with all of us? Do not destroy Spain as a punishment for our sins. For her to be destroyed on our account would be an evil act, and the like of it would not be acceptable to good Christians.

(551) 'Father, Lord of the earth, true Christ: you have not kept your part of the bargain as it was stated to me. You made a pact with me that you would come to my aid: when I have in no way failed you, why have you failed me?

(552) 'Lord, since the Count has been abandoned by you, and since in some way you are displeased with him, take, O Lord, his county as your fief; if not, it will be very soon dragged down.

(553) 'But I will not die here abandoned in this way; rather, the Moors shall have a rough deal from me. This my suffering body will first do such things to them that, while the world lasts, it will be spoken of.

(554) 'If you would grant me sufficient grace for me to get close to al—Mansur I do not think he could escape alive from me; I would try myself to avenge my death.

(555) 'All those of my vassals who lie dead here would this day be avenged by their lord, and all would be brought together with me in

todos en paraiso   conmigo ayuntados;
farie muy grande honra   el conde a sus criados.'

(556) Querellando se a Dios   el conde don Fernando,
los finojos fincados,   al Criador rogando,
oyo una grande voz   que le estava llamando:
'Fernando de Castiella,   oy te creçe grand bando.'

(557) Alço suso los ojos   por ver quien lo llamava,
vio al Santo apostol   que de suso le estava:
de caveros con el   grand conpaña llevava,
todos armas cruzados,   commo a el semejava.

(558) Fueron contra los moros,   las sus fazes paradas,
− ¡nunca vio omne nado   gentes tan esforçadas! −
el moro Almançor,   con todas sus mesnadas,
con ellos fueron luego   fuerte miente enbargadas.

(559) Veien d'una señal   tantos pueblos armados,
ovieron muy grand miedo,   fueron mal espantados;
de qual parte venian   eran maravillados;
lo que mas les pesava:   eran todos cruzados.

(560) Dixo el rey Almançor,   'Esto non puede ser;
¿do l'recreçio al conde   atan fuerte poder?
Cuidava yo oy sin duda   le matar o prender,
è avra con estas gentes   el a nos cometer.'

paradise; the Count would do very great honour to his liegemen.'

(556) As the Count lifted his plaint to God and prayed to him on bended knee, he heard a great voice calling to him: 'Ferdinand of Castile, a great increase of strength comes to you today.'

(557) He raised his eyes to see who was calling him, and saw the holy Apostle standing over him. He had a great company of knights with him, all bearing the emblem of crusaders, it seemed to him.

(558) They moved towards the Moors in battle—lines: no man born ever saw such brave soldiers! The Moor al—Mansur and all his host were immediately locked in fierce fighting with them.

(559) The Moors, seeing so many troops all wearing the same emblem, were greatly afraid, and marvelled where they could have come from. What most disturbed them was that they were all crusaders.

(560) Said King al—Mansur: 'This cannot be. Where did the Count obtain such a vast increase of his strength? I thought that I would today kill or capture him; now he with these new soldiers will attack us.'

## 14. Niceties of diplomacy (953—56)

*In about 950 Otto I 'the Great', Holy Roman Emperor, sent an embassy to the Caliph Abd—al—Rahman III in Cordova. Its object was probably to ask the Caliph to assert control over the base maintained by Muslim forces at Fraxinetum (near St Tropez?), from which they raided far into the Emperor's north Italian lands, and elsewhere. The Caliph sent a reply with a bishop, but the terms of the letter were highly offensive to Christianity, and for three years the emissaries were held in Germany as virtual prisoners. Eventually Otto released them and sent a further letter to the Caliph. This was prepared by Otto's brother Bruno, Archbishop of Cologne, and was insulting to Islam. It was carried by John, a monk of the monastery of Görz near Metz, who — knowing the contents — apparently hoped for martyrdom at the hands of the infidels. John was accompanied by a brother monk, Garamannus. They reached Cordova in 953 or 954; our extracts start from this point.*

*The account was written by another John, Abbot of St Arnulph in Metz. It is incomplete and it is thought that the writer's death, about 983, prevented its conclusion; we do not know the outcome of the negotiations about Fraxinetum.*

*We have no reason to doubt the total accuracy of the account, which at all points has the ring of truth. The presence of the Jew Hasdeu and*

(121) Rex undique meticulosus ancepsque, periculum sibi posse imminere considerans, artibus omnis generis quo evadat pertemptat. Et primo quidem Judeum quendam, cui nomen Hasdeu, quo neminem umquam prudentiorem se vidisse aut audisse nostri testati .sunt, ad eos misit, qui de omnibus ab eis ipsis penitus exploraret. Is quoniam fama perferente dispersum fuerat, regii eum baiulum esse mandati, uti animum Johannis sibi conciliaret primo, quo sollicitabantur metu eum erigit, nihilque mali quemquam eorum ibi passurum, sed cum honore patriae remittendos edicit. Multa de ritu gentis, et qualiter se coram eis observare deberent, commonuit. Ipsi iuniores a quibuscumque vanis lascivis motibus locutionibusve compescerent; nihil tam parvum fore, quod non mox regiae notitiae perferretur. Si copia sibi egrediendi pateret, ne qua scurrilitate feminis saltem nutu se applicarent, nullam sibi pestem truculentiorem futuram; legem sibi propositam nullatenus excederent, quo nullo observatius notarentur, deprehensique nihili penderentur. Johanne ad ea prout competebat respondente, atque acceptissime monitorem ferente, suosque ex contrariae partis homine suffundente, post plura invicem conserta, pedetemptim Judaeus causam ingreditur. Quid missi ferant, sollicite disquirit.

*of 'a certain bishop John' (of Cordova?) in the negotiations is an indication of the extraordinarily cosmopolitan and tolerant nature of high—level Cordovese society at the time. The clash between John of Görz and 'bishop John', who surely speaks for all the Christians of al—Andalus in their simple need to survive, seems to be a unique record. Unique also is the very personal portrait of Abd—al—Rahman III, greatest of the Caliphs and at the height of his power, sketched by the Christian visitors. The only disappointment is to find that at the second audience of John of Görz with the Caliph, what had been planned as a meeting of minds by the Caliph in section 134 turns out to be an occasion for mere schoolboy boasting (continued in 136, not included). At any rate, faces had been saved all round, and nobody was martyred: the refined and worldly Caliph saw no reason to assist Christian fanatics towards this goal, but even so, John of Görz — who died in 974 — was later canonized.*

*Of Recemundus, who played a key role, it should be noted that he was a Cordovese who held a post in the Caliphal administration, being better known under his Arabic name of Rabi ibn Sa'id. On returning from his mission to Germany he claimed as his reward the bishopric of Eliberri, Granada, just then providentially vacant, and he was ordained for this purpose. Later he went on important missions to Byzantium, Syria, and Jerusalem.*

*The text is taken from Vázquez de Parga, pp. 73—88.*

(121) The Caliph, always timid and uncertain, considered what danger might threaten him, and sought contrivances of all kinds by which he might avoid it. First he sent to them [the Christian emissaries] a certain Jew, Hasdeu by name, than whom none more wise was ever seen or heard of, as our people testified, in order that he should discuss everything thoroughly with them. On account of his reputation for patience, he had it put about that he was the bearer of the royal commission, so that he could first win John's confidence, thereby giving him cheer and freeing him from fear, assuring him that no harm would come to him and that they would be sent home with honour. He reminded them of many things concerning the customs of the people and how they should behave in their presence. As young men they should refrain from all manner of idle and lewd gestures or words; nothing would be so slight but that it would be reported at once to the Caliph. If there should be ready opportunities for going out, they should not even show any inclination for light—hearted joking with the women, for the sternest punishment would be inflicted upon them. They should in no way depart from the guidance being offered them, for they would be most carefully watched, and would be thought guilty of the smallest fault. After John had replied to all this as best he could, and had most willingly listened to his adviser, securing the agreement of his companions for their part, and after much else had been added to the above, the Jew cautiously began on the main matter. What, he earnestly

Dum paululum cunctari videt Johannem — nam tunc secreto inter eos agebatur — sui dat fidem silentii, immo si opus sit tuti opem consilii. Johannes cuncta ordine digerit. Dona regi missa, epistolam praeterea auribus regis inferendam; absque ea neque dona exhibenda, neque praesentiam sibi regis fas esse conveniendam. Sententiam simul epistolae verbis aperit. 'Periculosum', inquit Judaeus, 'cum hac regem videre. Cauti certe sitis, quid nuntiis vobis missis regi respondeatis. Legis enim severitatem iam vobis innotuisse non dubito, eique declinandae prudenter oportet consulere.'

(122) Illo tunc discedente, post aliquot menses episcopus quidam Iohannes ad eos missus est, qui post multa mutuae confabulationis rogata et reddita, ut fit inter fideles, colloquia, mandatum regis subinfert, ut cum muneribus solummodo in conspectu regis adveniant. 'Quid ergo', Iohannes ait, 'de litteris imperatoris? Nonne earum maxime causa directus sum? quia ipse blasphemas praemisit, his etiam vana erroris sui commenta destruentibus confutetur.' Ille ad haec temperatior: 'Considerate', ait, 'sub qua conditione agamus. Peccatis ad haec devoluti sumus, ut paganorum subiaceamus ditioni. Resistere potestati verbo prohibemur apostoli. Tantum hoc unum relictum est solatii, quod in tantae calamitatis malo legibus nos propriis uti non prohibent; qui quos diligentes christianitatis viderint observatores, colunt et amplectuntur, simul ipsorum convictu delectantur, cum Iudaeos penitus exhorreant. Pro tempore igitur hoc videmur tenere consilio, ut quia religionis nulla infertur iactura, cetera eis obsequamur, iussisque eorum in quantum fidem non impediunt obtemperemus. Unde tibi multo satius nunc de his reticere, et epistolam illam omnino supprimere, quam scandalum tibi tuisque, nulla instante necessitate, pernitiosissimum concitare.'

(123) Iohannes paulum commotior: 'Alium', inquit, 'quam te, qui videris episcopus, haec proferre decuerat. Cum sis enim fidei assertor, eiusque te gradus celsior posuerit etiam defensorem, timore humano a veritate praedicanda nedum alios compescere, sed nec te ipsum oportebat subducere; et melius omnino fuerat, hominem christianum famis grave ferre dispendium, quam cibis ad destructionem aliorum consociari gentilium. Ad hoc, et quod omni catholicae ecclesiae detestabile est et nefarium, ad ritum eorum vos

asked, had they been sent to do? Since he saw that John was hesitating somewhat — even though the discussion between them was taking place in private — he gave a promise of confidentiality, especially if the matter carried a need of total secrecy. John set it all out in good order. Once the presents had been given to the Caliph, the letter must also be brought to the Caliph's attention; without that there should be no presents offered, nor would it be right for him to enter the Caliph's presence. Then he disclosed the message of the letter in his own words. 'It would be dangerous', said the Jew, 'for you to see the Caliph with this. Surely you must be careful about what reply you make to the Caliph's messengers when they come to you. I do not doubt that the severity of the law is already well known to you, and you must consider how you can act carefully and avoid that.'

(122) The Jew left, and after a few months a certain bishop John was sent to them. He, after many discussions of mutual interest (as between members of the same faith), both asked for and offered back, brought the Caliph's order: that the Christian ambassadors should be brought into the royal presence with their gifts alone. 'What then', asked John of Görz, 'about the letters from the Emperor? Was I not ordered to make a most important issue of them? For if the Emperor sends insults, he, by having these rejected, as the empty fabrications of his error, will be confounded.' Bishop John answered this in measured tones. 'Consider', he said, 'under what conditions we live. We have been driven to this by our sins, to be subjected to the rule of the pagans. We are forbidden by the Apostle's words to resist the civil power. Only one cause for solace is left to us, that in the depths of such a great calamity they do not forbid us to exercise our own laws. They can see that we are diligent followers of the Christian faith, and so they cultivate us and associate with us, just as they delight in their own society, while they thoroughly detest the Jews. For the time being, then, we keep the following counsel: that provided no harm is done to our religion, we obey them in all else, and do their commands in all that does not affect our faith. So I advise you now to leave most of these things unsaid, and altogether to suppress that letter, rather than to bring about a most dangerous clash for yourself and for your people when there is absolutely no need to do it.'

(123) Somewhat angered, John of Görz replied: 'It would be fitting for someone other than you, a bishop, to utter such sentiments. But since you are a propagandist for the faith, your superior rank should have made you a defender of it, and still less should you obstruct others in preaching the truth out of any human fear, nor should you yourself hold back from doing that. It would be altogether better for a Christian man to suffer the harsh burden of hunger, than to join in the banquets of the gentiles and thus favour the destruction [of the faith?] of others. In this regard — and this is a thing most hateful to the whole Catholic Church, and evil — I hear that you are circumcised according to the custom of Islam, when the

audio circumcisos, cum fortis sententia apostoli reclamet: "Si circumcidamini, Christus vobis nihil proderit".   Itemque de cibis, quos gratia communionis eorum abhominamini: "Omnia munda mundis", et: "Erunt doctores vaniloqui et seductores docentes illa et illa, et inter cetera abstinere a cibis, quos Deus creavit percipere cum gratiarum actione fidelibus", et: "Sanctificatur enim per verbum Dei et orationem".'   At ille: 'Necessitas', inquit, 'nos constringit; nam aliter eis cohabitandi nobis copia non esset; quin et a maioribus longeque antiquitus traditum observatumque ita tenemus.' 'Numquam', Iohannes inquit, 'id approbauerim, ut metu, amore, vel favore mortali, divina transgrediantur statuta.   [...]   Quoniam eis vos necessitate constrictos assentire fatemini, mihi procul his necessitatibus Christi gratia libero, fixus Domino miserante stat animus, quod nullo terrore, allectione vel gratia, ab his quae imperatoris suscepi mandatis deflectar.   Nam nec sine epistola imperiali, nullis inde demptis vel commutatis usque ad unum apicem litteris, eum conveniam, et si quid contra ea quisquam oblataverit, quae sanae et catolicae fidei ferimus, et diversus ad haec asserta obvenerit, palam resistam, nec ipsius amore vitae ab attestatione veritatis diffugiam.'

(124) Haec regi clam nuntiantur.   Nam necdum illa publice a rege, quibus item publice responderet, mandata directa fuerant, sed episcopus ille disquirendi tantum gratia advenerat.   Rex callidis, quibus omnibus mortalibus praestare dicebatur, consultationibus mentem hominis modo hac modo illac attemptare excogitat, et tanquam muro praevalido diversa arte impulsis machinis, ita firmitatem pectoris eius, si quo pacto daretur, certat concutere. Cumque post mensem aut sex vel septem ebdomadarum spatium ei regii nuntii mitterentur, atque ex ipso quid apud se praefinierit quaererent, nihilque inmutatum a primis initiis renuntiarent, rex miraculo tantae constantiae in diversa agebatur; et primo quidem terrere eum plus metu christianorum, qui regno eius libere divinis suisque rebus utebantur, posse credens, die quadam qua dominica erat ei epistolam plenam minarum misit. His enim tantum diebus dominicis, aut si qui festae nostrae religionis erant maximi, natalis Domini, epiphaniorum, paschae, ascensionis, pentecostes, sancti Iohannis, apostolorum, aut nominatorum erant sanctorum, ad aecclesiam proximam, quae erat in honore sancti Martini, permittebantur accedere, custodibus hinc inde duodecim quos sagiones vocant, se deducentibus.   Cum ergo ea dominica ad aecclesiam processisset, in ipso itinere epistola ei porrecta est.   Et quia cartae magnitudo — nam quadra pellis vervecis erat — terrebat, ne a communione sacrorum quo tendebat

forthright statement of the Apostle is: "If you circumcise yourselves, Christ will not help you." I hear the same of your foodstuffs, some of which you reject for the sake of keeping on good terms with the Moslems: "All things are clean for those who are clean in soul"; "There will be prating sages who will teach this and that in a beguiling way, among other things abstinence from certain foods, even though God created them to be prepared with thanksgiving by His faithful"; and "Let it be made blessed by the Word of God and by prayer".' But Bishop John answered: 'Necessity constrains us, for otherwise there would be no way in which we could live among them. Indeed, we hold it so as something handed down to us and observed by our ancestors from time immemorial.' 'Never', said John of Görz, 'could I approve of that: that the divine laws should be transgressed out of fear, or for friendship, or on account of some human favour. [...] Even if I accept that you, constrained by necessity, fall in line with them, I, by the grace of God free from such necessity, and with my mind firmly made up, will in no way be deflected by any fear or enticement or favour from those orders of the Emperor which I undertook to obey. So I will not agree to suppress or alter one iota of these letters, and if anyone should have any objection to make against those things which we state concerning our firm Catholic faith, or comes up with some contrary view of our claims, I will publicly oppose him, and will not for the sake of life itself run away from the task of witnessing to the truth.'

(124) These remarks were secretly reported to the Caliph. The messages not having been sent publicly by the Caliph, John of Görz could not reply publicly, and the bishop had come into the matter solely in order to make exploratory inquiries. The Caliph, in careful consultations (such as are said to be advisable for all mortals), tried to determine how by one means or another he might influence the emissary's mind, believing that — just as the strongest wall can be shaken by driving siege—engines against it — he would manage to shake John's firmness of purpose. When after a month or a period of six or seven weeks of sending messengers to him, and trying to secure some concession within the limits the Christians had set for themselves, it became clear that the latter would not make any change from their original position, the Caliph in amazement at such constancy turned to other possibilities. First, one Sunday, he sent a letter to John full of threats, thinking he could fill the Christians with fear, since they were freely practising their religious rites in his realm. They were allowed to go only to the nearest church, St Martin's, and that only on Sundays or for the important feast—days of our religion, that is Christmas, Epiphany, Easter, the Ascension, Pentecost, St John, and the days dedicated to the Apostles and the Saints, being accompanied there and back by twelve guards of the sort they call 'sagiones'. As John was going to church that Sunday, a letter was handed to him. Because the size of the letter — it was a square of parchment — alarmed him, lest it should call him away from holy communion, to which he was going, he deferred opening it for the time

avocaretur, interim distulit aperire, donec sacris peractis ad diversorium remearent. Ut revolvit, terrentia quaedam quae sibi contingere posset invenit, nec umquam alias ita se ullis terroribus percitum confessus est. (125) Nam post multa, quae ei nisi iussis regis assentiretur comminabantur, quibus tamen nullo modo se motum fuisse testatus est, ad haec ultimum insertum est, quod si ipsum interimeret, nullum in tota Ispania christianum vitae relinqueret, sed omnes gladio trucidaret. Addens hoc: 'Cogita', inquit, 'quot animarum propter te interfectarum apud Deum reus eris, qui nisi contentione tua, a quo pacem et salutem magis sperare debuerant, nullo alio reatu peribunt, quique pro eis quaecumque velles optinere a nobis posses, sin tanta obstinatione nobis adversus persisteres.' His in ipsa qua ab aecclesia hospitium repetebant via tacite perlectis, dum magnis animi aestibus aliquando agitatur, ut vel quod contra ea consilii caperet, vel qualiter ad haec regi rescriberet, quia non satis litteris respondendi usum habebat, repente sententiae illius caelitus, ut sepe nobis fatebatur, memoria menti terrorem omnem metumque proterruit: 'Iacta', inquit, 'in Domino curam tuam', et alterius: 'Quis fecit os hominis? none ego?' [...]

(127) Haec regi perlata, non in iram, ut prius, mentem incendit, sed consilio regio perlata sunt. Iam pridem enim a suis, quibus res nostrae iam fuerant pervulgatae, abstrudendas eas commonitus erat, ne imperatori nostro obluctari temptaret. Eum belicosissimum multarum gentium victorem, iniurias omnes, praecipue legatorum, quo nunquam alias seviore animo repetiturum, ac plurimorum copiis regnorum coactis, Ispaniam totam postquam variis calamitatibus vastavisset, forte tandem iure victoris sibi subiecturum. Pluribus ita iactatis, quidam forte suggessit, ut quia vir ille tantae videbatur constantiae, ac non minoris arbitrari posset prudentiae, quem etiam tanti temporis mora in lege sua tam fixum monstrasset, ac proinde fidem mortalibus non denegaret, is ipse super hoc, quid facto sibi opus esset, consuleretur. Ita nuntiis se convenientibus postquam ultima haec mandata percepit: 'Tandem', inquit, 'sapientiore consilio rem tractastis. Si mox initio id esset quaesitum, non tantas vobis vel nobis tedii et anxietatis molestias tot spatia temporum protraxissent. Nunc citum id facile extat consilium. Mittatur domino nostro imperatori legatio a rege vestro, ut mihi, quid de commissis agere debeam, describat. Eius litteris iterum visis, ad universa oboediam.'

being, until (their holy duties being performed) they returned to their lodging. When he read it, he found certain alarming things which might happen to him, and owned that he had never been so disturbed before by other kinds of fears.

(125) For, after many things with which he was threatened if he refused to obey the Caliph's commands, by which he declared he was in no way moved, the following was finally stated: that if he should be killed, he [the Caliph] would not leave any Christian in the whole of al — Andalus alive, but would slaughter them all. He added: 'Think of your responsibility before God for the death of so many souls, of people who, were it not for your obstinacy, will not perish on account of any other charge, and who ought to be able to hope for peace and salvation from you. You are at liberty to ask on their behalf for any concession you like, rather than persisting so obstinately in opposition to us.' John of Görz turned these things over in his mind as he re — read the letter while walking from the church to his lodging, his mind being torn by great doubts as he tried to decide what to do, and what sort of reply he should make to the Caliph, for he had little experience of such things. But he was suddenly reminded of that axiom — as he often told us — by which all terror and fear might be banished from the mind: he said 'Cast thy burden upon the Lord' [Psalms 55.22], and again, 'Who hath made man's mouth? Have not I the Lord?' [Exodus 4.11].

[In 126, John dictates an uncompromising letter to the Caliph.]

(127) When this letter reached the Caliph, it did not rouse his mind to anger, as had happened before; instead he referred it to his council. The Caliph was first advised by his councillors, to whom our affairs were already known, to suppress his wrath, lest there should be a risk of a confrontation with our Emperor. He, a most warlike victor over many peoples, bringing together the forces of many realms, might ravage all al — Andalus with divers disasters, and would perhaps take control of it all by right of conquest, in retaliation for all the wrongs done to him, especially to his emissaries, for no wrong was ever received with greater indignation than this. After much discussion of these matters, someone by chance suggested that since the man [John of Görz] seemed to be so firm in his purpose, and could not be thought to be any the less in good sense, and had shown himself to be so constant in his faith after such a long period, and would not therefore deny his faith under any merely human pressures, he should himself be asked what he considered should be done. So John heard this final resolution from carefully — chosen emissaries. He replied to them as follows: 'At last, thanks to sound counsel, you have made some progress. If that sound counsel had been taken at the start, much tedium and anxiety for you and for us might have been avoided. Now a swift and easy plan presents itself. Let an embassy be sent by your Caliph to our Emperor, so that it can bring me back word about what I should do with my orders. As soon as I have letters from the Emperor, I will obey in all things.'

(128) His regi nuntiatis, acceptoque consilio ut a prudente suggesto, quaeri iubetur, quis iter tantum vellet assumere, cum rarus aut fere nullus palam se ostendendo proferret, propositumque esset, ut quisquis illuc iret honore quovis petito et cuiuscumque generis muneribus rediens potiretur. Tandem extitit inter palatina offitia Recemundus quidam, adprime catholicus, et litteris optime tam nostrorum quam ipsius inter quos versabatur linguae Arabicae institutus. [...]

(131) Ita cunctis expletis, Iohannes trium iam fere annorum claustris solutus, regiis mandatur apparere conspectibus. Cum a legatis ei diceretur, ut crine detonso, corpore loto, veste lautiore se appareret, uti regiis conspectibus praesentandum, illeque renueret, rati illi non ei vestium mutatoria subesse, regi nuntiant. Ille mox decem libras ei mittit nummorum, unde illa quibus decenter oculis regis indueretur, conquireret. Non enim fas esse gentis, ut vili habitu regiis aspectibus praesentaretur. Iohannes primo cunctatus utrum susciperet, tandem cogitans, usui pauperum id melius esse expendi, gratias munificentiae regiae reddit, quod sui tam sollicitus esse dignatus sit. Deinde responso monachi dignum subiunxit: 'Regia', inquiens, 'dona non spernor, vestes vero alias praeterquam quibus monacho uti licet, nec pallia prorsus nec eas qui alicuius coloris sunt nisi nigro tantum tinctas aliquatenus induam.' Hoc regi relato: 'Hoc', inquit, 'responso eius constantem animum recognosco. Sacco quoque indutus si veniat, libentissime eum videbo, et amplius mihi placebit.'

(132) Post haec, die praefixa qua praesentandus erat, apparatus omni genere exquisitus ad pompam regiam demonstrandam conseritur. Viam totam ab hospitio ipsorum usque ad civitatem, et inde usque ad palatium regium varii hinc inde ordines constipabant; hic pedites hastis humo stantes defixis, longe inde hastilia quaedam et missilia vibrantes manuque crispantes, ictusque mutuos simulantes; post hos mulis quidam cum levi quadam armatura insidentes; deinde equites calcaribus equos in fremitu et subsultatione varia concitantes. Mauri praeterea forma insolita nostros exterrentes ita variis proludiis, quae nostris miraculo arbitrabantur, itinere numium pulverulento, quem per se ipsa quoque temporis siccitas — nam solstitium erat aestivum — sola concitaret, ad palatium perducuntur. Obvii proceres quique procedunt, in ipso limine exteriori pavimentum omne tapetibus pretiosissimis aut palliis stratum erat.

(133) Ubi ad cubiculum, quo rex solitarius, quasi numen quoddam nullis

(128) When these developments were reported to the Caliph, he accepted the suggestion as a wise one, and ordered that someone willing to undertake such a long journey should be sought; and since very few or almost none would be willing to come forward, it was proposed that anyone willing to go should be able to claim, on his return, any honour he chose, and all manner of rewards. Eventually a certain Recemundus — a Catholic, moreover, and exceptionally learned in both Arabic and Latin literature — presented himself from among the palace staff.

[... 129, 130: Recemundus journeyed to Görz in ten weeks, staying there and in Metz and eventually being received by the Emperor in Frankfurt. 'Litterae mitiores', 'more diplomatic letters', were there prepared for the Caliph. Recemundus left on Palm Sunday 956 with a companion, Dudo of Verdun, and reached Cordova in early July.]

(131) When all these matters were explained to him, John, released from almost three years of cloistered seclusion, was ordered to appear in the royal presence. When he was told by the messengers to make himself presentable to royalty by cutting his hair, washing his body, and putting on clean clothes, he refused, lest they should tell the Caliph that he had changed in his essential being beneath a mere change of clothes. The Caliph then sent John ten pounds in coin, so that he might purchase clothing to put on and be decent in the royal eyes, for it was not right for people to be presented in slovenly dress. John could not at first decide whether to accept the money, but eventually he reasoned that it would be better spent for the relief of the poor, and sent thanks for the Caliph's generosity and for the solicitude he had deigned to show him. The monk added in his reply: 'I do not despise royal gifts, but it is not permitted for a monk to wear anything other than his usual habit, nor indeed could I put on any garment of a colour other than black.' When this was reported to the Caliph, he remarked: 'In this reply I perceive his unyielding firmness of mind. Even if he comes dressed in a sack, I will most gladly receive him.'

(132) On the day which had been agreed for John's presentation at court, all the elaborate preparations for displaying royal splendour were made. Ranks of people crowded the whole way from the lodging to the centre of the city, and from there to the palace. Here stood infantrymen with spears held erect, beside them others brandishing javelins and staging demonstrations of aiming them at each other; after them, others mounted on mules with their light armour; then horsemen urging their steeds on with spurs and shouts, to make them rear up. In this startling way the Moors hoped to put fear into our people by their various martial displays, so strange to our eyes. John and his companions were led to the palace along a very dusty road, which the very dryness of the season alone served to stir up (for it was the summer solstice). High officials came forward to meet them, and all the pavement of the outer area of the palace was carpeted with most costly rugs and coverings.

(133) When John arrived at the dais where the Caliph was seated alone

aut raris accesibile, residebat, perventum est, undique insolitis cuncta velaminibus obtecta, aequa parietibus pavimenta reddebant. Rex ipse thoro luxu quam poterat magnifico accumbebat. Neque enim more gentium ceterarum soliis aut sellis utuntur, sed lectis sive thoris colloquentes vel edentes, cruribus uno alteri impositis, incumbunt. Ut igitur Iohannes coram advenit, manum interne osculandam protendit. Osculo enim nulli vel suorum vel extraneorum admisso, minoribus quibusque ac mediocribus numquam foris, summis et quos praestantiori excipit pompa, palmam mediam aperit osculandam.

(134) Inde, sella parata, manu, ut sedeat, innuit. Longa deinde utrimque silentia. Tunc rex prior: 'Tuum', inquit, 'cor mihi plurimum diu cognosco fuisse infensum, quadiu te demum aspectu meo suspendi. Sed tu ipse penitus nosti, quod aliter fieri non potuit. Tuam virtutem, sapientiam expertus sum; aliena, ne viderem te cum epistola distulerunt, sed quod non odio tui id factum sit, volo cognoscas; et non solum te nunc libenter excipio, verum de quibuscumque postulaveris impetrabis.' Iohannes ad haec, qui, sicut nobis postea referebat, aliquid fellis tam diutino angore contracti in regem evomere cogitabat, tam placidus repente effectus est, ut nihil animo ipsius umquam aequabilius esse potuisset. Inde ad singula respondit se quidem negare non posse, primo tot acerbitate nuntiorum fuisse permotum; inter ipsa tamen tacitum crebrius cogitasse, simulatis potius quam veris minarum intentionibus haec erga se agitari; postremo quoque cuncta dilationum obstacula ex superioribus totius triennii actis vel dictis rescisse, nec esse quicquam reliqui, quod merito odio sui factum suspicari deberet: unde si qua ea essent, se penitus animo depulisse, gratiae tantum, quam tam clementi magnificentia obtulisset, gratulari, et quod regii pectoris in hoc et robur constantiae et moderationis mediae pervidisset temperamentum satis egregium. Rege his in multam gratiam delinito pluribusque eum compellandi parante, munera imperatoria primum excipi postulavit. Quo facto, reditus indulgentiam e vestigio obsecravit. Rex ammirans: 'Quomodo', inquit, 'haec tam repentina fieri possit divulsio? Tanto temporis spatio alterutrum expectati, modo vix visi, ita abrumpemur ignoti? Nunc interim mutuo semel conspectu aperuit, iterum visi iam amplius, tertio tota iam plenitudo notionis vel amicitiae firmabitur. Inde domino tuo remittendus, digno eo teque deduceris honore.' His Iohanne assentiente, secundi legati iubentur intromitti, eoque praesente munera quae deferebant oblata.

(135) Tunc demum utrisque ad hospitia remissis, post aliquantum tempus Iohannes a rege revocatus, familiaria multa cum eo conseruit. De nostri

— almost like a godhead accessible to none or to very few — he saw everything draped with rare coverings, and floor—tiles stretching evenly to the walls. The Caliph himself reclined upon a most richly ornate couch. They do not use thrones or chairs as other peoples do, but recline on divans or couches when conversing or eating, their legs crossed one over the other. As John came into his presence, the Caliph stretched out a hand to be kissed. This hand—kissing not being customarily granted to any of his own people or to foreigners, and never to persons of low and middling rank, but only to the high—born and to those of exceptional dignity, the Caliph none the less gave John his hand to kiss.

(134) Then the Caliph signed to John to be seated. A lengthy silence ensued on both sides. Then the Caliph began: 'I know your heart has long been hostile to me, and that is why I refused you an audience till now. You yourself know that I could not do otherwise. I appreciate your steadfastness and your learning. I wish you to know that things which may have disturbed you in that letter were not said out of enmity towards you; and not only do I now freely receive you, but assure you that you shall have whatever you ask.' John — who, as he later told us, had expected to utter something harsh to the Caliph, since he had long harboured such resentment — suddenly became very calm and could never have felt more equable in spirit. So he answered that he could not deny he had at first been greatly exercised by the harsh tone of the emissaries, and had thought it better to remain silent for a long period than to torment himself by feigned rather than true statements of threats in response to the Caliph's threats; but eventually all the obstacles placed in his way by deeds and words over three years had been removed from above, and now no obstacle based on justified enmity remained to make him doubtful of his status. This being so, he had dismissed these things completely from his mind, and was only glad that he had won such generosity and favour, and that in this matter he had perceived such strength of purpose and moderation in the royal heart, and a most noble character. The Caliph was greatly pleased with these remarks, and addressed John on other subjects. Then he asked him to hand over the presents from the Emperor. When this was done, John instantly requested permission to leave. The Caliph asked in surprise: 'How does this sudden change come about? Since both of us have waited so long for a sight of each other, and since we have now scarcely met, is it right for us to part as strangers? Now that we are together, there is an opportunity for each of us to acquire a little knowledge of the other's mind, and we could meet again at greater length, and on a third occasion forge a truly firm bond of understanding and friendship. Then, when I send you back to your master, you could bear yourself thither with all due honour.' John agreed to this. They ordered the other emissaries to be brought in, and the presents which they were carrying were handed over to the Caliph.

(135) The Christians returned to their lodging, and when after a time John was again called to see the Caliph, he conversed with him on a

imperatoris potentia atque prudentia, de robore et copia militum vel exercitus, de gloria et divitiis, de bellorum industria et successibus, multaque id generis. Sua econtra iactare, quanto exercitus robore omnes seculi reges excelleret. Ad haec Iohannes pauca respondit, ut possint qualitercumque regis animum mitigare, tandemque addit: 'Illud vere fateor, regem me hoc seculo neminem nosse, qui nostro imperatori terra armis aut equis possit aequari.' [...]

number of subjects of mutual interest: the power and wisdom of our Emperor, the strength and numbers of his army, his glory and wealth, events of war, and many things of that kind. The Caliph for his part boasted that his army exceeded that of any other of the rulers of the world in strength. John made but little answer to this, saying only what might serve to pacify the Caliph's mind, but eventually he added: 'I speak the truth when I say that I know of no monarch in the world who can equal our Emperor in lands or arms or horses.'

## 15. Two miracles concerning al—Mansur (997)

*In August 997 al—Mansur, in the most devastating of all his raids, laid waste large areas of the Kingdom of León and penetrated as far as Compostela, destroying the city and the Cathedral, and removing its bells to serve — inverted — as oil—lamps in the Great Mosque at Cordova. He respected only the tomb of the Apostle St James. The text which follows is one of three gathered into an appendix to the* Historia Turpini *(on which see text 8), and is headed in the MSS 'Calixtus papa' in line with the spurious attribution of other elements to Calixtus II. In view of the deformation suffered by the name of Almanzor, al—Mansur, it is not likely that this text was written in Spain even if the story originated there. That al—Mansur and his men suffered divine vengeance in the form of*

Quid patrie Gallecie post Karoli necem accidit, nobis est memorie tradendum. Cum igitur post Karoli necem Gallecie tellus per multa tempora in pace temporali quiesceret, demonis instinctu surrexit quidam Sarracenus Altumaior Cordube, dicens quod terram Gallecianam et Yspanicam quam Karolus ab antecessoribus suis olim abstulerat, ipse sibi adquireret legibusque Sarracenicis subiugaret. Tunc, coadunatis sibi exercitibus multis, terras et patriam huc illucque deuastando, usque ad beati Iacobi urbem peruenit, et quicquit in ea inuenit totum ui rapuit. Similiter basilicam apostolicam indigne totam deuastauit, codices et mensas argenteas et tintinnabula et cetera ornamenta ab ea abstulit. Cumque in ea Sarraceni ipsi cum equis suis hospitati essent, gens dira digestionem circa etiam ante altare apostolicum agere cepit. Quapropter alii ex illis diuina ulcione operante solucione uentris commoti quicquit in corpore continebant per posteriora foras eiciebant. Alii uero occulorum lumina, per basilicam et urbem ut ceci errantes, amittebant. Quid plura? Hac egritudine idem Altumaior tactus, omnino etiam execatus, consilio cuiusdam capti sui eiusdem basilice sacerdotis cepit inuocare Deum Christianorum in auxilium his uerbis dicens: 'O Deus Christianorum, Deus Iacobi, Deus Marie, Deus Petri, Deus Martini, Deus omnium Christianorum, si me ad pristinam sanitatem reuocaueris, Mahummet deum meum abnegabo et Iacobi magni uiri ad patriam rapacitatis causa amplius non ueniam. O Iacobe, uir magnus, si uteri meo et occulis meis salutem dederis, quicquit a domo tua abstuli restituam.' Tunc post quindecim dies, omnibus dupliciter ecclesie restitutis, ad pristinam salutem Altumaior reuocatus a patria sancti Iacobi recedit, promittens se non amplius uenire in horis eius causa rapacitatis, et predicans Deum Christianorum esse magnum, et Iacobum magnum esse uirum. Postea uero horas Yspanicas deuastando peruenit ad uillam que uulgo dicitur Orniz, in qua beati Romani basilica obtima ac pulcherrima erat, palleis et codicibus obtimis et crucibus argenteis et textis aureis decorata. Ad quam cum iniquus Altumaior uenit,

*dysentery, many dying of it, is recorded pleasurably by several Spanish chronicles.*

*The text is taken from the same source as text 8, pp. 395—97.*

*In the second miracle, no 'Orniz' can be identified in Spain. There are many churches dedicated to St Romanus (Román), and there are several saints of that name. The writer might have chosen the name because the famous church at Blaye, north of Bordeaux on one of the pilgrim routes into Spain, and rich in relics of Roland, was dedicated to him; however, possible candidates are San Román de Tobillas, east of León, where there was an early monastic church, and San Román de Entrepeñas near Saldaña (Palencia), where there was a priory known to have passed to the reforming Cluniacs and thus having French connections when this text was composed in about 1140.*

It is our duty to record what happened to the land of Galicia after Charlemagne's death. It remained at peace for a long time after this, but then, by the devil's prompting, there arose in Cordova a certain Saracen, al—Mansur, who proclaimed that he would conquer for himself all the lands of Galicia and Spain which Charlemagne had long ago taken from his predecessors. He gathered all his numerous forces and, ravaging the lands on all sides, eventually reached Compostela, and took as booty all that he found therein. In the same way he shamefully sacked the whole church of the Apostle, removing from it manuscripts and silver tables and bells and other ornaments. The Saracens had lodged themselves and stabled their horses in the church, and this foul people began to digest their meal before the very altar of the Apostle. By divine retribution, some of them were afflicted by looseness of the bowels, and shot whatever they had in their bellies out through their back passages. Others lost the sight of their eyes and wandered blindly about the church and the city. What next? Al—Mansur himself was afflicted with this complaint and, completely blinded, on the advice of one of his prisoners who was a priest of that same church, began to call upon the aid of the God of the Christians with these words: 'O God of the Christians, God of St James, of St Mary, of St Peter, of St Martin, of all Christians, if you will restore me to my earlier state of health, I will renounce my god Muhammad and will not come again to the land of great St James bent on taking booty. O St James, the Great, if you restore health to my belly and my eyes, I will hand back all that I have stolen from your shrine.' After a fortnight, everything having been handed back doubled in value to the church, al—Mansur was restored to health and departed from the land of St James, promising never to return to those parts on expeditions for booty, and proclaiming the greatness of the God of the Christians and of St James. After that he ravaged other parts of Spain, and coming to a place called Orniz, in which there was a splendid and very beautiful church dedicated to St Romanus, rich in copes and fine manuscripts and silver crosses, and adorned with hangings worked

rapuit quicquit in ea inuenit, et uillam similiter deuastauit. Cumque in eadem uilla cum suis exercitibus hospitatus esset, quidam dux exercituum eius, ingressus in eandem basilicam, uidit columnas pulcherrimas lapideas, que eiusdem ecclesie tecta sustentabant que etiam in summitate deargentate et deaurate erant, nequicie et inuidie stimulo tactus, quendam cuneum ferreum inter basses cuiusdam columne et eandem columnam infixit. Cum itaque cuneum illum malleo ferreo fortiter magnis etiam ictibus feriret, totamque basilicam precipitare temptaret, diuino operante iudicio idem homo lapis efficitur. Qui etiam lapis usque hodie in effigie hominis in eadem basilica perstitit, habens talem colorem qualem eiusdem Sarraceni tunica tunc gerebat. Solent etiam peregrini enarrare qui illuc precum causa tendunt, quod lapis ille fetorem emittit. Quod ut Altumaior uidit, ait domesticis suis: 'Magnus est reuera et glorificandus Deus Christianorum, qui tales habet alumnos, qui cum sint ab hac uita migrati tamen uiuos sibi rebelles ita iustificant, quod uni occulorum lumen auferunt, de alio lapidem mutum faciunt. Iacobus lumen occulorum a me abstulit: Romanus de homine lapidem fecit. Sed Iacobus magis clementissimus est quam iste Romanus. Iacobus enim occulos meos reddidit mihi misertus, sed hominem meum reddere non uult Romanus. Fugiamus ergo ab his horis.'

Tunc confusus abscessit paganus cum suis exercitibus. Nec fuit postea per multum tempus qui beati Iacobi patriam debellare auderet. Sciant igitur se dampnandos in euum, qui eius tellurem amplius inquietauerint. Qui uero a potestate Sarracenorum illam custodierint celesti munere remunerabuntur.

in gold, this unspeakable al—Mansur stripped it of all that he found in it, and likewise destroyed the settlement. While he was lodging in the place with his army, one of his commanders saw, on entering the church, most beautiful stone columns which, covered in gold and silver, held up the church roof. Goaded on by evil and greed, he inserted a metal wedge into the base of one of the pillars. When he drove the wedge in, with mighty blows of a heavy hammer, he tried to make the whole church collapse, but by divine intervention the man was turned to stone. The stone in the shape of a man still stands today in the church, coloured in precisely the same way as the Saracen's uniform he was then wearing. Pilgrims who go there to pray say that the stone gives out a stench. When al—Mansur saw this, he said to his servants: 'The God of the Christians is greatly to be praised, having such followers; for when they have departed from this life they deal justly with the living who offend them, in one case taking away a man's sight, in another turning him into a mute stone. St James took away my sight; St Romanus turned a man into stone. But James is more merciful than this Romanus. James in compassion for me restored my sight, but Romanus refuses to give me back the man he turned to stone. Let us therefore depart quickly from this place.'

So the pagan left in confusion with his forces. Afterwards it was a long time before he dared to attack St James's land again. Let those who would disturb that land know that they would be damned for evermore. Those who protect that land from the power of the Saracens will be rewarded with favours in heaven.

### 16.   St James announces the capture of Coimbra (1064)

*Tales of miracles and saintly apparitions are often conventional, formulaically related, and tedious to the modern mind.   The following seems to have qualities of drama and human interest which make it exceptional.   The hint that the King in his 'corruptible flesh' had led a less than fully virtuous life should not be missed: he felt unworthy to approach the Deity directly and needed the intercession of St James, and even then, had to pray with extra devoutness.   For St James as Patron of Spain and a warrior—saint, compare text 13.   Only a 'greculus', translated as 'a Greek' but perhaps better 'an ignorant little Greek', and a newcomer, could be allowed to show himself unaware of the Apostle's martial qualities.   On the theme of St James in medieval Spain, especially as Santiago 'Matamoros', see Américo Castro, chapter 4.   A general account of the cult and the pilgrimage is that of T.D. Kendrick, St James in Spain (London, 1960), and of great interrest is R.A. Fletcher, St James's Catapult: The Life and Times of Diego Gelmírez ... (Oxford, 1984), concerning the Bishop and eventually Archbishop of Santiago de Compostela under whose rule the cult and propaganda for it reached their height (1100—40).   The present writer's guarded word when introducing the matter of St James in Spain, 'dicitur', 'it is said', is exceptional in Spain at the time, when there was normally unquestioning belief in the early preaching*

Quibus triunphatis, ut Coynbria illarum partium maxima ciuitas, que istis prefuerat, in cultum christianitatis redigeretur, limina beati Iacobi apostoli, cuius corpus per diuinam nostri Redemptoris visitacionem ad Yspaniam delatum dicitur, rex flagitando petiit.   Ibique, suplicatione per triduum facta, vt id bellum prosperos ac felices haberet euentus, apostolum ad diuinam magestatem pro eo intercessorem fore postulabat.   Adorato itaque venerando loco, Fernandus rex, diuino fretus munimine, Coynbriam audacter accelerat, castrisque supra eam positis, consedit.

Ceterum, vt deuotissima eius oratio qualiter Deo accepta fuerit omnibus clareat, exprimere dignum duxi.   Conpleta namque extitit in deuocione Fernandi regis rata sententia nostri Saluatoris: 'Amen', inquiens, 'dico vobis quodcumque petieritis Patrem in nomine meo dabit vobis.'   In hoc enim quod ciuitatem illam a ritibus paganorum erui et ad fidem christianorum reuerti flagitabat, profecto in nomine Ihesu, quod saluator interpretatur, Deum Patrem pro eius salute rogabat.   Sed quoniam adhuc Fernandus, in corruptibili carne positus, familiarem se diuine gratie esse per meritum vite nesciebat, apostoli sufragia postulat, quatinus ad intercedendum piissimi magistri familiarem notissimum accedat.   Pugnat itaque Fernandus rex apud Coynbriam materiali gladio, pro cuius uictoria capescenda Iacobus Christi miles apud magistrum intercedere non cessat.

*mission of the Apostle to the Peninsula, the miraculous transfer of his remains to Galicia, and the discovery of these by divine revelation at what became Compostela early in the 9th century.*

*Ferdinand began to besiege Coimbra on 19 March 1064 and entered it on 9 July. The fate of the inhabitants is uncertain. An entry in the Annals of Compostela says that 5,050 persons were enslaved. An Arabic source says that after the commanding Muslim general had surrendered with his wives and children, other defenders fought on until exhausted by hunger; when they surrendered, the men were killed and the women and children enslaved. What is stated about this in our text, even though only a proposal by the defenders, was in reality the norm of the times when cities or castles surrendered on terms to besiegers of either religion in Spain.*

*This miracle is recounted in the* Liber Sancti Jacobi *(II, 19), where the pilgrim is a Greek bishop, no less, named Stephen; and in a hymn 'Ad honorem Regis summi', in which the same bishop is mentioned (respectively pages 283–85 and 398 of the Whitehill edition).*

*The text is taken from the* Historia Seminensis *(on which see text 12), pp. 190–93 (with* perparvum *four words from the end as in the reading of Vázquez de Parga replacing the meaningless* per parium *of the edition: he has this text on pp. 91–95).*

After these victorious campaigns, waged in order that Coimbra, the chief city of those parts and superior to them all, should be restored to the Christian faith, the King went with all haste to Compostela, to which the body of St James the Apostle is said to have been taken by the divine aid of our Redeemer. There, having prayed for three days that the campaign should have a successful outcome, he begged the Apostle to act as intercessor for him with the Lord. From that holy and venerated place King Ferdinand, trusting in divine protection, confidently set out for Coimbra and besieged it, setting up positions all round.

For the rest, in order that it should be clear to all that his most earnest prayer was acceptable to God, I consider it worth quoting the following: while he was in a state of intense devotion, the firm declaration of our Saviour was repeated to King Ferdinand: 'Verily, verily, I say unto you, whatsoever ye shall ask the Father in my name, He will give it to you' [John 16.23]. Since he was seeking to tear the city from pagan rites and restore it to the Christian faith, he set out in Jesus's name (this being interpreted as 'Saviour'), and prayed to God for their safety. But since up to this time Ferdinand had no experience of divine grace through any merit of his life, being a man of ordinarily corruptible flesh, he prayed to the Apostle, begging him to intercede as a close associate of most merciful God. So King Ferdinand fought on at Coimbra with his earthly weapons, while James the soldier of Christ did not cease to intercede for him with the Lord in favour of his victory.

Tandem Fernando serenissimo regi celitus concessum triumfum hoc modo beatus apostolus Conpostelle innotuit: venerat a Ierosolymis peregrinus quidam greculus, ut credo, et spiritu et opibus pauper, qui in porticu ecclesie beati Iacobi diu permanens, die noctuque vigiliis et orationibus instabat. Cumque nostra loquela iam paulisper vteretur, audit indigenas templum santum pro necessitatibus suis crebro intrantes, aures apostoli bonum militem nominando, interpellare. Ipse uero apud semetipsum, non solum equitem non fuisse, ymo etiam nec vsquam equum ascendisse asserens, supereminente nocte, clauditur dies tunc ex more, cum peregrinus in oratione pernoctaret, subito in extasi raptus ei apostolus Iacobus, velud quasdam claues in manu tenens, aparuit, eumque alacri vultu aloquens ait: 'Heri', inquid, 'pia vota precancium deridens, credebas me strenuissimum militem numquam fuisse.' Et hec dicens, allatus est magne stature splendidissimus equus ante fores eclesie, cuius niuea claritas totam apertis portis perlustrabat ecclesiam, quem apostolus ascendens, ostensis clauibus peregrino innotuit Coymnbriam ciuitatem Fernando regi in crastinum circa tertiam diei horam se daturum.

Interea, labentibus astris, cum die dominica sol primo clarum patefecerat orbem, grecus tanta visione atonitus omnes clericos et omnes ville primores in vnum conuocat, atque huius nominis et expeditionis ignarus, eis ordine rem pandendo, Fernandum regem hodie Coinbriam ingressum dicit. Qui denotato die legatos cum festinatione ad castra inuictissimi regis dirigunt, qui solerter iter agentes percipiant, utrum ex Deo hec visio procederet, ut ad laudem nominis sui ministri manifestari huic mundo debuisset. At legati, postquam maturantes in Coymbriam peruenerunt, ipso die, quem apostolus Iacobus Conpostelle significauerat, regem agressum hora tertia ciuitatem inuenerunt.

Siquidem, cum per aliquot temporis spatia Coynbrienses infra menia inclusos teneret, positis in giro arietibus, murum ciuitatis in parte fregerat. Quod uidentes barbari, legatos cum supliciis ad regem miserunt, qui sibi liberisque vitam tantummodo postulantes, et urbem et omnem substantiam preter viaticum perparvum stipendium regi tradiderunt.

Eventually the Blessed Apostle of Compostela informed noble King Ferdinand of the triumph granted to him by heaven in the following way. There arrived from Jerusalem a certain Greek pilgrim, as I am told, meek in spirit and poor in worldly goods, who stayed a long while at the door of the Cathedral of St James, praying and keeping vigil by day and night. Being after a short time acquainted with their speech, he was able to listen to the local people as they repeatedly went into the church on their business, addressing the Apostle and calling him 'the good soldier'. This man declared that not only was James not a knight, but had never even mounted a horse. With night coming on and as the pilgrim stayed praying in a sort of trance in the darkness, the Apostle St James appeared to him, holding what seemed to be keys in his hand and, with a cheerful countenance, addressed him: 'Yesterday', he said, 'you mocked the pious words of those at prayer, denying that I had ever been a soldier (and a very active one at that).' As he said this, a most magnificent horse of great stature appeared at the doors of the church, and — since the doors were open — his shining brightness illuminated the whole building. The Apostle mounted him and, brandishing his keys, told the pilgrim that the city of Coimbra would surrender to King Ferdinand about the third hour the following day.

Meanwhile time moved on and the early brightness of Sunday began to light the world. The Greek, amazed at such a vision, called together all the clergy and principal men of the town and, knowing nothing of the name of Coimbra nor of the campaign, explained the matter to them, telling them that on that day King Ferdinand would enter Coimbra. Messengers were sent with all speed to the headquarters of the invincible monarch to find out if the vision had proceeded from God, so that due praise of the name of His minister [St James] could be given for having so shown himself to us in this world. The messengers, having reached Coimbra at speed that very day, found that what St James of Compostela had told them was true: the King had entered the city at the third hour.

Indeed, the King had already for some time kept the inhabitants of Coimbra penned inside the defences, with battering—rams in position all round, and had broken down a section of the city walls. When the barbarians realized this they sent representatives to the King to appeal to him to spare the lives of themselves and their children, promising to hand over to the King the city and all their possessions except for very modest provisions needed for their journey [to a place of refuge].

## 17.  The capture of Barbastro (1064)

*The narration of Amatus of Monte Cassino (Aimé de Montcassin) of the French expedition to Barbastro in 1064 is an episode in his* Historia Normannorum, *written from about 1080 to 1083. The Latin original is lost, and we know the text only from the anonymous Old French translation made in the 14th century. The episode remained famous enough to form the theme, in the late 12th century, of the French epic* Le Siège de Barbastre.

*Barbastro was an important town and fortress in the line which ran from Lérida to Saragossa, in the lands of the Muslim ruler of the latter city. He seems to have abandoned it to its fate. The siege lasted for forty days from 6 July to mid–August (from late May or early June to mid–July, according to Ubieto). It seems that Amatus was not exaggerating when he attributed the subsequent loss of the place to the sins of the conquering knights. While no other Christian writer says anything about Barbastro at this time (except to note that the Muslims recovered the city in April 1065), the Cordovese historian Ibn Haiyan has an extensive account (translated by Dozy, Recherches, II, 335, and again by Ubieto, pp. 56–59: see below) based on a contemporary eye–witness report, and there is another in the work of al–Bakri transmitted by the later writer Ibn 'Idari (in Ubieto, 60–61). Among the immense quantities of booty taken by the Christians, Crespin took for himself 1,500 young women and 500 cartloads of furnishings, ornaments, clothing and coverings, while some 50,000 Muslims were killed or taken away as prisoners.    On leaving*

(5) Et à ce que la religion de la Foi christiane fust aëmplie, et macast detestable folie de li Sarrazin, par inspiration de Dieu, s'acorderent en una volenté li roy et li conte et li prince en uno conseill.  C'est que fust assemblée grant multitude de gent, et grant chevalerie de Françoiz et de Borguegnons et d'autre gent, et fussent en compaignie de li fortissime Normant, et des deüssent aler combatre en Espaingne, à ce que la chevalerie de li Sarrazin, laquelle il avoient assamblée, fust occupée et subjette a li Chretien.  Et à ceste choze faire fu eslit un qui se clamoit Robert Crespin.  Et quant il fu eslut, il se appareilla d'aler à la bataille oùillec estoit comman d'aler.  Et clamerent l'ayde de Dieu; dont Dieu fu present en l'aide de ceux qui l'avoient demandé.  Dont li fidel de Dieu orent victoire de la bataille, quar une grant part de li Sarrazin furent mort. Et rendirent grace à Dieu de la victoire qu'Il presta à son pueple.

(6) Et alore fu prese le cité qui se clamoit Barbataire, molt grant tere, et plene de grant ricchesce, et molt garnie.  Et tout l'ost voust que Robert Crespin la feïst garder, à ce que en lo secont an retornast o tel axercit ou plus grant, pour prendre des autres cités d'Espaingne.

(7) Et lo dyable, armé de subtillissime malice, pour invidie de lo bon commencement de la Foi, pensa de contrester, et metre en lo penser de li

*Crespin installed a garrison of 1,500 knights and 1,000 foot—soldiers, but these were evidently insufficient to outweigh — here one returns to the view of Amatus — God's punishment for the sins of the Christians. Crespin, the son of Gilbert Crespin, a Norman lord, was evidently an energetic wanderer and soldier of fortune like others of his extraordinary race at the time. He is recorded in Byzantium from 1069, where two chroniclers listed his deeds at length. Eventually he died in Armenia, poisoned.*

*Amatus makes Crespin out to be the sole leader, but others may have had equal status: Count Ermengol III ('de Barbastro', since he was killed there), with a force of Catalans; Duke William VIII of Aquitaine; and William of Montreuil, the Pope's standard—bearer* (gonfalonier). *The evidence about this is reviewed, with much else of interest, by A. Ferreiro in* Journal of Medieval History, *9 (1983), 129—44. Ferreiro makes it clear that the oft—cited letter of Pope Alexander II (1061—73) to the clergy of Castel Vulturno in Campania, which does indeed promise remission of sins to those going to fight the Muslims in Spain, cannot be taken as referring directly to the Barbastro expedition nor taken as a fully 'crusading' statement which in some way antedates the true call to the First Crusade made at Clermont in 1095 by Urban II.*

*The text is taken from that published by V. de Bartholomaeis in* Fonti per la Storia d'Italia *(Rome, 1935), pp. 13—16. On the episode, see, in addition to Ferreiro, Defourneaux, pp. 131—35, and A. Ubieto Arteìa,* Historia de Aragón *(Saragossa, 1981), pp. 54—66.*

(5) In order to assist the spread of the Christian faith, and destroy the hateful folly of the Saracens, the King and the princes and the nobles agreed, under God's inspiration, on an objective. It was that a great number of fighting men, and knights from among the French and Burgundians and others, should assemble and go together with the mighty Normans to campaign in Spain, in order to bring down Saracen military power and make it subject to the Christians. For this purpose Robert Crespin was chosen as commander. On being chosen, he began to make all preparations for going to war. They prayed for divine aid, and this was granted to those that sought it, for God's faithful secured victory and a great number of the Saracens were killed. All gave thanks to the Lord for the victory He granted to His people.

(6) Then the city of Barbastro was captured: it was very extensive, full of enormous wealth. The whole army wished Robert Crespin to retain it, and that he should return the following year with the same army or with a larger one, in order to take other cities in Spain.

(7) But the devil, full of subtlest evil, out of envy of this happy progress by the Christian faith, tried to turn it back, putting lustful thoughts

chevalier de li Christiens feu d'amour. Et, qué se hauchassent, chaïrent en bas. Pour laquel choze Christ fu corrocié, car lo chevalier se donna à lo amor de la fame. Adont, pour lor pechié, perdirent ce qu'il avoient acquesté; et furent secuté de li Sarrazin. Et, perdue la cité, une part furent occis, et une part furent en prison, et une part foyrent et furent delivré.

(8) Crespin, pour la vergoigne, non vouloit puis retorner en son païz; mès vint en Ytalie à ceus de sa contrée. Et là demora par alcuns ans. Et pour faire chevalerie souz lo pooir de lo Impereor, ala en Costentinoble, où il ot molt de triumphe et molt de victoire. Et puiz fu mort.

into the minds of the Christian knights. Those that had risen high were to be cast down. The knights gave themselves over to the love of women, and Christ was angered. So, for their sins, they lost what they had won, and were defeated by the Saracens. Once the city was lost, some of them were killed and others captured; some fled and managed to escape.

(8) Crespin in his shame did not care to return to his homeland; instead, he went to join his countrymen in Italy, and stayed there for some years. Then, hoping to do knightly deeds under the Emperor's banner, he went to Constantinople, where he enjoyed many triumphs and victories. After this he died.

## 18. The mosque of Toledo (1085)

*The capture of Toledo by Alfonso VI of Castile—León in 1085 was the single most momentous event of the long centuries of warfare. Not only was it of immense strategic importance, since from it the roads to the south, towards the Muslim heartland, lay open, over relatively easy country; it had national importance as the old capital of the Gothic kingdom before 711, and had been the seat of the Primate of the nation's Church. Alfonso for several years had besieged the city and devastated its territory, trying also to use diplomatic means; it was these which were ultimately successful, in that the Muslim ruler, al—Qadir, was persuaded finally to capitulate on being promised that Alfonso would instal him as King of Valencia. The capitulation was on 6 May; Alfonso made his ceremonial entry on 25 May; and the episode recounted in the following extract is to be placed in July.*

*Among the terms of the capitulation was evidently a clause by which the Muslims — a particularly useful and even distinguished population — were guaranteed not only their lives and most of their property, but also continued possession of at least one mosque. Such conditions were normal enough in the Peninsula, but clearly unnatural and intolerable to the passionate and violent French and others from beyond the Pyrenees (as at Barbastro in 1064, our text 17, and even more plainly before Las Navas in 1212, text 40). In the present instance both intolerant protagonists were French. Bernard de Sédirac was a monk sent from Cluny in order to occupy the important abbacy of Sahagún in about 1080, and was an obvious choice for the archbishopric of Toledo and the primacy of Spain*

[...] Qui [Bernardus] mox veniens, factus Abbas, omnibus se exhibuit amabilem et benignum, adeo quod cum Deus omnipotens Toletum Christianae restituit potestati, mox ipse post modicum intervallum fuit electus in Archiepiscopum et Primatem. Cumque Rex ad partes Legionis ivisset, ipse electus, Regina Constantia hortante, adscitis militibus christianis, maiorem Mezquitam ingressus est Toletanam, et eliminata spurcitia Mahometi, erexit altaria fidei christianae, et in maiori turri campanas ad convocationem fidelium collocavit. Quod cum ad Regis notitiam pervenisset, indignatus animo, et dolore accensus, eo quod Sarracenis pactum firmaverat de Mezquita, a Sancto Facundo tribus diebus venit Toletum, proponens Bernardum electum et Reginam Constantiam incendio concremare. Cumque tanti furoris indignatio ad notitiam Toletanorum Arabum pervenisset, maiores et minores cum parvulis et uxoribus in pago qui Magam dicitur, Regi obviam exierunt. Cumque Rex ad eorum multitudinem pervenisset, existimans eos causa querelae venisse, sic respondit: 'Non vobis iniuria facta fuit, sed mihi, cuius fides fuit hactenus illibata; sed iam de cetero de fide non potero me

*when the city was captured. Queen Constanza was a Burgundian princess whom Alfonso married in 1079, his second wife. They evidently formed a powerful combination of Gallic intolerance, and seem to have had the support of the Christian troops; the governor whom Alfonso had installed in the captured city, the famous Sisnando Davídiz, a Christian nobleman born and raised under Muslim rule in what is now Portugal, would have been a firm supporter of the terms of the capitulation, but was clearly powerless to save the mosque. According to a note of M. Férotin in* Bibliothèque de l'Ecole des Chartes, *61 (1900), 340, the whole episode is legendary (though of early date); but the fact that Bernard was officially consecrated as Archbishop and the cathedral was endowed by royal charter on 18 December 1086 without reference to this episode hardly serves to stamp it a fiction.*

*Church bells are more important than might appear from the brief reference in our extract. The Muslims loathed the sound of them, and their ringing in churches in al—Andalus and elsewhere was forbidden. For the Archbishop to instal bells in the minaret of the mosque and to ring them was thus a peculiarly offensive sign of triumph and contempt for the defeated Muslims. It should be noted that nearly up to the moment when Alfonso captured the city, Toledo had a 'Mozarabic' Archbishop, Pascual, as it had had for centuries: he died during the siege, conveniently creating the vacancy for the new man. Bernard continued as Archbishop until his death in 1125.*

*The text is taken from* De rebus Hispaniae, *VI.24, for which see text 2.*

[...] When Bernard arrived soon after, he was made Abbot [of Sahagún], in which post he showed himself to be gentle and kindly to all, up to the time when Almighty God restored Toledo to the power of the Christians, and there after a short while he was elected to the archbishopric and primacy. When the King had gone off to León the Archbishop—elect, with Queen Constanza encouraging him, and with the approval of the Christian troops, entered the chief mosque of Toledo, and having purged it of the filth of Muhammad, set up an altar of the Christian faith, and placed bells in the main tower so that the Christians could be called to worship. When news of this reached the King, he was outraged and deeply grieved, because of the agreement he had made. with the Saracens concerning the mosque, and in three days he travelled from Sahagún to Toledo, proposing to have Bernard the Archbishop—elect and Queen Constanza burned alive. When news of the King's great anger reached the Moors of Toledo, the great and the small together with their wives and children went out to meet the King at Maga. As soon as the King reached the main group of them, he, realizing that they had come to make their protest, said: 'This outrage was not done to you, but to me, for up to this point my trustworthiness was unquestioned; now in other matters I shall not

iactare: mea autem intererit, et vobis satisfacere, et in praesumptores acrius vindicare.' Arabes autem, ut erant prudentes, elevatis vocibus, et flexis poplitibus, cum lacrimis audientiam postularunt. Tunc Rex aliquantum substitit, tenens equum, et Arabes in hunc modum perorare coeperunt: 'Bene novimus, quod Archiepiscopus dux et Princeps est legis vestrae, et si causa fuerimus necis eius, ob zelum fidei Christiani nos percutient una die, et si Regina perierit causa nostri, semini eius erimus perpetuo odiosi, et post dies tuos acrius vindicabunt. Unde petimus, ut parcas eis, et nos voluntarie te absolvimus a foedere iuramenti.' His auditis, ira Regis in gaudium commutatur, eo quod Mezquitam habere poterat sine fidei laesione, et ingressus est urbem regiam, omnia pacifice pertractavit.

be able to boast of that trustworthiness; now it will concern me both to give you satisfaction and to punish the offenders severely.' However the Moors, being prudent, raising their voices and on bended knees, sought an audience. Then the King stayed for a while, holding his reins, and the Moors began to address him as follows: 'We are fully aware that the Archbishop is the head of your faith, and if we were to be the cause of his death, there might come a day when the Christians out of zeal for their faith would strike at us; and if the Queen should perish on account of us, we shall be forever hateful to her descendants, and after your time they will take a bitter revenge. So we beg you to spare them, and we voluntarily absolve you from the bond of your oath.' When he heard this the King's rage turned to joy, since he could have the mosque without any breach of faith, and he went into the royal city where he dealt with all matters of business in a peaceful way.

### 19.  St Dominic of Silos frees a captive (1087)

*St Dominic was Abbot of the great monastery of Silos (Santo Domingo de Silos), near Burgos, from 1041 to 1073, and his sainthood was locally proclaimed soon after his death. A few years later the monk Grimaldo, whose name suggests that he was of French origin (Grimault), began to set down the Saint's* Vita *consisting of a prologue, a hymn, a life of the Saint, and numerous miracles worked by the Saint in life and after death. Of the three Books into which the work is divided, the first two seem to be Grimaldo's, the third a slightly later addition made as new miracles were recorded. The nature of the miracles is very diverse. Most relate to cures of the sick, but seven concern the release of captives held by the Moors. One (II.26) concerns Christian soldiers who had been justly imprisoned by King Alfonso VI because, setting off from Hita at a date which can be placed about 1088—91, they had attacked t<sup>h</sup>e Moorish inhabitants of Guadalajara then on terms of official truce. In I.16, it is a question of Moors held captive as slaves in the monastery of Silos: they escape, but the Saint in life receives a revelation about their hiding—place, and they are found and returned into captivity. In later times it was chiefly as a liberator of Christians held captive in Moorish lands that St Dominic was famous, as will appear in text 44 of Pero Marín; in this activity St James for a time offered competition (text 27).*

*Captives were taken and held by both sides with the expectation that*

Quidam miles, Petrus uocatus, de uico qui dicitur Plantata ortus, uir satis egregie strenuitatis et non infime nobilitatis, cum quodam optimate nostre prouincie quodam castrum, Alaietum uocatum, in terra Sarracenorum situm, comitante magna et ualida militari multitudine, perrexit.  In quo castro per dies aliquot cum aliis comilitonibus ad predandum exiuit; sed accidente graui infortunio, occulto Dei iudicio, omnes a Sarracenis capti sunt; et qui hostili prede iniabant, pro dolor!, hostium preda facti sunt.

De quibus captiuis facta inter Agarenos consueta partitione, prenominatus Petrus in cuiusdam militis partem deuenit.  Qui miles eum ad domum suam perduxit et, quia domus illius carcere carebat, in altissima uoragine lutulendi lacus eum demersit.  In quo lacu per duos annos miseram uitam et omnino infelicem omnique dira mortem deteriorem in luctu et in totius generis afflictione, sine omnis uiuentis consolatione, duxit.  Sed miserante Domino, qui, ueraci Sacre Scripture testimonio, peccata hominum in se confidentium in tribulatione dimittit, infelicem captiuum in infelicitate sua non despexit neque neglexit, sed per beatum patronum nostrum, Dominicum, ab infestissime captiuitatis iugo clementer eripuit et optatissime libertati mirabiliter restituit.

Cuius ereptionis series hec est.  Petro milite in castro quod uocatur Murcia, litoris maris proximo, in horribilis lacus detruso uoragine, in ipso

*they would ultimately be ransomed; there was a well—organized trade in this. While prisoners they were made to work hard in the craft industries or on the land, and the many who had no financial resources might do so until they died; but for these, Silos and other charitable bodies on the Christian side tried to raise money with which to purchase their freedom. Perhaps it was only when this failed, and it must have been often, that divine aid was invoked. In all these stories, as in those of Pero Marín later, there is great insistence on the brutality of Moorish owners and jailers. In Pero Marín's accounts,* penas *is translated throughout as 'hardships' rather than 'torments' or 'tortures', and this seems right, but doubtless there was starvation and there were beatings, in order to speed the ransoming process, or in rare instances to secure conversion to Islam. Transfer of captives 'beyond the sea' to N. Africa was much feared, since this greatly reduced the chances of ransom or escape. We have no independent testimony about any of this.*

*In many respects, here and in the writings of Pero Marín, there is a certain conventional structure in the stories and a rather formulaic repetition of motifs which make one guarded about accepting the literal truth of each case.*

*The text which follows is II.25, datable by the reference to the Aledo campaign to about 1087. It is taken from the edition and study by Vitalino Valcárcel,* La 'Vita Dominici Siliensis' de Grimaldo *(Logroño, 1982), pp. 370—75.*

A certain soldier named Peter, from the village of Llantada, known for his courage and of good family, set off for Aledo in the lands of the Saracens, as a member of a large and strong force commanded by a nobleman of our region. When they reached the castle he and some of his comrades spent some days taking booty; but, by the inscrutable will of God, they suffered a great misfortune, and all were captured by the Saracens. Those who were keen to take booty from the enemy themselves became, alas, the enemy's booty.

When the Agarenes divided up the captives in their usual way, Peter fell to the lot of a soldier who took him to his house and, since he had no proper prison, cast him into a very deep watery pit full of slime. In this pit he lived for two years wretchedly and altogether abominably, suffering grief and all manner of afflictions: a state worse than death, and without consolation from any living soul. But God who, according to the true testimony of the Scriptures, pardons the sins of those who trust in Him and cry out to Him in their tribulations, mercifully did not scorn or neglect the wretched prisoner in his misery; instead, through the agency of our blessed Patron, Dominic, He released him in his clemency from the yoke of cruel captivity and restored him to the liberty he so greatly desired.

His liberation occurred as follows. When the soldier Peter had been cast into the depths of his terrifying pit in the city of Murcia, not far from

conticinio noctis IIII ferie ebdomadis, missus a piissimo et omnipotente Domino, beatus Dominicus adest cum magno splendore luminis, in habitu monachali, regens suos gressus sustentatione baculi, diligenter obseratis foribus domus, que undique circumdabat lacum retinentem captiuum. Ad cuius introitum continuo patefactum est obstrusum illius lacus claustrum, omni ex parte munitum ac proprio nomine captiuum intro iacentem uocauit. Cui et ait: 'Miser, cur teipsum neglegis? Et quamobrem hunc teterrimum lacum non egrederis? Et quare te pristine libertatis ignauia pressus, minime conaris?' Qua uoca audita, captiuus intremuit et arbitratus esse dominum suum se decipientem ut egrederetur et sic, inuenta occasione fuge, puniretur aut etiam morti traderetur, hoc responsum reddidit: 'Impossibile est michi, domine, quod mones implere: undique certe strictis coartor uinculis ac miserabiliter detineor altis huius tetri lacus angustiis.' Cui beatus Dominicus: 'Noli', inquid, 'desperare de misericordia Domini, qui semper se inuocantes adiuuat et peccata oppressorum afflictorum in tribulatione relaxat; et ideo tu, in hac tua intolerabili afflictione ad eum in tuo toto corde clama et mee humilitati crede quia in proximo aderit tibi ipsius clementia et, tibi benigne succurrendo, non solum reuocabit ad propria, sed etiam concedet meliora pristinis beneficia.' Ad hanc uocem miserabilis captiuus, lacu clausus, aliquantulum recepta fiducia, contra retulit talia: 'Rogo te, per omnipotentissimam maiestatem, domine, ut indicare michi digneris quis es qui mecum loqueris uel si sunt credenda que prosequeris.' Cui uir sanctus respondit: 'Quod dico, intellige et firmiter tue menti trade nec insit tibi aliqua hesitatio, si uis frui salubri tui corporis et anime comodo; me scito esse Dominicum peccatorem, quondam Exiliensis monasterii abbatem, sed a Domino sum misericordiam consequutus et ego ei obtuli tuas preces et gemitus et ab eo ad te liberandum sum missus; et tu meis ammonitionibus assensum prebe consiliisque, remota omni dubitatione, crede. Et sic omne opus tuum prosperabitur et prosperitatem felix perseuerantia subsequetur. Sagaciter ergo age et quod agis, prudenter dispone. Post hoc biduum erit dies qui uocatur dies Veneris, in quo die dominus tuus educet te de hoc ergastulo et ad excolendum ortum mittet cum duobus aliis sodalibus; ipse uero, uobis solis relictis, uacabit ocio cum suis ciuibus. Scias ergo quia in ipso die succurret tibi pietas Dei Omnipotentis et excutiet a te iugum tue intolerabilis capituitatis et reducet te ad securitatem pristine nobilitatis atque libertatis.' His dictis, sanctus uir disparuit et, ut uenerat, omnibus diligenter clausis ianuis, rediit.

Superueniente ergo die prefato, ille captiuus a lacu est eductus et, domino eius ocio uacante, ad culturam orti est missus. Et uno laborante, ab alio ut resideret est ammonitus; at ipso in gremio illius obdormiente, leniter caput eius de sino suo deposuit; leuissimo conatu ferreos compedes de

the coast, and was sleeping during the first hour of the night one Wednesday, the blessed Dominic — sent by merciful Almighty God — appeared to him in a great glow of light, dressed in his monk's habit and supporting himself on a stick as he walked. At the time all the doors of the house, which surrounded the pit in which the prisoner was held, were firmly locked. On the arrival of the Saint, the locks around the pit flew open, closed as it had been on all sides, and the Saint called out by name to the prisoner who lay within. He said: 'Why, wretched man, have you abandoned yourself? Why do you not climb out of this most foul pit? Why, forgetful of your earlier freedom, do you not at least try to get out?' On hearing this, the prisoner was afraid, and thinking that it was his master who was deceiving him into trying to escape so that, accusing him of trying to flee, he could punish him or even kill him, he replied: 'My lord, it is impossible for me to do what you suggest: I am strongly shackled all round and am wretchedly imprisoned in the deep confinement of this vile pit.' St Dominic said to him: 'Do not lose faith in the mercy of the Lord, who always helps those who call upon Him and pardons the sins of the oppressed and afflicted in their tribulations. Call upon Him, then, with your whole heart in your intolerable suffering, and believe me when I humbly say that His mercy will soon be with you: he will take pity on you and come to your aid, and will not only return you to your home but will also grant you greater benefits than those you enjoyed before.' On hearing this the wretched prisoner, enclosed in his pit, recovered some of his faith, and said: 'In the name of Almighty God I beg you, my lord, to tell me who you are and how I can believe what you are saying.' The Saint replied: 'Listen carefully to what I say and fix it in your mind without the slightest doubt, if you wish to enjoy health in body and mind: know that I am sinful Dominic, formerly Abbot of the Monastery of Silos. I made your prayers and complaints known to God, obtaining His mercy for you, and I have been sent by Him in order to set you free. Listen willingly to my advice and, banishing all doubts, trust in my counsel. In this way your affairs will go forward smoothly and happily. Act wisely, therefore, and carefully plan what you do. In two days' time it will be Friday [*dies Veneris, viernes*, day of Venus], when your master will take you out of this prison and will set you, with two companions, to work his garden. He will leave you alone while he takes his ease with his friends. Know, then, that that day the mercy of Almighty God will come to your aid and will strike the insufferable yoke of captivity from you and will restore you to the security of your former noble status and freedom.' After saying this, the holy man disappeared, leaving just as he had come with all the doors properly locked.

Then, on the stipulated day, the prisoner was taken out of the pit and, while his master took his ease, set to work the garden. While one laboured, Peter was called by the other to rest; but Peter, while the other man was sleeping on his breast, gently moved his head aside, and almost

suis pedibus abstulit et, preeunte gratia uiri Dei, Dominici, prospere duodecimo die Toletum regiam urbem peruenit. Quo perueniens, omnibus omnia que circa se gesta erant per beatum Dominicum retulit; certissimis indiciis esse uera que dixerat manifestauit.

Ergo hic dies sextus ebdomade errore infidelium paganorum est Veneri consecratus et a nomine ipsius dies Veneris uocatus. In quo die infausta et insana religione et nefanda atque abhominabili traditione uacat inreligioso ocio et execrebili cultura omnis atra gens Ysmaelitarum; hanc nempe inutilem et omnino uituperabilem legem tradiderunt eis pseudoprophete eorum. Denique, iuxta ueracem Scripturarum relationem, scimus Venerem fuisse impudicam meretricem; et quia illa spurcissima Ysmaelitarum gens omnino est soluta a iugo omnis pudicicie, idcirco ipsius nomine uocauerunt sextam feriam septimane; quam diem colunt suo miserrimo errore cessando inutiliter ab omni opere. Qui dies sexta sabbati uocatur hebraica ueritate. Sed omissis omnibus inutilibus, ad ordinem redeamus.

Igitur insigne miraculum omnes qui audierunt mirati sunt. Deum glorificauerunt, beati Dominici merita magnis laudibus extulerunt et ut ad monasterium sepulture eius ueniret et ut hoc omnibus predicaret hortati sunt. Quod fideliter compleuit: ad monasterium Exiliense uenit, magnum miraculum de se factum retulit, gratias Deo et ereptori suo, beato Dominico, egit et incolumis atque gaudens ad propria rediit.

Cuius exemplo prouocati, omnes corporaliter seu spiritualiter afflicti, Deum et beatum Dominicum in tribulationibus uestris inuocate pura cordis conpunctione; si enim fideliter et, secundum apostolicum dictum, sine hesitatione postulaueritis, impetrabitis quod petieritis. E contra, nil mirum est si quidam accedunt et non merentur accipere quod petunt: non apostoli nempe testimonio, nemo sine fide potest placere Deo.

effortlessly took the iron fetters from his feet and, with the grace of the man of God, Dominic, going before him, in twelve days of good progress he reached the royal city of Toledo. When he got there, he told everybody all that had happened to him on St Dominic's account, giving clear proof that all he had said was true.

This sixth day of the week was consecrated by the error of the pagan unbelievers to Venus, and thus is called day of Venus, *viernes*. On this day the whole black Ishmaelite people, following their accursed and senseless religion and their vile and abominable tradition, abandons itself to irreligious ease and to its unspeakable religious practices; for their false prophets gave them this useless and altogether damnable law. Indeed, according to the true account in the Scriptures, we know that Venus was a shameless whore; and since the utterly filthy Ishmaelite people is completely free of the yoke of any sense of shame, it was natural that they should give her name to the sixth day of the week. In their wretched state of error they celebrate this day, uselessly abstaining from doing any work at all. This sixth day is called, in the true Hebrew tradition, 'of the Sabbath'. However, leaving less important matters aside, let us return to our story.

All who heard this marvellous miracle were amazed: they praised God, were loud in their appreciation of the merits of St Dominic, and encouraged Peter to go to the monastery where the Saint's tomb was and there to tell all that had happened. This he duly did, and in the monastery of Silos narrated the great miracle from which he had benefitted, gave thanks to God and to his liberator, and safely and joyfully went home.

All of you, if you suffer in body or in spirit, should be moved by this example, and with pure hearts should call upon God and St Dominic in your tribulations. If in good faith and without hesitation (as the Apostle tells us) you ask, you shall have what you seek. On the other hand, it will not be surprising if some come and do not deserve to receive that which they seek: they are not asking in good faith and so do not deserve to receive what they seek; for according to the Apostle's testimony, without faith none can be pleasing to God.

### 20. Campaigns and politics in and around Valencia (1088)

*After his capture of Toledo in 1085, Alfonso VI at once kept his promise to place its dispossessed ruler, al—Qadir, on the throne of Valencia. But it proved difficult to maintain him there, as the following text — complicated, but reasonably self—explanatory — shows. Alfonso sent Alvar Fáñez as 'strong man' to help al—Qadir. He was Alfonso's chief general and figured prominently in many missions and military expeditions at this time, becoming both a figure of legend in his own right and a major literary figure as the principal lieutenant of the Cid in the Poema de mio Cid of the early 13th century. From 1109 he commanded the troops of Toledo and withstood a famous siege of the city by the Almoravids (our text 28), and was killed — still in the royal service, of Queen Urraca — in a brush with insurgents in Segovia in 1114.*

*The situation of Valencia after 1088 grew ever more insecure as*

(877) Assi acaesçio que pues que Yahia Alcadir rey de Toledo, nieto del rey Almemon, dio Toledo al rey don Alffonso — por pleyto quel fizo quando el rey don Alffonso çerco la çibdad, et porque los moros de Toledo reçibieran por sennor al rey de Badaioz yl metieran consigo en la villa, et desi enuiaran por el rey don Alffonsso que uiniesse çercar la villa como es ya contado todo — et assi fue la pleytesia que este Yahia nieto de Almemon et rey de Toledo ouo con el rey don Alffonso: que echado de Toledo el rey de Badaioz, que Yahia dexasse la çibdad al rey don Alffonso, et el rey don Alffonso quel ayudasse a ganar Valençia que fuera de su padre et era del regno de Toledo et deuie seer suya, et el rey don Alfonsso que ouiesse a Toledo. Et este pleyto puesto entrellos, salio de Toledo Yahia Alcadir et fuesse pora Valençia, assi como dixiemos aqui. Segund cuenta la estoria, las achaques por que este Yahia Alcadir, nieto del rey Almemon, ouo a dexar Toledo fueron muchas; et la una fue la trayçion quel fizieron los toledanos que metieron en la villa otro sennor sobrel, la otra porque el rey don Alffonso le apremio mucho en los çercos en quel touo, la otra porque esse rey don Alffonso mostro grand sabor que auie de auer a Toledo, la otra por que se le alço Abenhabeth et alçaronse con el muchas de las villas que fueran del rey Almemon su auuelo que eran çerca de su tierra de Abenhabeth, et con estos otros muchos logares que eran del su sennorio. Et aquel Yahia Alcadir nieto de Almemon, quando uio que tan mal se le paraua su tierra et se le assi alçaua toda, demando estonçes al rey don Alffonso quel ayudasse a cobrar Valençia por la postura que con ell auie, et quel diesse a Aluar Hannez que fuesse con el, que si los moros le non quisiessen reçebir que gela ayudasse ell a ganar et la entrassen por fuerça o por qualquier pleyto. [...] Salio de Toledo este nieto del rey Almemon en la era de mill et C XX annos [...] et aun diz quel prometiera el rey don Alffonso quel ayudarie a auer Denia et Santa Maria de Aluarrazin, ca diz que bien tenie el rey don Alffonso que por esta carrera

*diverse Christian powers sought to control and take it, facing after 1091*
*the threat of the incoming Almoravids, the Islamic revolutionaries who had*
*a substantial party of followers in the city (see text 23). Eventually the*
*Cid took the city in 1094 (texts 22, 23).*
    *The text is from Alfonso X's* Estoria de España, *chapters 877, 881,*
*and 882. Their source here, providing an unwontedly detailed and lively*
*account, as in this whole section of the* Estoria *concerning Valencia, was a*
*now lost Castilian translation of a history of the Christian conquest of*
*Valencia (entitled 'An eloquent account of the great calamity') by Ibn*
*al—Qama, for long a resident in the city (born 1036 or 1037, died 1116).*
*His Arabic original is lost also, so that the long passages adapted into the*
Estoria *and others quoted by later Arabic historians are of great*
*importance. For the edition used, see text 1. The date Era 1120 = AD*
*1082 is incorrect; probably Era 1125 = AD 1087 was intended, and a V*
*was omitted by a copyist.*

(877) It turned out that when Yahia al—Qadir, King of Toledo,
grandson of King al—Ma'mun, handed Toledo over to King Alfonso — in
accordance with the agreement he made when King Alfonso surrounded the
city, and because the Moors of Toledo had received the King of Badajoz as
their lord and had taken him into the place, sending then for King Alfonso
to say that he should come and besiege it, as we have already told — the
terms of the agreement reached between al—Qadir and Alfonso were as
follows: that once the King of Badajoz had been expelled from the city,
Yahia al—Qadir could hand the city over to King Alfonso, and Alfonso
would help him to take the throne of Valencia which his father had earlier
possessed, which formed part of the Kingdom of Toledo, and which ought
to be his again; King Alfonso was to remain in possession of Toledo. This
agreement being made between them Yahia al—Qadir left Toledo and went
to Valencia. The story says that the troubles which caused Yahia al—Qadir
to leave Toledo were numerous: one was the treachery of the Toledans to
him when they brought another lord into Toledo to place over him, another
was that King Alfonso pressed him so hard in his sieges, another was that
the same King was so desperately anxious to take the city; while, finally,
al—Mu'tamid [of Seville] turned against him, together with many of the
towns that had belonged to King al—Ma'mun his grandfather and were
adjacent to his [al—Mu'tamid's] lands, and together with many other places
in his [al—Qadir's] lordship. Al—Qadir, when he saw his kingdom in such
a state of open revolt against him, besought King Alfonso to help him to
take over Valencia as had been agreed, lending him the services of Alvar
Fáñez, so that if the Moors would not receive him, Alvar Fáñez could help
him to take it either by force or by some pact. [...] Al—Qadir left Toledo
in Era 1120 [= AD 1082], [...] and it is said that King Alfonso had
promised that he would help him to take Denia and Santa María de
Albarrazín also, for it was held that King Alfonso thought that in this way

serie toda la tierra suya et se apoderarie el della solamientre que Alcadir ouiesse los logares que auemos dichos, porque ueye que los moros estauan todos desacordados, et tenie que todo lo que començasse que lo acabarie, et non aurie y ninguno que se le amparasse por la discordia que era grand entrellos. [...]

(881) En estos fechos, auenosse Aluar Hannez con el rey de Valençia que fincasse con ell, et heredol y et diol muy buenas heredades. Et quando uieron los moros que aquel poder auie Aluar Hannez, llegauanse a ell quantos malfechores et garçones et trauiessos auie en la villa; et tornosse estonçes Valençia fascas en poder de cristianos, de guisa que fueron todos desesperados de meiorar en su fazienda, et punnauan de se yr de la villa quanto podien con sus muebles, et non preçiauan nada las heredades, ca ninguno non estaua seguro de su auer nin de su cuerpo. Estonçes fizo Aluar Hannez una caualgada por tierra de Abenhut, et enuio sus algaras a tierra de Burriana; et fueron con el grand companna daquellos moros malfechores que se le acogien et de otros almogauares. Et crebantaron villas et castiellos et aduxieron muchos ganados, vacas, oueias, yeguas et muchas ropas et muchas otras cosas preçiadas que fallauan en aquellos logares que crebantauan, et aduxieronlo a Valentia, et fizieron y almoneda dello, et uendieron y todo lo que quisieron. [...]

(882) Aquel fijo de Abubecar Abneabdalhaziz de que auemos ya dicho, pues que pleyteo por si con el rey de Valençia, puso su amor con Aluar Hannez, et daual sus presentes et sus donas; et sobresso puso otrossi su amor con un judio que era mandadero del rey don Alffonso, et con Aboeça Abenlupon. Et enuiaron todos rogar al rey don Alffonso por aquel fijo de Abubecar quel reçibiesse por suyo, et quel amparasse del rey de Valençia quel non fiziesse tuerto, et que ouiesse el sus heredades et sus rentas como solie; et el que diesse al rey don Alffonso XXX mill marauedis cada anno. Et el rey don Alffonsso reçibio su ruego dellos, et tomo en comienda a aquel fijo de Abubecar, et enuio rogar al rey de Valençia quel non fiziesse tuerto nin passasse a sus cosas por ninguna guisa. Et desi tornosse este judio a Valençia por coger estos XXX mill maraudedis por el rey don Alffonso et por otras cosas que auie y de recabdar. Et dalli adelante onrraron mas a aquel fijo de Abubecar Abneabdalhaziz por amor del rey don Alffonso; pero estauasse ell en su casa muy guardado que non salie fuera. Et non se assegurando ell aun en esto, forado de noche la paret de su casa, et salio por alli fuera en uestiduras de mugier et estido todo el dia en una huerta; et quando fue en la noche, caualgo en un cauallo, et fuesse por el castiello que dixiemos Muruiedro a Aboeça Abenlupon que era y. Estonçes aquel judio que dixiemos del rey don Alffonso, priso a un su fijo et dexol sobre fiadores en casa de un su tio que dizien Abenhueget, et fue

all the land would be his and he would have control over it, leaving to al—Qadir only the places we have mentioned; Alfonso could see that the Moors were all at odds among themselves, and believed that he could finish what he had begun, there being none to stand against him on account of the discord existing among them. [...]

(881) While this was going on, Alvar Fáñez came to an arrangement with the King of Valencia to stay with him, the King for his part giving him some very rich properties. When the Moors realized that Alvar Fáñez was so powerful, all the criminals and idle youths and evildoers of the city flocked to him. Valencia was then virtually in the hands of the Christians, to such an extent that the inhabitants despaired about the chance of ever seeing any improvement in their affairs, and tried to get out of the city as quickly as they could with their movable property, ceasing to value their estates, for no-ye could be certain of the safety of his wealth or of his life. Then Alvar Fáñez made a cavalry raid into the lands of Ibn Hud [ruler of Denia and Tortosa], sending his scouts into the lands of Burriana. They were accompanied by a great number of those criminally—inclined Moors who had joined him, and by other Moors from the frontier regions. They destroyed settlements and castles and returned with many flocks, cattle, sheep, mares, a good deal of clothing and many other valuable items which they found in the places they destroyed, and brought it all to Valencia, where they held an auction and sold all they wished. [...]

(882) The son of Abu—Bakr Ibn Abd—al—Aziz [the King of Valencia who had died in June 1085] whom we mentioned earlier, once he had come to an arrangement about his own interests with the King of Valencia [now al—Qadir], ingratiated himself with Alvar Fáñez, giving him presents; also with a Jew who was the ambassador of King Alfonso, and with Abu Isa Ibn Lebbon [governor of Valencia]. These together sent a message to King Alfonso on behalf of Abu—Bakr's son to ask him to take the young man into his guardianship, and to protect him from the King of Valencia so that no wrong should be done to him, and to ensure that he should have his properties and rents as before; for his part, he [Abu—Bakr's son] would pay Alfonso 30,000 *maravedís* each year. King Alfonso received this request, and took Abu—Bakr's son into his guardianship, sending word to the King of Valencia that he should do the man no harm and in no way interfere with his affairs. Then the Jew went back to Valencia in order to receive the 30,000 *maravedís* due to King Alfonso, and in order to attend to certain matters he had to pursue there. Thenceforward Abu—Bakr's son was held in greater honour, on account of King Alfonso; but he stayed in his house closely protected, and was not able to go out. Since he did not feel safe even there, he escaped from the house in women's clothing after making a hole in the wall, and hid all day in a garden; when night came, he rode off to Ibn Lebbon at Murviedro [Sagunto]. Then the Jew we mentioned, King Alfonso's man, took one of his sons and left him with due guarantees in the house of an uncle of his called Ben Hueget, and went

a Muruiedro demandar aquell auer; et ouo muchas razones con aquel fijo de Abubecar, et abenieronse quel diesse luego la meatad, et quando se fuesse a Valençia et estidiesse seguro et ouiesse sus heredades et sus rendas quel darie la otra meatad. Et pagol luego los XV mill marauedis en plata et en sortijas de oro et en pannos et en sartales preçiados, et este judio tornosse con esto poral rey don Alffonso. [...] Estonçes muchos de los ricos omnes de la villa de Valençia fuxieron, et fueronse pora Muruiedro por que se non assegurauan alli nin eran seguros de los cuerpos nin de los aueres. [...]

himself to Murviedro to ask for the money. After he had spent a long time talking to Abu—Bakr's son, they agreed that he would hand over half, and would give him the other half after he was able to return to Valencia and was safely in possession of his properties and rents. So he paid over 15,000 *maravedis* in silver and golden jewels and cloths and valuable necklaces, and the Jew returned with all this to King Alfonso. [...] Then many of the wealthy classes of Valencia fled and went to Murviedro, for in Valencia they were no longer safe as to their lives or their properties. [...]

## 21.  A romantic interlude (1091 or 1092)

*The following extract is self—contained, at least as a literary construct forming chapter 883 of Alfonso X's* Estoria de España *(see text 1). We do not know its source.* Rodrigo Jiménez de Rada in *De rebus Hispaniae (see text 2) says of Alfonso VI that 'Habuit etiam aliam uxorem [wife] quae Ceida, postea Maria fuit dicta' (VI.20), and Menéndez Pidal insisted that there had existed a now lost epic* Cantar *(poem) de la mora Zaida, but there is no evidence for this, and the story in the* Estoria, *while it seems to be based on a prose tale in the vernacular perhaps composed in the 13th century, shows no obvious poetic traces in the form of remaining rhymes or turns of phrase.  The elements in the tale were on all scores ripe for literary development, but as so often* history *and* story, *if etymologically the same, call forth very different developments.*

*In history, it is not likely that Alfonso, however strongly sexed, would have allowed any romantic attachment to influence his military and political needs; although in the present instance, it seems that he gained not only a*

La razon de la passada de los moros almorauides de Affrica a Espanna fue esta: Contado uos auemos ante desto de como este rey don Alffonsso caso con estas çinco mugieres que ouo una empos otra: donna Ynes, donna Costança, donna Berta, donna Helisabeth, la quinta donna Beatriz natural de Françìa.  Pues muertas todas estas mugieres fincaua el rey don Alffonso por casar.  Et en esta sazon otrossi regnaua en Seuilla Abenabeth, un moro de muy buenas costumbres por si et muy poderoso et auie aca en Castiella las çibdades et villas et castiellos que auemos suso dicho ante desto: Cuenca, Ocanna, Vcles et Consuegra et los otros logares que dichos son.  Et auie estonçes aquel rey Abenabeth una fija donzella grand et muy fermosa et de muy buenas costumbres, et amauala el mucho; et por meioria della et uenirle meior casamiento por y, diol Cuenca et todas las otras villas et castiellos que auemos contados, et otorgogelos por suyos con buenas cartas et bien firmes.  Et el rey don Alffonso que siempre fue muy esforçado rey et muy auenturado et de grandes fechos, pero que a Toledo auie ganado, por tod esso non quedaua de contender en fecho de armas, tanto que moros et cristianos auien que ueer en ell.  En tod esto, sonando la su muy grande fama deste rey don Alffonso, ouolo a oyr et saber aquella donzella donna Çayda; et tanto oyo deste rey don Alffonso que era cauallero grand et mui fermoso et libre en armas et en todos los otros sus fechos, que se enamoro dell; et non de uista ca nunqual uiera, mas de la su buena fama et del su buen prez que cresçie cada dia et sonaua mas, se enamoro dell donna Çayda, tanto que fue ademas.  Assi que ella muy enamorada dell, como las mugeres son sotiles et sabidoras pora lo que mucho an a talent, ouo ella sus mandaderos — et de como el rey don Alffonso andaua estonçes por Toledo et por las conquistas que fazie estonçes en las villas de aderredor della et era açerca de la tierra dessa donna Çayda — ouo ella sus mandaderos con

*lover but also castles and lands of strategic importance on the southern approaches to Toledo, recently acquired. Princess Sa'ida was not the daughter of al—Mu'tamid of Seville, but his daughter—in—law, wife of al—Mu'tamid's son al—Ma'mun, killed when the Almoravids took Cordova in March 1091. She did not bring castles with her as a dowry, nor as a present from al—Mu'tamid as guarantee of any pact with Alfonso against the Almoravids: they were simply her possessions. She did not become Alfonso's wife, despite the efforts of later historians to make her so, but official concubine — a recognised and respected status — and bore him a son, Alfonso's only male offspring, who despite his illegitimacy might well have succeeded as King, but he was killed in the great Christian rout at Uclés in May 1108. Sa'ida seems to have died giving birth to Sancho, probably in September 1093. On joining Alfonso she — probably with children she already had — became Christian, as was normal enough, with María or (in other texts) Isabel as her baptismal name. She was buried in the Abbey of Sahagún to which Alfonso had a special devotion.*

The reason for the crossing of the Almoravids from Africa to Spain was as follows. We have earlier told you that this King Alfonso [VI] was married to five women in succession: Inés, Constanza, Berta, Elizabeth, and the fifth Beatrice, who was French. Since all five died, King Alfonso was free to marry again. At this time there reigned in Seville al—Mu'tamid, a Moor of goodly habits in himself, and very powerful, since he possessed here in what we now call Castile the cities and places and castles we mentioned earlier: Cuenca, Ocaña, Uclés, Consuegra, and all the other places listed. This King al—Mu'tamid had a daughter, fully grown and very beautiful, unmarried and of a goodly style of life. The King loved her dearly, and in order to improve her lot and improve her chances of marriage, he gave her Cuenca and all the other places and castles we have mentioned, granting them to her under firm agreements. King Alfonso, ever energetic and successful and known for great deeds, even though he had won Toledo, did not for all that cease in military endeavours, to the extent that both Moors and Christians had to take account of him. With King Alfonso's great fame so widely known, this lady Princess Sa'ida came to hear of it; and so much did she hear about King Alfonso being a great knight and very handsome and strong in arms and in all else that he did, that she fell in love with him; not by seeing him (for she never did), but on account of his good reputation and his high honour which grew day by day and was more talked of, this kind of love being stronger than the other. She being so deeply in love, and since women are clever and wise when they put their minds to a matter that closely concerns them, she sent her messengers to speak to the King and ask that she should meet him, for she was mightily impressed by the reputation and handsomeness in him that all spoke of, adding that she loved him and wanted to see him; this being easy for the messengers, since King Alfonso was at the time in the area of

quien le enuio dezir et rogar que ouiesse ella la uista del, ca era muy pagada del su prez et de la beltat quel dizien dell, et qual amaua et quel querie ueer. Et aun por llegar el pleyto mas ayna a lo que ella querie, enuiol dezir por escripto las villas et los logares que su padre le diera, et que si el quisiesse casar con ella quel darie Cuenca et todos aquellos castiellos et fortalezas quel el padre diera. El rey don Alfonso quando este mandado le uino, plogol mucho con aquellas nueuas, et enuiol dezir que uiniesse ella do touiesse por bien, et el que la uernie ueer de tod en todo. Et unos dizen que ueno ella a Consuegra que era suya et açerca de Toledo, otros dizen que a Ocanna que era suya otrossi, otros dizen que las uistas que fueron en Cuenca. Mas las uistas ayan seydo o quier, ca el fecho de lo que la Çayda querie acabosse; et nos uayamos por la cuenta de nuestra estoria que dize assi: Pues el rey don Alffonsso tomo su caualleria grand et buena, et guardandose todauia muy bien que enganno nin trayçion non andidiesse y, fue ueer a donna Çayda. Et desque se uieron amos, si ella era enamorada et pagada del rey don Alffonso, non fue el menos pagado della, ca la uio el grande et muy fermosa et ensennada et de muy buen contenente, comol dixieron della. Et ouo luego sus fablas con ella, et demandol que si ella tal pleyto querie dell que si se tornarie cristiana. Ella respondiol que se tornarie cristiana et quel darie luego Cuenca et todo lo al que su padre le diera, et que farie todas las cosas del mundo que el mandasse de mejor mient que otra cosa, sol que con ella casasse. El rey don Alffonso ueyendo como era nueua la conquista que el fiziera de Toledo, et lo que la Çayda auie serie grand ayuda pora auer Toledo meior parada, ouo su conseio con sus condes et sus ricos omnes, et tornola cristiana como lo auemos contado ya suso ante desto, et caso con ella, et fizo luego en ella un fijo. Et ella entrego de Cuenca al rey et de todo lo al. Et al fijo mando el rey poner nombre, et con su sobrenombre llamaronle don Sanch Alfonso; et diol el rey luego a criar al conde don Garçia de Cabra. Empos esto el rey don Alffonso de Castiella et de Leon, catando ya el debdo que auie con Abenhabeth rey de Seuilla padre de donna Maria la Çayda su muger, ouo dalli adelante su connoçençia con ell et sus amores muy grandes.

Toledo and was then capturing places around the city and also adjacent to the lands of Princess Sa'ida. Also, in order to bring the matter more quickly to the conclusion she desired, she sent him in writing a list of the places her father had given her, saying that if Alfonso would marry her, she would hand over to him Cuenca together with all those castles and fortresses she had received from her father. When King Alfonso received this message he was very pleased with the news, and sent to ask her to come to him at whatever place she might choose, and that he promised to be there. Some say that she came to Consuegra, which was hers and which was not far from Toledo, others say that it was Ocaña which was also hers, others again say that the meeting was in Cuenca. Wherever the meeting took place, the fact is that what Princess Sa'ida wished was achieved. Let us continue with the narration of the text we are following: King Alfonso called out the flower of his cavalry, and taking care in case any deceit or treachery should be planned in this matter, went to meet Princess Sa'ida. Once they were together, if she was already much in love and delighted with King Alfonso, he was no less delighted with her, for he found her full−grown and very beautiful and well−educated and very attractive, just as people had said she was. Then the King asked her formally whether, since she was asking for an agreement [to marry] from him, she would be willing to become a Christian. She replied that she would, and that she would give him Cuenca and all the other places that her father had given her, and that she would do anything else in the world that he might order, provided only that he would marry her. King Alfonso, aware that his capture of Toledo was recent, and that the lands in the possession of Sa'ida would be of the greatest help in making Toledo more secure, took counsel with his counts and nobles. Then he had Sa'ida baptized, as we mentioned earlier, and married her; and a son was born to them. She handed over Cuenca and all the other places to the King. The King ordered that his son should be called Sancho Alfonso, and he handed him over to be brought up by Count García of Cabra. After this King Alfonso of Castile and Leon, realizing how much he owed to al−Mu'tamid King of Seville, the father of Princess María 'la Zaida' his wife, was thenceforth on terms of close friendship with him. [...]

## 22. Lament for the loss of Valencia (1094)

*Chapter 910 of the* Estoria de España *(see text 1) is a transcript of the translation of Ibn al—Qama's history of Valencia from which our text 20 was drawn. It is put in the mouth of 'Alhuacaxi alfaqui', that is, religious leader. In the previous chapter of the* Estoria, *909, also from Ibn al—Qama, is the verse lament said to have been spoken by 'a Moorish sage' from the battlements of Valencia as the Christians began their final attack: the Arabic verse is transliterated into Spanish, and each stanza is followed by a Spanish translation.* A.R. Nykl *undertook the task of reconstructing the possible Arabic original in* Hispanic Review, 8 (1940),

'Ay pueblo de Valençia! Venidos son sobre uos muchas tribulationes et muchos quebrantos del grant poder de nuestros enemigos que nos cuydan astragar et an ende el poder, ca estamos en ora de peresçer, et sera grant marauilla si desto pudieremos estorçer; et todos aquellos que nos desta uez vieren libres desta cuyta, lo que non puede seer, lo ternan por cosa estranna mucho. Por ende pido yo merçed a Dios que assy commo el fizo otros muchos miraglos et muy grandes en tan marauillosos fechos commo este en que nos estamos, que assy nos libre esta uez del poder de nuestros enemigos en este lugar en que nos dio grant folgura et alegria et solaz, en que todo el pueblo de Valençia viuiemos a grant plazer de nos. Ca de todo en todo non vernie sobrel pueblo de Valençia esta tribulation nin los vençrien sus enemigos, sinon por los sus grandes pecados et por la muy grant soberuia que mantouieron; et por este pecado auran a perder tan noble çibdat commo Valençia, en que eran apoderados. Por las quatro piedras cabdales digo yo en el mi coraçon que se querien ayuntar por fazer duelo et non podien; esto digo yo: por la primera piedra cabdal sobre que Valençia fue formada, es por nuestro sennor el rey que te mucho preçiaua; la segunda piedra es el infante fijo de nuestro señor el rey que cuydaua heredar Valençia et seer sennor della; la terçera piedra es el rey de Çaragoça que era mucho amigo et conseiero de nuestro sennor el rey, que se sintia tanto de Valençia como si la el perdiese; la quarta piedra es el muy noble arrayaz vassallo et conseiero de todos sus fechos de nuestro sennor el rey; et por cada vno destos nonbro yo fuerte piedra cabdal sobre que estaua Valençia bien segura et bien guardada. Por el noble muro que sobre estas quatro piedras fue leuantado digo yo el noble pueblo et grande que en Valençia era, de las muchas gentes et muy escogidas que eran fuertes et rezias et seruian su sennor et anparauan a Valençia, et agora con astragadas. Por las muy altas et muy nobles torres digo yo por los muy ricos omnes et muy nobles et mucho onrrados defendedores de nuestro sennor el rey et de ti, Valençia, siempre con grant lealtad; et assy eras tu, Valençia, entorrada de los que son agora muertos et derramados. Por las muy blancas almenas et resplandesçientes al rayo del sol digo yo por las palabras destos muy nobles sennores que las dizien con muy noble

*9—17.*

*While Arabic texts of Spain form the substance of a companion volume to this, in the case of Ibn al—Qama it can be argued in favour of inclusion here that his Arabic original is lost, and more positively, that what he wrote has been mediated through Castilian of a period only slightly later than his own. Christian chroniclers valued text 20 (and much else like it) as a sound historical record superior to anything they had available in Latin. They valued this Lament for Valencia perhaps with some sympathy for what their permanent enemies had suffered, and also doubtless as an evocation of the splendours of a great city. The Cid and his womenfolk gazed upon Valencia and marvelled in the same way (Poema de mio Cid, 1610—17), and Alfonso X as Prince was enraptured by Seville when it fell to the Christians (text 47).*

'Alas, people of Valencia! There have come upon you great troubles and tribulations from the immense power of our enemies, who intend to destroy us and who have the power to do so. We are about to perish, and it will be a great marvel if we are able to turn this aside; all those who might see us freed from this trouble — which can hardly be the case — will think it a near impossibility. So I beg God's mercy, so that, just as He worked many other miracles in situations very like that in which we find ourselves, He may release us this time from the power of our enemies, here in this place in which He gave us such great ease and joy and pleasure, in which we, all the people of Valencia, have lived so happily. For, all things considered, this tribulation would not have come upon the people of Valencia, nor would our enemies have overcome us, if it were not for their great sins and on account of the overweening pride that they showed; for this sin they will lose the noble city of Valencia in which they held power. I say in my heart that it was on account of the four great stones that they wanted to come together to express their grief and were not able to. The first great stone on which Valencia was built represents our lord the King who so valued her. The second stone is the Prince, son of our lord the King, who expected to inherit Valencia and be the lord of her. The third stone is the King of Saragossa who was a close friend and adviser of our lord the King; who felt the loss of Valencia as keenly as if it were his own. The fourth stone is the most noble commander—in—chief, the vassal of our lord the King and his adviser in all things. Each of these I name as a strong and principal stone on which Valencia stood secure and well protected. The noble wall which was raised upon these four stones is the great and noble people which dwelled in Valencia, made up of many different and very select elements that were strong in the service of their lord and of Valencia, and that are now destroyed. The lofty and most noble towers represent the chief citizens and the noble and most honourable defenders of our lord the King and of the city; in this fashion you, Valencia, were towered about by those that are now dead and scattered.

entendimiento, de que se aprouechaua el tu pueblo et era mas apuesto en
los fueros et en las otras cosas que por estos sennores nos daua nuestro
sennor el rey; et por que las sus palabras eran dichas con derecho et con
razon, paresçian bien a todo el pueblo, et assi eran resplandesçientes et
blancas de muy grant apostura, por que semeiauan menas del tu pueblo; et
bien assy commo esta çibdat non podrie seer apuesta sin menas, assy ningun
pueblo non podrie seer apuesto sin las merçedes et sin los demostramientos
de tan nobles sennores, ca Dios, que es rayz de iustiçia, se tenie por
seruido de quanto en ti fazien, Valençia.    Por el tu rio cabdal Guadalhiar
digo yo por el muy noble libro de los nuestros fueros que en ti eran,
Valençia; ca bien assy commo los arbores et las otras cosas por que los
omnes an gouierno de vida se non podrien mantener sin agua, assi el tu
pueblo, Valençia, non puede seer mantenido sin este libro de nuestra ley
onde salien muchos buenos gouiernos pora ti et a todo tu regno en commo
deuiemos obrar, de que agora andamos desdennados et obramos de lo que
non deuriemos obrar.    Et por las tus açequias claras et muy fermosas de
que te tu aprouechauas cada dia, digo yo por los muy buenos alcalles que
en ti eran que dauan muy buenos juyzios — que es cosa muy clara juyzio
derechurero — de que el tu pueblo era muy bien gouernado et mantenido
en justiçia et en derechura de egualdat, cada vno en su derecho, et eramos
muy bien gouernados de derecho gouierno.    Por las muy nobles huertas
dizia yo et digo de todo mio coraçon por las muy grandes alegrias que
resçibiemos de cada dia en el muy noble pueblo de ti, Valençia, de los
grandes viçios que auiemos entre nos cada vno con sus compannas, en los
muy nobles casamientos que faziemos auer a nuestros fijos et a nuestros
parientes de que resçibiemos despues grandes onrras et acresçimiento de
linaie que es muy buen fructo de huerta, et con los otros plazeres que se
allegan a estos que se leuantan por esta razon.    Et por el lobo rauioso que
cauo las rayzes a las tus huertas, por que non pueden dar flores, digo yo
por el muy fuerte enemigo que auemos en el Çid que es muy poderoso et
nos astraga cada dia con su poder, corriendonos et leuandonos los nuestros
bienes cada dia con poder de su caualleria.    Por los tus muy nobles prados
digo yo las muy grandes riquezas del tu pueblo, Valençia, de que ellos eran
abondados et siempre andauan conplidos de alegria, que agora todo lo an
perdido manteniendo guerra.    Et por las muy nobles flores que en el prado
eran, digo yo por los muy sabios omnes que entre el tu pueblo morauan,
que son muertos.    Por el tu noble puerto de mar digo yo por nuestro
sennor el rey que nos aduzie al pueblo de Valençia muchas merçedes et
libertades en todas las cosas que merçed le pediemos pora onrra del pueblo
de Valençia, onde eramos ricos et libres et bien aforados et sin ninguna
mala subgeçion, de las quales subgetiones non deuen auer fijos dalgo; ca por
este puerto nos solien venir siempre tan grandes merçedes que nunca se nos
pueden oluidar mientre que biuamos.    Por el tu muy grant termino digo yo
en el mio coraçon por la muy grant fama de la grandez et del poder del
pueblo de Valençia, et por el grant saber que en ellos era que siempre se

The white battlements that shine in the rays of the sun represent the words of these most distinguished gentlemen who spoke them with proper understanding, words which you the people made use of and as a result became the more elegant in its laws and in the edicts which our lord the King gave us through these gentlemen. Since their words were spoken with justice and reason, they seemed good to the whole people, and hence they seemed to shine in their elegant purity, for they looked like veins [of bright ore in the rock] of the people. Just as this city could not seem elegant without those veins, so no people could seem handsome without the favours and demonstrations of goodwill from such noble gentlemen, for God, who is the fount of justice, considered Himself well served by all that they did in Valencia. Your river Guadalaviar represents the most noble book of the laws that were observed in Valencia; for just as the trees and other things by which men maintain life could not survive without water, your people, Valencia, cannot survive without this book of our law from which have come many good rulings for the city and all the realm concerning how we should act, even though we now scorn them and act in ways we should not. The waterways so clear and beautiful by which the city supplies itself each day represent the good judges the city had, who issued excellent judgements (rightful judgement being a most precious thing), by which the people was well governed and justly ruled on a proper basis of equality, each man having his rights, and we were well ruled in a proper spirit. The most noble market — gardens represent the great pleasures we received each day in Valencia, and the great joys we had among ourselves, each one with his companions, and the honourable marriages which we made for our children and relatives from which we later received great honour and enhancement of our lineages, as one takes goodly fruit from a garden, together with other pleasures of similar kinds from the same source. By the ravening wolf that dug up the roots of the plants in your gardens, so that they no longer produce flowers, is meant the powerful enemy we have in the Cid, who with his immense power attacks us every day, raiding us and carrying off our goods each day with his cavalry. By your most lovely meadows is intended the great wealth of your people, Valencia, from which everyone was supplied and was always full of happiness, all now lost in times of war. The beautiful flowers that grew in the fields represent the most learned men that dwelled among you, and are now dead. Your fine harbour represents our lord the King who brought to the people of Valencia many favours and liberties whenever we asked him for them for the good of Valencia, for thanks to them we were rich and free and well provided with laws and free of any evil subjection, for noble citizens should not have to bear any forms of subjection. Through this harbour great favours came to us, and we shall never forget them as long as we live. The great extent of your lands represents the fame of the greatness and power of the people of Valencia, and the great learning that there was in the city, for the Valencians always

solien defender con sabiduria et con poder a todos aquellos que contra el pueblo de Valençia vinien. Por que a la tu grant enfermedat non pueden fallar melezina de guarimiento et que los fisicos te an ya desenparado, aquellos que te solien guarir et non pueden, esto digo yo por la muy noble mesnada de la tu caualleria, que te non pueden ualer et manteniendo esta guerra son astragados. Et todas estas cosas que yo he dichas, son muy grant quebranto que yo tenia et tengo en el mi coraçon por la muy grant coyta en que esta Valençia et nos todos con ella.'

knew how to defend themselves with learning and with power against all those who came to attack the city. When I talk of your great sickness and the fact that no medicine can be found to cure it, and the fact that the doctors have already given up hope for you, those doctors who used to ease your pain and can do so no longer, I mean by this the glorious host of your cavalry, which can no longer save you and which is being destroyed in this war. All these things that I have said, are said with a great sense of doom that I have in my heart, and out of the immense distress into which Valencia is plunged and all of us with her.'

### 23. The Cid's speech to the Moors of Valencia (1094)

*After years of military and diplomatic campaigning, the Cid, Rodrigo
Díaz de Vivar, entered Valencia on 15 June 1094. The final siege had
lasted twenty months, and the Cid, eager to take over the great city in
running order, starved it into capitulation rather than trying to storm it.
Valencia was the weakest of the* taifa *kingdoms of al—Andalus and, as a
great trading and industrial centre surrounded by the richest land in Spain
(the famous* huerta)*, was an immense prize. The Cid took the city and
kingdom as his personal possession (as is clear in the poem when he invites
his family to view it: 'entrad comigo en Valençia la casa, / en esta
heredad que vos yo he ganada', 1606—7), and if he had lived longer he
might have ruled as a* taifa *king himself. He was certainly not going to
hand his conquest to King Alfonso VI as a possession of the Castilian
crown (as Antonio Machado wishfully thought: 'cuando Myo Cid Rodrigo el
de Vivar volvía, / ufano de su nueva fortuna y su opulencia, / a regalar
a Alfonso los huertos de Valencia').*

*Clearly if the Cid wished to rule Valencia permanently, he had to win
the support of the inhabitants by fair treatment as he promises in the
remarkable text which follows, again recorded by Ibn al—Qama (Estoria de
España, chapter 918: see text 1). Not only had the people suffered
starvation and loss of life during years of fighting, and seen their trade
and rich farms and estates all around laid waste by the Cid; they had also
been riven by religious dissent as the party of Islamic revolution, backed
by the Almoravids who were taking over al—Andalus, took power at times
inside the besieged city. The leader of this faction was Ibn Yahhaf,
mentioned in our text, now a prisoner of the Cid. In the present extract
it is clearly the principal men from among the 'Spanish' Moors of
Valencia whom the Christian leader is addressing, of whose support he
could be fairly sure when it was a question of eliminating the Almoravid
'fifth column' in the city, and later of defeating the Almoravid army
from Seville when it tried to retake the place (battle of Cuarte, late*

[...] Et a cabo de quatro dias que el Çid ouo la villa, echo pregon por
la villa que se llegassen todos en la huerta del Çid. Et vinieron y los de
la villa et los de los castiellos que eran en derredor; et quando se ayuntaron
todos, sallio el Çid a ellos a vn logar que estaua aguysado con tapetes et
con estolas, et mando a los omnes buenos et onrrados que posassen cabel;
et començoles a dezir et de retraerles vnas cosas, et desi dixoles: 'Yo so
omne que nunca oue regnado, nin omne de mi linage non lo ouo; et del
dia que vin a esta villa, pagueme della mucho et cobdiçiela, et rogue a
Nuestro Sennor Dios que me la diesse, et veet qual es el poder de Dios
que el dia que yo pose sobre Juballa non auia mas de quatro panes, et

*October 1094). The Cid put Ibn Yahhaf before a mixed
Christian—Moorish court: he seems to have been charged not with ordering
the murder of the deposed King of Valencia, al—Qadir, in October 1092,
but with perjury to the Cid in the matter of the concealment of
al—Qadir's treasure, and he was burned at the stake, perhaps the only
severe (if legally justified) act of the Cid's rule. The hero died in the
summer of 1099. His wife Jimena and the army held the city against
increasing Almoravid pressure until 1102, when they sent for Alfonso VI's
aid: he came with an army but after studying the situation realized that
Valencia was untenable, and evacuated the garrison and Christian settlers,
burning the city as he withdrew.*

*Juballa (modern Cebolla) was taken by the Cid in 1093. Alcudia is a
northern suburb of Valencia, outside the walls, where the Cid had
established himself from July 1093. The matter of the* diezmo *is not the
small detail it might seem: the Cid promises not to take in taxes more than
the basic amount authorized by the Koran, since one of the factors aiding
the Almoravids — Islamic revolutionaries and strict adherents to the Koran
— was the excessive taxes imposed by the* taifa *rulers of al—Andalus.*

*One problem remains. In which language did the Cid speak? Ibn
al—Qama naturally wrote his text in Arabic. Since, while careful to give
other details about the setting, he makes no mention of language or
interpreters, we might assume that the Cid spoke in Arabic, the only
language which his hearers would understand. This is by no means
impossible: the Cid spent many years from 1081 in Muslim Saragossa as
mercenary commander of the royal army, and for years before 1094 had
been immersed in the affairs of Arabic—speaking lands.*

*The basic work on the history of the time (giving credence to some
aspects of poetic and legendary origin) remains that of R. Menéndez
Pidal,* La España del Cid *(Madrid, 1929 and later eds, 2 vols); abbreviated
and translated by H. Sutherland,* The Cid and his Spain *(London, 1934).
A very readable account is that of S. Clissold,* In Search of the Cid
*(London, 1965).*

[...] Four days after he took the city, he proclaimed throughout it that
everybody should gather on the estate which he was occupying. People
from the city and from the castles and settlements round about assembled.
When they were all present, the Cid came out to meet them, seating
himself in a spot which had been prepared with carpetings and drapes, and
ordering that the principal men should sit near him. He began to speak by
making them a few reproaches, and then continued: 'I am a man who
never ruled, and none among my ancestors was a ruler either. From the
day that I came to this city I was much pleased with it and wanted it for
myself, and prayed to our Lord God to give it to me: you can see how
powerful God is from the fact that on the day I began to besiege Cebolla I
possessed no more than a few crusts of bread, but now God has bounteously

fizome Dios merçed que gane Valençia et so apoderado della. Pues si yo derecho fiziere en ella et aderesçar sus cosas, dexarmela a Dios; et si yo y mal fago a tuerto o a soberuia, bien se que mela toldra. Et desde oy mas, vaya cada vno a sus heredades et ayalas assy commo las solien auer; et el que fallare su huerta o su vinna o su tierra vazia, entrela luego; et el que fallare su heredad labrada, de a aquel que la labro quantol costo et la espensa que y fizo, et tomele assy commo manda la ley de los moros. Et otrossi mando a los que an de tomar los derechos de la villa que non tomen mas del diezmo, assy commo manda la ley de los moros. Et yo he puesto de veer uuestras faziendas dos dias en la selmana: el lunes et el jueues; et si algunos pleitos otros ouieredes que sean apresurados, venit qual dia quisieredes a mi, ca yo uos oyre, ca yo non me aparto con mugeres nin a cantar nin a beuer, commo fazien uuestros sennores que los non podiedes veer; et yo por mi quiero veer todas uuestras cosas et seeruos assy commo compannero, et guardar vos he assy commo amigo a amigo et pariente a pariente; et yo quiero seer alcalle et alguazil, et cada que alguna querella quierdes vnos dotros yo uos fare luego emendar.' Et despues que todo esto les ouo dicho, dixoles assy: 'Dixieronme que Abeniaf fiziera tuerto a algunos de uos, que uos tomo los aueres pora enpresentar a mi, et que gelo tomo por razon que vendieran el pan muy caro; et yo non gelo quise tomar, nin querria yo tomar tal auer nin tal presente. Et quando yo tal auer quisiesse, yo lo tomaria, ca non lo demandaria a el nin a otro ninguno; mas non mande Dios que yo tal cosa de mala parte tome a ninguno nin sin razon. Et quantos alguna cosa vendieron o ganaron lo suyo muy bien, Dios les ponga pro en ello; et a quantos alguna cosa tomo, vayan a el, que yo mandare que uos lo torne todo.' Despues desto dixoles: '¿Viestes el auer que yo tome de los mandaderos que yuan a Murçia? Mio era por derecho, ca gelo tome en guerra, et tomelo de aquellos que falsaron el pleito que pusieran comigo; et pero que por derecho lo tome, quiero gelo dar luego fasta el postremer dinero, que non pierdan dello poco nin mucho. Et quiero que me fagades pleito et omenaie de las cosas que uos yo dire, et que me non salgades nin vos tiredes dello, et que obedescades mio mandado, et que non me falgades en ninguna postura que pongades comigo, et quanto que yo dier et fizier que sea tenido, ca yo amovos et quierouos bien, et quiero tornar sobre uos et pensar de vos, et duelome de quanto mal et de quanta lazeria leuastes de grant fambre et de mucha mortandat. Et si lo que agora fiziestes ouierades fecho antes, non legaredes a lo que llegastes, nin conprarades el cafiz del trigo por mill marauedis; mas yo uos lo tornare por vn marauedi. Pues seed agora en uuestra tierra muy segurados, ca yo defendido he a mis omnes que non entren en uuestra uilla a mercar nin a vender nin a comprar, ca yo les he mandado que merquen

given me Valencia and I rule it. If I conduct myself justly here and put affairs in order, God will leave me in possession of the city; but if I do wrong here by injustice or out of pride, I know full well that He will take it from me. From today, let each one go to his estate and possess it as was his wont. If anyone finds his irrigated plot or his vineyard or his land empty, let him take possession of it at once. If he finds that his estate has been worked, let him compensate the occupier for whatever he has spent, and resume ownership of it as the law of the Moors requires. Furthermore I order that those who collect the city's taxes should not take more than the proper tithe [tenth part], as your law stipulates. I have designated two days of the week, Monday and Thursday, for attending to your business; but if you have other matters which are urgent, come to me on whatever day it may be, for I will listen to you. It is not my habit to go off with women or to spend time singing and drinking, as your former masters did, making themselves unavailable to you. For my part, I wish to hear about all your affairs and to become a sort of companion to you, behaving towards you as friend to friend or relative to relative. I wish to be both judge and minister, and whatsoever dispute you have amongst yourselves, I shall try to resolve it.' After he had said this, he continued: 'They told me that Ibn Yahhaf wronged several of you, in taking from you possessions in order to present them to me, and that he took these from you because food was being sold at very high prices. I did not care to accept such presents from him, nor would I wish to take such goods or presents. If I should wish to take such things, I would do so, without asking him or anybody else; but may God not allow me to take such things improperly or unreasonably. Those of you who traded their own goods properly, may God give you a fair return from it. Those from whom Ibn Yahhaf took anything should approach him, for I shall order that he should return it all to you.' After this he said to them: 'Did you see the property that I took from the messengers who were going to Murcia? It was mine by right, for I took it from them in war, and I took it from those who had broken the agreement they had made with me. But even though I took it from them by right, I intend to return it to them, down to the last farthing, so that they should not suffer the slightest loss. Now I want you to make me a solemn promise concerning matters I will explain to you. You are not to back out of it or get round it. You will obey my commands, and will not deceive me in any agreement that you make with me. Everything that I grant or do is to be respected, for I respect and love you well, and wish to give due attention to your needs and welfare, and I grieve at how much harm and suffering you endured from all the terrible starvation and great slaughter. If you had only done earlier what you are doing now, you would not have reached the state you did, and would not have had to pay a thousand *maravedís* for a measure of corn; but I will restore it to you at a single *maravedí*. Return to the possession of your lands, then, in safety, for I have forbidden my men to enter your city to trade or to buy and sell,

en el Alcudia quanto ouieren de mercar. Et esto fago por tal de uos non enoiar, et mando que non meta ninguno en la villa catiuo, et sil y metier, tomad el catiuo et soltadle, et matat al quel y metier sin calonna ninguna.' Et dixo avn mas: 'Yo non uos quiero entrar en uuestra villa nin quiero morar en ella, mas quiero fazer sobre la puente de Alcantara vn lugar en que me depuerte a las vezes et que lo tenga presto, si mester me fuere, pora quequier que me acaezca.' Et despues que todo esto les ouo dicho, mandoles que fuessen cada vnos a veer sus cosas; et partieronse del los moros por muy sus pagados, et marauillaronse de quanta promessa les prometiera et de quanto bien les mostrara, et seguraronse sus coraçones et perdieron el miedo que auien, et cuydaron seer conbrados et arribados de quanto mal ouieran, et tenien por uerdat quanta promessa les fiziera. [...]

ordering them to do all their trading in the Alcudia. I do this in order to avoid disturbance to you. I further order that nobody should bring any captive into the city, and if any should do so, take the captive and free him, and kill the man who brought him in without this counting as any crime.' He further said: 'I do not propose to enter your city or dwell in it, but will build, close to the Alcántara bridge, a place in which I may take my ease at times and which I shall have ready, if needs be, for whatever may befall.' After he had said all this to them, he ordered them all to go about their business. The Moors left well content with the Cid, marvelling at the promises he had made to them and at the kindness he had shown them. They felt at ease in their hearts and lost the fear they had had, feeling that they had left behind all the evils they had suffered; and they felt sure the Cid would honour all the promises he had made to them.

120

## 24. Moorish honour, Christian treachery (about 1098)

*Although the* Poema de mio Cid *is available in several translations, including one in the present series, it is hardly possible to exclude an extract from it here. Although Christian—Muslim warfare is less than a prime theme of the poem, the Moors are present as permanent enemies whom the Cid several times defeats and from whom he takes the prize of Valencia (text 23). Conquest, in history and in literature, did not have to mean dispossession and slaughter, and the tradition in the Peninsula on both sides was often of relatively kindly treatment, so that for long before the fall of Granada in 1492 Castile—León and Aragón had a very substantial population of* mudéjares, *Muslims in lands of the Christian crowns. There are many instances of the same kind of acceptance and tolerance across borders in times of formal or informal truce, as in the following extract concerning the Cid at Valencia and Avengalvón, Muslim ruler of Molina in what is now Aragón. Each man needed the alliance of the other: Avengalvón for his survival, the Cid for an important staging—post on the road between Valencia and Castile.*

*The* Poema *was composed probably in 1207 or a little before. Its author created a partially historical but mainly convincingly pseudo—historical framework for his literary creation: thus it is known that Avengalvón existed and ruled Molina, but at a date later than that of the Cid of history. The poet may have intended (as he did in other respects) an object—lesson for those who would lead the campaign which culminated in the great victory at Las Navas de Tolosa in 1212 (text 40) then in preparation: that however great their religious zeal (fortified by the*

'¡Oyas, sobrino, tu, Felez Muñoz!
2635      Por Molina iredes, i yazredes una noch,
saludad a mio amigo    el moro Avengalvon;
reciba a mios yernos    commo el pudier mejor.
Dil que enbio mis fijas    a tierras de Carrion.
De lo que ovieren huebos    sirvan las a so sabor,
2640      desi escurra las fasta Medina    por la mi amor;
de quanto el fiziere    yol dar[e] por ello buen galardon.'
Cuemo la uña de la carne    ellos partidos son.
Hyas torno pora Valençia    el que en buen ora nasçio.
Pienssan se de ir    los ifantes de Carrion;
2645      por Santa Maria d'Alvarrazin    fazian la posada,
aguijan quanto pueden    ifantes de Carrion;
felos en Molina    con el moro Avengalvon.
El moro quando lo sopo    plogol de coraçon,
saliolos reçebir    con grandes avorozes;
2650      ¡Dios, que bien los sirvio    a todo so sabor!

*proclamation of the campaign as a full papal crusade in 1206), they should not, when trying to drive the alien Almohads out of Spain, forget that useful allies might be found among the local rulers of al—Andalus, the Spanish Moors of whom Avengalvón was one. Within the plot of the poem, the extract relates to the moment at which the Cid sends off from Valencia to their home in Carrión his two young daughters and their husbands, Diego and Fernando González, the Infantes de Carrión. The Cid already has cause to doubt the Infantes' trustworthiness, and sends with the party his own 'man', Félez Muñoz, outwardly so that he should return with a report about the properties settled upon the wives (lines 2620—22), in fact as protector; his role turns out to be a vital one. The Infantes are the villains of the poem, and indeed part of the poet's purpose seems to have been to blacken the name of their powerful family of about 1200 by attributing gross villainies to these (purely literary) predecessors; in the present episode they are false to a more than generous host. The poet perhaps implies that men are men the world over, and that an honourable Moor (with the name of God — whose God? — in his mouth, and naturally so, 2684) is a better man than the most blue—blooded Christian noble if he is evil. Avengalvón is then the model for what would be a long line of idealized 'noble Moors' who flourished particularly in Spanish literature of the 15th and 16th centuries, that is, when their people had ceased to be a military threat.*

*For the full text of the poem and a translation, see P. Such and J. Hodgkinson,* The Poem of My Cid, *in this series (1987), with ample bibliography. The extract is taken from the edition of Colin Smith (Oxford, 1972).*

|   | 'Hear me, nephew, Félez Muñoz! |
|---|---|
| 2635 | Go to Molina and rest there one night, |
|   | greeting my friend the Moor Avengalvón for me; |
|   | let him receive my sons—in—law with all due honour. |
|   | Tell him that I am sending my daughters to Carrión. |
|   | He should serve them well with whatever they need. |
| 2640 | From there he should escort them as far as Medina for my sake; |
|   | I will reward him well for all that he does.' |
|   | As the nail is drawn from the flesh, they were parted. |
|   | Now he who was born in a propitious moment returned to Valencia. |
|   | The young lords of Carrión start on their journey. |
| 2645 | They rested one night at Santa María de Albarrazín, |
|   | and set off from there with all speed: |
|   | here they are in Molina with the Moor Avengalvón. |
|   | When the Moor heard of their coming he was greatly pleased, |
|   | and went out to greet them with a great show of joy: |
| 2650 | Lord, how well he served them and put them at their ease! |

Otro dia mañana   con ellos cavalgo,
con dozientos cavalleros   escurrir los mando;
hivan troçir los montes   los que dizen de Luzon.
A las fijas del Çid   el moro sus donas dio,
2655    buenos seños cavallos   a los ifantes de Carrion.
Troçieron Arbuxuelo   e legaron a Salon,
o dizen el Anssarera   ellos posados son.
Tod esto les fizo el moro   por el amor del Çid Campeador.
Ellos veyen la riqueza   que el moro saco,
2660    entramos hermanos   conssejaron traçion:
'Hya pues que a dexar avemos   fijas del Campeador
si pudiessemos matar   el moro Avengalvon
quanta riquiza tiene   aver la iemos nos.
Tan en salvo lo abremos   commo lo de Carrion,
2665    nunqua avrie derecho   de nos el Çid Campeador.'
Quando esta falssedad   dizien los de Carrion
un moro latinado   bien gelo entendio;
non tiene poridad,   dixolo [a] Avengalvon:
'Acayaz, curiate destos,   ca eres mio señor;
2670    tu muert oi conssejar   a los ifantes de Carrion.'
El moro Avengalvon   mucho era buen barragan,
con dozientos que tiene   iva cavalgar.
Armas iva teniendo,   paros ante los ifantes;
de lo que el moro dixo   a los ifantes non plaze:
2675    'Dezid me: ¿que vos fiz   ifantes de Carrion?
¡Hyo sirviendo vos sin art   e vos conssejastes pora mi muert!
Si no lo dexas   por mio Çid el de Bivar
tal cosa vos faria   que por el mundo sonas
e luego levaria sus fijas   al Campeador leal;
2680    ¡vos nunqua en Carrion   entrariedes jamas!
Aquim parto de vos   commo de malos e de traidores.
Hire con vuestra graçia,   don Elvira e doña Sol;
¡poco preçio las nuevas   de los de Carrion!
Dios lo quiera e lo mande,   que de tod el mundo es señor,
2685    d'aqueste casamiento   que[s] grade el Campeador.'
Esto les ha dicho   y el moro se torno;
teniendo ivan armas   al troçir de Salon,
cuemmo de buen seso   a Molina se torno.

Next day he rode out with them
and ordered that they should be escorted by two hundred
    horsemen.
They crossed the Luzón mountains.
The Moor presented gifts to the Cid's daughters,
2655    and gave a good horse each to the young lords.
They passed Arbujeulo and reached the River Jalón,
stopping for the night at Ansarera.
All this the Moor did for them out of respect for the Cid.
The two brothers saw the wealth which the Moor displayed,
2660    and between them plotted a crime:
'Since we are to abandon the Cid's daughters,
if we could also kill the Moor Avengalvón
we should become masters of all his wealth;
we should have it as firmly as we do our lands of Carrión,
2665    and the Cid would have no right to proceed against us.'
When the two young lords discussed this treacherous plan
a Moor who understood Spanish overheard all that they said.
He did not keep it secret, but told Avengalvón:
'Master, beware of these men, as you are my lord:
2670    I heard your murder plotted by the lords of Carrión.'
The Moor Avengalvón was a goodly tough man,
and rode out with two hundred of his troops.
He made a display with his weapons, and halted in front of the
    lords.
What he had to say was not to the young lords' liking:
2675    'Tell me: what have I done to you, my lords of Carrión?
I served you honourably and you plotted to murder me!
If I were not to leave it aside for the sake of the Cid of Vivar
I would punish you in such a way that would resound through
    the world
and then take his daughters back to the noble Cid;
2680    you would never see Carrión again!
I take my leave of you, as of villains and traitors.
I depart with your leave, doña Elvira and doña Sol.
How low the reputation of the lords of Carrión has fallen!
May God who is lord of all the world grant
2685    that the Cid may still have some satisfaction from these
marriages.'
When he had said this the Moor went off;
he made a display with his weapons as he crossed the Jalon,
and prudently returned to Molina.

124

## 25. The Cid takes Murviedro (1098)

*Murviedro, 'ancient wall', is ancient Saguntum and modern Sagunto, a major fortress built in a superb defensive position (as can still be appreciated today) on the coast north of Valencia. In 1098 the Cid, only a year before his death, was still strengthening his grip on his kingdom of Valencia by further conquests. As was customary, the fortress was starved into submission rather than stormed. The agreement by which the defenders were allowed to send for help within a fixed term was normal enough too; but so were the Cid's savage threats as his patience was exhausted. The varied sources from which the Murviedrans tried to get help well illustrate the complexities of the political situation of the time, and all in different ways might have had reason to detest the Cid and therefore to send help to the besieged. Their best prospect was their co—religionary Joseph, that is Yusuf ibn Tashufin, Emperor of the*

His autem gratia Dei sic peractis, cum sua militia egreditur de Almenara, dicens et fingens se uelle ire in Ualentiam, cum ille in corde suo secreto Murum Uetulum circumdare et debellare disposuisset; jnterim manibus ad celum extensis orauit ad Dominum, dicens: 'Deus eterne, qui scis omnia antequam fiant, quem nullum latet secretum, tu scis, Domine, quia Ualentiam prius nollem intrare, antequam Murum Uetulum obsidere et debellare, et debellatum in fortitudine gladij, tua potentia operante, obtinerem, et te donante, iam adepto atque sub imperio nostro habito et possesso, ibidem tibi Deo uero missam te laudando facerem celebrare.' Finita itaque huiuscemodi oratione, oppidum Muri Uetuli ilico obsedit, atque gladijs, sagittis, telis et omnium armorum generibus et machinamentis expugnauit, et defensores castelli et habitatores qui ibi erant grauiter afflixit et coegit, atque eisdem egressum a castello et ingressum ad castellum omnino prohibuit.

Defensores autem castelli et habitatores, perspicientes se undique inpugnatos nimiunque afflictos et coactos, locuti sunt ad inuicem: 'Quid miseri faciemus? Rodericus iste tyrannus in castro isto nullo modo nobis uiuere uel habitare permittet; faciet etenim nobis, quod habitatoribus de Ualentia et de Almenara eidem resistere non ualentibus nuper fecit. Videamus ergo quid acturi simus. Jam enim nos et uxores nostre et filij atque filie fame proculdubio moriemur; nullus quidem erit qui de manibus suis nos eripere ualeat.' Quod cum cognitum esset, Rodericus fortius et instantius solito more eos debellare inchoauit, eosque grauissime constrinxit. Cum igitur sentirent et uiderent se positos in tanta amaritudine, clamauerunt ad Rodericum dicentes: 'Quare infers nobis tanta et tam importabilia mala? Cur interficis nos et lanceis et sagittis et gladijs? Mollifica et mitiga cor tuum, et miserere nostri. Tibi unanimiter supplicamus, quatinus pietatis intuitu dierum aliquorum nobis indutias dones. Jnterea nuntios nostros ad regem et dominos nostros mittemus, quod nobis succurrere ueniant. Si uero

*Almoravids, but he was occupied elsewhere.*
     The passage is taken from the Historia Roderici, *edited by R.*
*Menéndez Pidal in* La España *del Cid (Madrid, 1929, and later eds, 2*
*vols), II, pp. 963—67.* This work was composed in the mid—12th century
*possibly by a cleric of Salamanca who had access to what remained of the*
*Cid's documentary archive, since this may have been deposited in the*
*Cathedral there (see text 26).* It is a vital source for our knowledge of
*the hero's life, well based on fact but not without legendary accretions and*
*also, of course, much rhetorical development in direct speech and in other*
*ways.* It was a source for the author of the Poema de mio Cid *(text 24),*
*and in particular, its section on Murviedro gave the poet some motifs for*
*his description of the Cid's siege of Valencia.* A recent discussion of the
Historia *is that of G. West, 'Hero or Saint? Hagiographic elements in the*
*life of the Cid',* Journal of Hispanic Philology, *7 (1983), 87—105.*

     These objectives being achieved, by the grace of God, the Cid left
Almenara with his army, putting it about that he was returning to Valencia,
when he was secretly intending to besiege and take Murviedro.  With hands
uplifted he prayed to God: 'Eternal God, who know all things before they
are done, and from whom no secret is hidden, you know that I am
unwilling to set foot in Valencia again until I have besieged and taken
Murviedro.  As soon as I have taken it at swordpoint and if, with the aid
of your power, you grant it to me, I will have Mass said there in praise of
you, O Lord, once the place is firmly taken into our rule.'  In this way he
finished his prayer, and immediately began the siege of the fortress of
Murviedro, attacking it with swords, arrows, missiles, and all manner of
weapons and engines.  He gave the defenders of the fortress and its
inhabitants a very hard time, and totally prevented people from leaving or
entering the place.
     The defenders and inhabitants of the fortress, seeing that they were
under attack and being so hard pressed on all sides, said to each other:
'What can we wretched people do?  The tyrant Rodrigo will in no way
allow us to continue to live in the fortress.  He will do to us what he
recently did to the people of Valencia and Almenara when they proved too
weak to resist him.  Let us therefore consider what we should do.  Now we
and our wives and children will surely die of hunger; there will be none
strong enough to save us from his hands.'  When he heard of this Rodrigo,
as was his wont, began to attack them still more fiercely, and pressed them
very hard.  Then when the people realized the full tragedy of their
situation, they called aloud to Rodrigo, saying: 'Why are you bringing so
many and unbearable evils down upon us?  Why are you killing us with
spears and arrows and swords?  Soften your heart and take pity on us.  All
together we beg you, as far as your compassion allows, to grant us a truce
for some days.  In the meantime we will send messengers to our King and
other rulers, to see if they will come to our aid.  If nobody has come

nullus uenerit ad presignatum placitum, qui nos de manibus tuis liberare ualeat, erimus tui et seruiemus tibi. Scias sane uera ueritate, quia oppidum Muri Uetuli tanti nominis et tante fame est in cognitione omnium gentium, quod illud tibi tam cito nullatenus dabimus. Prius utique quam sine indutijs nobis concessis detur, nos omnes prius mori ultro proculdubio scias. Nobis itaque omnibus interemptis, postea illud habere poteris.' Rodericus autem plane perpendens quia nichil eis hoc ualeret, indutias .XXX. dierum eisdem dedit.

Jlli autem miserunt nuntios suos ad regem Iuzeph et ad moabitas et ad regem Aldefonsum et ad Almuzahen regem Cesaraguste et ad Albarrazin regem atque comitem barcinonensem, quatinus usque .XXX. dies eis succurrere uenire omnino minime desisterent. Quod si facere nollent, diebus .XXX. iam transactis, Roderico oppidum proculdubio darent et eidem ulterius tanquam domino fideliter seruirent. Cum rex Aldefonsus uidisset at audisset nuntios Muri Uetuli, sic eis respondit: 'Vera certitudine mihi credatis quia uobis non sucurram, quoniam malo quod Rodericus habeat oppidum Muri Uetuli, quam quilibet rex sarracenorum.' Nuntij autem hoc audito, sine ullo consilio ad propria sunt reuersi. Nuntijs uero qui ad Cesaraugustam missi fuerant, Almuzahen huiusmodi dedit responsum: 'Ite et quantum potueritis confortamini, et estote fortes eidem debellando resistentes, quia Rodericus dure ceruicis est et preliator fortissimus et inuincibilis, et ideo ego cum eo prelium comittere penitus pertimesco.' Nam paulo ante Rodericus ad eum nuntios miserat, dicens: 'Scias utique, Almuzahen, quod si cum exercitu tuo contra me uenire temptaueris et mecum bellum commiseris, tu et nobiles tui aut mortui aut captiui de manibus meis nullo modo euadetis.' Sic uero Roderici pauore perterritus, non fuit ausus uenire. Rex autem Albarrazin nuntijs super hoc presentatis inquit: 'Quantum plus potueritis, confortamini et resistjte ei, quia ego non ualeo uobis succurrere.' Moabite autem nuntijs sibi missis dixerunt: 'Si Iuzeph rex noster uenire uoluerit, nos omnes ibimus simul cum eo, et uobis libenter succurremus; sin autem, sine illo cum Roderico bellare minime audebimus.' Comes autem barcinonensis, qui ab eis inmensum acceperat tributum, nuntijs sibi missis ait: 'Scitote quia cum Roderico bellare non audeo, sed uadam citjus, et circundabo castrum suum quod dicitur Aurepensa, et dum ille ad me uenerit mecumque pugnare conatus fuerit, uos interim ex alia parte cibariam, in uestrum castellum sufficienter mittite.'

Comes itaque, ut predixit, mox castellum obsedit. Quod audiens, Rodericus pro nichilo penitus hoc habens, ad succurrendum castro suo ire renuit. Interea uero quidam miles comiti super castellum iacenti ait: 'Comes nobilissime, ueritate certissima audiui Rodericum contra te uenire tecumque bellum comitere uelle.' Quo audito, rei ueritatem probare nolens, continuo de castro circundato recessit, et Roderici pauore ad terram suam pauidus fugit.

within the designated period to free us from your hands, we will surrender to you and serve you. But you should surely know that the fortress of Murviedro has such a great name and fame in the minds of all peoples that there is no way in which we shall hand it over to you quickly. Rather than hand it over without a truce being granted to us, you must know that we will all gladly die. After we have all been slain, you will be able to have the place.' Then Rodrigo, absolutely certain that none of this would do them any good, granted them a truce of thirty days.

They meanwhile sent messengers to King Joseph and his Almoravids, and to King Alfonso, and to al—Mu'tamin the King of Saragossa, and to the King of Albarrazín and the Count of Barcelona, begging them on no account to fail to come to their aid within thirty days; adding that if these rulers were unwilling to help, they would certainly after thirty days hand the fortress over to Rodrigo, and would thereafter serve him faithfully as their lord. When King Alfonso heard the messengers from Murviedro, he answered them as follows: 'Believe me, I shall not help you, since I prefer Rodrigo to have Murviedro, rather than any ruler of the Moors.' When the messengers heard this, they went home disconsolate. To the messengers who had been sent to Saragossa, al—Mu'tamin gave this answer: 'Go, and be strengthened as best you may, and be firm in resisting his attacks, for Rodrigo is very powerful and a fierce and invincible fighter, and I am very fearful of engaging in battle with him.' Shortly after, Rodrigo sent ambassadors to him, who said: 'You should know, al—Mu'tamin, that if you try to come against me with your army, and engage in battle with me, there is no way in which you and your nobles might escape death or captivity at my hands.' Being mightily afraid of Rodrigo, King al—Mu'tamin did not dare to come. The King of Albarrazín said to the messengers: 'Be strong and resist him as far as you are able, for I can do nothing to help you.' The Almoravids said to the messengers sent to them: 'If Joseph our King is prepared to come, we will all go with him, and will gladly help you; but without him we will not in any way venture to fight Rodrigo.' The Count of Barcelona, who had received an immense amount of tribute from them, gave the following reply to the messengers sent to him: 'You know that I will not venture to fight Rodrigo, but I will go at once to surround his fort called Oropesa, and while he comes to me and prepares to fight me, you in the meantime can get a sufficiency of food supplies into your fortress from the other side.'

The Count soon besieged the fort as he had promised. On learning this Rodrigo, considering the matter of little account, declined to go to the aid of his fort. A certain soldier said to the Count at the siege: 'Most noble Count, I have heard it said as a matter of absolute truth that Rodrigo is coming against you and is disposed to engage you in battle.' On hearing this, and not caring to check the truth of this report, the Count at once withdrew from the siege of the fort and, full of fear of Rodrigo, fled away home.

Transactis igitur .XXX. dierum indutijs, Rodericus barbaris qui intus in castello Muri Uetuli erant, dixit: 'Vt quid tardatis michi tradere oppidum?' Jlli autem sub dolo eidem sic responderunt: 'Domine: nuntij, quos direximus, nondum ad nos reuersi sunt; quamobrem adhuc nobilitati tue unanimiter supplicamus, quatinus indutias aliquantulas nobis dones.' Cum igitur Rodericus dolo et fraude eos sibi loqui perpenderet, et propter aliquod spatium habendum eosdem sibi hoc fjcte dicere plenius cognosceret, ait eis: 'Vt omnibus pateat hominibus quod nullum regum uestrorum timeo, adhuc .XIJ. dierum indutias uobis concedo, quatinus uenire et uobis succurrere nullam habeant excusationem. Transactis itaque .XIJ. diebus, uobis in rei ueritate dico, quod si castrum protinus mihi non dederitis, quoscunque uestrum capere uel habere potero, uiuos igne cremabo et gladio non sine tormentis trucidabo.' Venit itaque dies presignata, in qua eisdem qui intus erant in castro dixit Rodericus: 'Cur tantas interponitis moras, et non traditis mihi castrum iam promissum?' Jlli responderunt: 'Ecce Pascha uestrum, quod dicitur Pentecostes, iam proximum est; jn die Pasche trademus tibi omnino castrum; non enim reges nostri succurrere uolunt. Tu autem cum tuis tucius ingredere illud, habetoque secundum libitum tuum.' Jlle uero ait ad eos: 'Jn eadam sane die Pentecostes non ingrediar castellum, sed do uobis adhuc indutias usque ad festum sancti Iohannis. Jnterim accipite uxores uestras et liberos et familias atque omnem substantiam, et cum omnibus rebis uestris ite in pace, quocunque uolueritis. Euacuate itaque castrum, quod liberum sine impedimento mihi relinquatis. Ego autem, diuina clementia operante, in natiuitate sancte Iohannis Babtiste intrabo castrum.' Sarraceni uero, propter tantum talemque miserationis amorem, plures et deuotas sibi retulerunt grates.

Jn natale itaque sancti Iohannis Babtiste, Rodericus ad intrandum castrum milites suos premisit, quibus castrum ascendere ac intrare omnino precepit. Jlli uero castrum continuo intrauerunt, et summitatem castri iam obtinentes, Deo gratias exultantes retulerunt. Mox nimirum castrum ipse Rodericus ingrediens, in eo missam celebrare et munus oblationum offerre statim deuota mente iussit. Jdibem sancti Iohannis ecclesiam miro construi opere fecit.

Portas ciuitatis et omnium murorum munitiones, et cuncta que intus in urbe et in castro erant, militibus sollicite custodire precepit. Jn ipso autem castro, quamuis euacuato, multas inuenerunt diuitias. Muri Uetuli quidam habitatores sarraceni tunc in urbe adhuc permanebant; post triduum uero capti oppidi Rodericus ait illis: 'Nunc uobis omnibus modis precipio, ut cuncta que meis hominibus abstulistis, et ea que contra me et ad meum dedecus et meum dampnum mohabitis contulistis, mihi reddatis; quod si facere nolueritis, uos in carcerem intrudi, et uinculis ferreis dire illaqueari nequaquam dubitetis.' Jlli uero quesita redere non ualentes, diuitijs suis omnino nudati et uinculis uincti, ad Ualentiam protinus Roderici mandato sunt directi.

After the thirty days' truce had expired, Rodrigo said to the barbarians inside Murviedro: 'Why are you delaying in handing over the fortress to me?' They craftily replied to him as follows: 'Lord: the messengers we sent out have not returned to us yet. With one voice we beg of your noble nature to grant us some little extension of the truce.' Rodrigo realized that they were speaking deceitfully, and fully aware that they had said this in lying fashion in order to gain time, he said to them: 'In order that it should be plain to all men that I fear none of your rulers, I grant you a truce for a further twelve days, so that there shall be no excuse for their being unable to come and help you. When twelve days have passed, I tell you in all truth, if you do not then instantly hand the fortress over, I will put to death all of your people I can capture, burning some alive and finishing others off with the sword after torturing them.'

When the stipulated day came, Rodrigo said to those inside the fortress: 'Why are you causing such delays, and why are you not handing the fortress over to me as you promised?' They answered: 'The feast of Pentecost which your people keep is now close at hand. On the day of Pentecost we will hand the fortress completely over to you; for our rulers do not wish to help us. You may then safely enter it with your men, and possess it at your pleasure.' He then said to them: 'I will not enter the fortress on the day of Pentecost, but I grant you a truce until the feast of St John. Meantime, take your wives and children and relatives and all your belongings, and go in peace wherever you wish. Evacuate the fortress, which you are to hand over to me undisturbed without delay. And I — God willing — will enter the fortress on the day of St John the Baptist.' The Moors, since Rodrigo had shown such compassion for them, gave him great and heartfelt thanks.

On St John's day, Rodrigo sent his men to take over the fortress, ordering them to occupy it completely. They entered the place forthwith, and on occupying its topmost point joyfully gave thanks to God. Rodrigo, himself entering the fortress soon after, ordered that Mass should be said at once and offerings devoutly made. Later he had the church of St John built in a splendid style.

He ordered the gates of the town and all the defensive works on the walls, and everything within both the town and the fortress, to be carefully guarded by his men. In the fortress itself, even though it had been evacuated, they found considerable riches. Up to that time certain Moorish inhabitants of Murviedro stayed on in the town. Rodrigo said to them three days after the place was occupied: 'Now I order you: you are to hand over to me all those things which you kept back from my men, and those things which to my shame and detriment you gathered from the Almoravids. If you refuse to do this, I will imprison you, and do not doubt that you will be chained up in cruel fashion.' Those who proved unwilling to give up what he sought were stripped completely of their belongings and, loaded with chains, were sent at once by Rodrigo's order to Valencia.

## 26.  The Cid endows the Cathedral of Valencia (1098)

*There could be no firmer sign of the intended permanence of Christian conquerors in their conquest than the establishment there of a bishop with his cathedral and all the many elements of worship, Church feasts, administration, etc., which accompanied him.  Hieronymus was French, Jérome, from Périgord, and was a Cluniac monk who was probably recruited for service in Spain (with many others at the time) when Archbishop Bernard of Toledo returned from a visit to Rome through S. France in 1096, and he was sent to Valencia probably in 1097.  The chief mosque of the city was converted into a cathedral, dedicated to Santa María (de las Virtudes).*

*The purpose of the charter which follows is to settle upon Bishop and Cathedral estates near Valencia, whose rents would maintain them.  But this section has a lengthy preface in which the writer, with a broad view of history and biblical allusions, sees Rodrigo the Cid as a literally heaven—sent leader and avenger of Christianity.  In content and style this passage is unique in its time.  Set down far from the chancery practices*

XPS.  Cum diuinam presentjam catholicorum nullus ambigat ubique potencialiter adesse, quedam tamen pre ceteris loca ad propiciandum fidelibus sibi legitur Omnipotens elegisse; israheletico namque populo legalibus ceremoniis obumbrato, et tabernaculo Silo, ubi Deus habitauerat in hominibus, ex filiorum Heli nequitja reprobato, in monte Syon domum oratjonis cunctis gentibus instituit, in cuius templi dedicatjone, ad roboranda simplicium corda, Domini gloria in nebula patenter apparuit, et Deo imperium qui premeditatus hoc fuerat in eternum permanere constituit.  Vt autem accedente plenitudine temporis, de terra orta est ueritas et mentita est sibi iudeorum iniquitas, atque in Sponsi et Redemptoris sui thalamum ingressa est redempta plenitudo gentjum, profecto claruit quod Sanctus Spiritus per Malachie predixerat uaticinium: A solis ortu usque ad occasum magnum est nomen meum in gentibus, et in omni loco sacrificatur et offertur nomini meo oblatjo munda.  Repulsa igitur primum ut oportuit iudea perfidia, apostolice sonus predicatjonis ab orientali Syon in fines orbis exiens, totam sub occiduo repleuit Hispaniam; que firmiter ad Dei cultum eruditissimis informata doctoribus, abiectis supersticionibus, extirpatis erroribus, nemine resistente, nonnullis in pace quieuit temporibus.  At ubi prorsus ex Dei dono abscessit aduersitas et ad uotum cuncta successit prosperitas, refriguit caritas, habundauit iniquitas, et sectando ocium orrendum Dei oblita iudicium, repentinum est perpessa exterminium, et

*of Christian lands, Bishop Hieronymus himself may well have been its author, bringing new French modes of thought to the routine of military operations and perhaps a new language to the routine of lawyers' jargon. That Rodrigo towards the end of this passage uses the first person would not of course invalidate this.*

*Hieronymus, Jerónimo, has a prominent role in the* Poema de mio Cid: *a Christian of the muscular kind who announces his wish to kill Moors in God's service, who in addition to his religious role with the Cid's army does indeed fight in battle and has the honour of striking the 'first blows': see especially lines 1287—1306, with mention of his election to the see of Valencia and his endowment (line 1304) as in the present extract. After the recovery of Valencia by the Muslims, he went to be Bishop of Salamanca and Zamora, and died in 1120.*

*The original charter of 1098 survives in Salamanca, where it would have been kept (with, I speculate, the rest of the Cid's archive) against the day when Valencia was again in Christian hands and the Church could resume possession of its rights granted by the Cid. (In fact, Valencia was not again taken until 1238, and then by the Aragonese.) It is published in* La España del Cid *(see text 25), II, pp. 866—67.*

No Catholic doubts that the divine presence is powerfully felt everywhere, but we read that the Almighty chose certain places in preference to all others for those that were faithful to him. The Israelites being in the darkness of the rites of their law, and the tabernacle of Shiloh, where God had dwelled among men, being condemned because of the evil of the sons of Eli, He instituted a house of prayer on Mount Zion for all peoples, at the dedication of whose temple, in order to strengthen the hearts of simple people, the glory of the Lord appeared to all in a cloud, believing that this dedication to God would remain for all time. But in the fullness of time, truth arose in the land and the iniquity of the Jews was denounced, and all peoples were redeemed by entering the marriage—bed of the Spouse and Redeemer, and surely then shone forth the prophecy which the Holy Spirit had made through Malachi: 'For from the rising of the sun even unto the going down of the same my name shall be great among the Gentiles; and in every place incense shall be offered unto my name, and a pure offering' [I.11]. Jewish perfidy therefore being rejected, as it had to be, the sound of apostolic preaching went out from Zion in the East to the ends of the earth, filling the whole of Hispania in the extreme West. Hispania, strongly drawn to the worship of God by most learned sages, after superstitions had been put aside and errors eradicated, lived quietly in peace for a long time. But when adversity departed straightway, by the gift of God, and as much prosperity as they wished succeeded it, charity grew cold, iniquity abounded, there was a pursuit of idleness forgetful of the terrible judgement of God, there was a sudden disaster to be borne, and the splendour of secular things together with that of the Church was overthrown

crudeli filiorum Agar gladio secularis dignitas funditus corruit pariter cum sanctuario: et qui liber seruire noluit Domino dominorum, iure cogitur fieri seruus naturalium seruorum. Itaque annorum ferme .CCCC.$^{orum}$ in hac calamitate labente curriculo, tandem dignatus clementissimus Pater suo misereri populo, inuictissimum principem Rudericum Campidoctorem oprobrii seruorum suorum suscitauit ultorem et christiane religionis propagatorem; qui post multiplices et eximias quas diuinutus assecutus est preliorum uictorias, diuiciarum gloria et hominum copia opulentissimam urbem cępit Ualentiam; necnon et innumerabili moabitarum et tocius Hispanie barbarorum exercitu superato, uelut in momento ultra quam credi potest sine sui detrimento, ipsam meschitam, que apud agarenos domus oracionis habebatur, Deo in ęcclesiam dicauit, et uenerabili Ieronimo presbitero, concordi et canonica acclamatjone et electjone per romani pontificis manus in episcopum consecrato et specialis priuilegii libertate sublimato, prelibatam eclesiam ex suis facultatibus tali dote ditauit: Anno siquidem incarnatjonis Dominice LXXXX° VIII°, post millesimum, ego Rudericus Campidoctor et principes, ac populos quos Deus quandiu ei placuerit meę potestati comisit, donamus ipsi Redemptori nostro, qui solus dominatur in regno hominum et cuicunque uoluerit dat illud, et matri nostrę ecclesie fedi uidelicet Ualentine, et uenerabili pastori nostro Ieronime pontifici, uillam que dicitur Pigacen, cum uillis et terris et uineis. [...]

by the cruel sword of the sons of Hagar; and he who as a free man had not wished to serve the Lord of Lords, was compelled by law to become a slave of those who were born to be slaves. Then, after the passing of a period of nearly 450 years since this disaster, the most merciful Father deigned to take pity on his people, and raised up the ever – victorious leader Rodrigo the Campeador as avenger of the shame of his servants and as a champion of the Christian religion; and he, after many famous victories in battles which he won by divine aid, with a thirst for riches and a great number of men, took the extraordinarily wealthy city of Valencia. This was after defeating a vast army of Almoravids and the barbarians of all Spain, and in a shorter time than anyone would believe possible, without loss to his men. He dedicated the mosque, which was a house of prayer for the Agarenes, to God as a church, and gave the aforementioned church with the following endowment from his own resources to the worthy priest Hieronymus, consecrated as bishop by unanimous and canonical approval and appointed by the hand of the Pope and raised up by the grant of a special privilege.

So in the year of our Lord 1098 I, Rodrigo the Campeador and my commanders, together with the peoples whom it has pleased God to place in my power for the time being, give to our Redeemer, who alone rules in the kingdom of men, and assigns that kingdom to whomsoever He will, and to our mother Church of Valencia, and our pastor the worthy Bishop Hieronymus, the village of Picasent, with its farms and its lands and vineyards [...]

[There follow other properties, seven in all; then the customary anathema clauses, etc.]

134

## 27.  St James frees a captive (1100)

*Text 19 has shown St Dominic of Silos freeing a Christian captive of the Moors in about 1087, and his reputation for doing this went on strongly in the 13th century (text 44).  But St James as Patron of Spain was not to be outdone, at least by those who compiled the* Liber Sancti Jacobi *in about 1140, where the following text (II.22) is given under the heading* 'Miraculum Sancti Iacobi a Domno Papa Calixto Editum' *('A Miracle of St James set down by Pope Calixtus', second of that name, 1119—24).  On the* Liber, *see text 8.  The extract is taken from the same source as text 8, pages 286—87.*

*Perhaps more startling than the wanderings of the captive are the details of the wild beasts encountered by the man somewhere between*

Anno dominice incarnacionis millesimo centesimo quemdam ciuem Barquinonensem sancti Iacobi baselicam horis Gallecie peregrinationis causa fertur aduenisse.  Qui cum ab apostolo tantum peteret, ut eum a captione inimicorum liberaret, si forte in ea caderet, ad propria reuersus, negotii causa Siciliam perrectus, a Sarracenis in mari captus est.  Quid plura?  Per nundinas et foros tredecies uenditur et emitur.  Qui uero eum emebant, beato Iacobo catenas et uincula eius conterente, tenere nequibant.  Primo uenditur in Corociana, secundo apud urbem Iazeram in Ysclauonia, tertio in Blasia, quarto in Turcoplia, quinto in Perside, sexto in India, septimo in Ethiopia, octauo in Alexandria, nono in Affrica, decimo in Barbaria, undecimo in Beserto, duodecimo in Bugia, tredecimo in urbe Almaria; in qua cum esset a quodam Sarraceno duplicibus catenis fortiter circa crura nexus, beatum Iacobum altissonis ei imploranti idem apostolus apparuit, dicens: 'Quia dum esses in baselica mea, tantum a me petisti deliberationem corporis tui, et non anime salutem, in his periculis lapsus es.  Sed quia dominus misertus est tui, misit me ad te, ut ab his ergastulis eruam te.'
Ilico disruptis cadenis eius per medium, ab occulis eius beatus apostolus disparuit.  Itaque homo ille solutis a uinculis per urbes et castella Sarracenorum, quandam partem catene in testimonio tanti miraculi manibus ferens, ad terram Christianorum, uidentibus Sarrecenis, palam cepit redire.  Cumque aliquis paganus illi obuiaret, eumque capere temptaret, ipse ostendebat ei partem catene, et statim aduersarius ab eo fugiebat.  Multa enim agmina leonum, ursorum, leopardorum et draconum illum gradientem per deserta loca deuorare appetebant, sed uisa catena, quam apostolus tetigerat, procul ab eo recedebant.  Hunc hominem ad beati Iacobi limina regredientem, catenam manibus ferentem, nudis etiam pedibus ac excoriatis, inter Stellam et Grugnum ueraciter egomet repperi, et hec omnia michi

*Almería and La Rioja, where Calixtus talked with him. Bears are still found in the Pyrenees and Picos de Europa, but the other faunistic items were extinct in the Peninsula from remote times.* A literary source for this passage is readily found, for the same animals figure with others in the dire dream which Charlemagne had (a vision of Gabriel) in the Chanson de Roland *about the perils facing the Frankish army in Spain: in version 'O' of the poem,*

*En grant dulor i veit ses chevalers,*

*Urs e leuparz les voelent puis manger,*

*Serpenz e guivres, dragun e averser,*

*Grifunz i ad plus de trente millers ... (2541—44)*

while in 2549 *the Emperor himself is attacked by a lion.*

In the year of our Lord 1100 a certain citizen of Barcelona is said to have come as a pilgrim to the cathedral of St James in Galicia. He prayed to the Apostle only that he should free him from captivity by his enemies, if perchance he should suffer that. Then he went home, and later, while sailing to Sicily on business, he was captured at sea by Saracens. What next? He was bought and sold thirteen times at marts and markets. Those who purchased him were unwilling to keep him, because St James always broke his chains and shackles. First he was sold in Kurashan, the second time in the city of Jezireh in Slav lands [probably al—Jazira 'the island', a province — not a city — between the Tigris and Euphrates, in the north—east part of what is now Syria; the reference to 'Slav lands' suggests confusion with the land of Chazar in what is now S. Russia, earlier settled by Turks], the third time in Blasia [unidentified], the fourth in Turkish lands [?], the fifth in Persia, the sixth in India, the seventh in Ethiopia, the eighth in Alexandria, the ninth in North Africa, the tenth in Barbary, the eleventh in Bizerta, the twelfth in Bougie, the thirteenth in the city of Almería. In this last place, when he was shackled by a certain Saracen by double chains drawn tightly round his legs, as he was praying to St James on high, the Apostle himself appeared to him, saying: 'Since, when you were in my church, you prayed only that I would set your person free, and not for the salvation of your soul, you have been cast into all these perils. But because the Lord has taken pity on you, He sent me to you, in order that I should free you from this prison.'

Thereupon his chains were broken, and the holy Apostle disappeared from his sight. The man began to make his way back to Christian lands without any concealment, carrying part of his chain as witness to this great miracle, and in full view of the Saracens. When some pagan stood in his path, and tried to recapture him, he held up part of the chain and the enemy fled away before him instantly. Many groups of lions, bears, leopards, and dragons tried to devour him as he passed through wild places, but on seeing the chain which the Apostle had touched, they drew back to a distance from him. I myself found this man between Estella and

enarrauit. A Domino factum est istud et est mirabile in oculis nostris. In hoc ergo exemplo illi sunt corripiendi, qui petunt a Domino sanctisque suis aut uxorem aut terrenam felicitatem, aut honores, aut censum, aut inimicorum letum, aut cetera his similia, que ad proficuum corporis solummodo pertinent, non que ad anime salutem. Si corporis necessaria sunt petenda, igitur anime uita, id est, bone uirtutis, fides scilicet, spes, caritas, castitas, pacientia, temperantia, hospitalitas, largitas, humilitas, obedientia, pax, perseuerentia et cetera his similis, magis sunt petenda, e quibus ipsa anima in sidereis sedibus sit coronata. Quod ipse prestare dignetur cuius regnum et imperium sine fine permanet in secula seculorum. Amen.

Logroño, returning anew to the shrine of St James, carrying his chain and with his feet bare and lacerated; and there he gave me a truthful account of all these events. In our eyes this is a miracle wrought by the Lord. In this story, therefore, there is a rebuke for those who pray to the Lord and His Saints for a wife or for earthly happiness, or estates, or property, or the death of their enemies, or like things which concern only the welfare of their bodily life, and not the salvation of their souls. If things necessary to the life of the body are to be sought, then so is the life of the soul, that is to say of goodly virtue: faith, hope, charity, chastity, patience, temperance, hospitality, generosity, humility, obedience, peace, perseverance, and other things of this order are to be sought in prayer, and that with them the soul may be crowned in its heavenly abode. May He whose kingdom and rule are everlasting deign to grant this. Amen.

## 28. Alvar Fáñez's defence of Toledo (1109)

*For Alvar Fáñez, see text 20. He commanded the troops in Toledo from 1109 and was lord of a large region to the south of the city. The Chronica Adefonsi Imperatoris of Alfonso VII of León–Castile (1126–57) was probably the work of Arnault, Bishop of Astorga (1144–52), a Frenchman who brought a knowledge of the classics and a superior feeling for biblical rhetoric to the task of writing Peninsular history, as is apparent in the following extract. The Chronica in its surviving form concludes with the Poema de Almeria relating to AD 1147; we do not know if it continued, in prose, beyond that point. The following account of the siege of 1109 is included as a deliberate digression: on mentioning Alvar*

(96) Omisso naturali ordine, ad ea quae olim christianis asperrima fuere bella, tractandi veniamus.   Post obitum regis domni Adefonsi, patris reginae Urracae, matris Adefonsi Imperatoris, rex Ali maximus Sarracenorum, qui rex Marrochiorum dominabatur Moabitis et ex ista parte maris Agarenis, longe lateque aliisque multis, et maris insulis et nationibus, sicut serpens aestu sitiens extulit caput, et quasi post mortem summi viri ibique triumphaturus, convocavit omnes principes et duces et milites Moabitarum et magnum exercitum conducticium Arabum, et multa milia militum et ballistorum et magnas multitudines peditum, sicut arena qui est in littore maris;   et habito usuque industrium consilio, congregavit exercitum et transfretando venit in Sibiliam et cum eo filius eius Texufinus; iussitque omnibus regibus, principibus et ducibus Moabitarum, qui erant super Agarenos, ut unusquisque eorum, parato agmine militum et ballistorum ac peditum pro posse suo, comportarent scalas et machinas et magna ingenia ferrea et lignea ad debellandum tam civitatem Toletum, ad quam properabat, quam alia oppida et civitates, quae sunt Trans Serram.

(97) Movitque castra de Sibilia et in paucis diebus venit ad Cordubam et ibi congregatae sunt ad eum omnes gentes, quae erant in terra Agarenorum, et moverunt castra de Corduba et venerunt per illam terram quae fuit de Alvaro Fannici, ceperuntque castella munita et civitates, quas partim destruxerunt, partim munierunt.   Deinde venerunt in Toletum et destruxerunt Sanctum Servandum et Azecha; deinde, ad ipsam civitatem proximantes, machinas in locis opportunis erexerunt eamque diu sagitta, lapide, lancea, telo igneque petentes oppugnaverunt.   Sed in civitate erat strenuus dux christianorum, Alvarus Fannici, cum magna multitudine militum

*Rodríguez, grandson or possibly great—grandson of Alvar Fáñez, and his status as governor of Toledo, in the* Poema de Almeria, *it occurred to Arnault to tell the story of his famous ancestor and the heroic defence of Toledo, either from some written source now lost, or from the account of an eye—witness. Despite the rhetoric and the biblical allusions, the narration is very circumstantial and the presence of vernacular words in Latin form (alcadrán, etc.) supports this.*

*'King Alí' is Ali ibn Yusuf, Emperor of the Almoravids, successor to his father Yusuf (1106—43). His decision to attack Toledo may have been occasioned by the news of the death of the warrior—king Alfonso VI on 30 June 1109.*

*The* Chronica Adefonsi Imperatoris *is edited by L. Sánchez Belda (Madrid, 1950). The extract consists of sections 96—101.*

(96) Departing from the natural order, let us come to those events which at an earlier time brought bitter battles to the Christians. After the death of King Alfonso [VI], father of Queen Urraca who was the mother of our Alfonso [VII] the Emperor, King Ali, greatest ruler of the Saracens, who as King of the Moroccans commanded the Almoravids and on this side of the sea the Spanish Moors, and many others far and wide, and the islands and nations of the sea, like a snake thirsting in the heat of summer raised his head, and as though he would triumph over our great King after his death, called together all the princes and commanders and soldiers of the Almoravids together with a great army of Arab mercenaries, and many thousands of horsemen and slingers and great companies of foot—soldiers, as many as the sands on the shore of the sea. After consultations, diligently undertaken, he formed up his army and, accompanied by his son Tashufin, crossed the Strait and reached Seville. He then gave orders to all the emirs, princes, and commanders of the Almoravids, who were in positions of authority over the Spanish Moors, that each one of them, once the lines of horsemen and slingers and foot—soldiers had been drawn up, should assemble — to the limits of his capacity — scaling—ladders and siege—towers and great engines of iron and of wood, for the purpose of storming the city of Toledo, for which he was setting off, together with other towns and cities of the region.

(97) He struck camp in Seville and in a few days reached Cordova. In that city there gathered to him all the forces of the lands of the Spanish Moors. They set out from Cordova, passing through the lands that had belonged to Alvar Fáñez, capturing castles and towns, some of which they destroyed and others of which they fortified. Thence they went to Toledo and destroyed San Servando and Aceca; then, approaching the city itself, they set up their engines in strategic places and over a long period attacked the city with arrows, stones, lances, missiles of every kind, and fire. However, Alvar Fáñez was in the city, as the energetic commander of the Christians, together with a great number of knights and archers and

et sagittariorum et peditum et robustorum iuvenum, qui sedentes super muros civitatis et super turres et portas, viriliter pugnabant contra Sarracenos, et multa milia Sarracenorum ibi postrata sunt, unde et virtute christianorum, fugati longe facti sunt a turribus civitatis, ut nichil nocere possent civitati neque eis, qui supra muros erant.

(98) Hoc videns rex Ali iussit peditibus ut adducerent multa lignea vinearum et arborum et per noctem ponere ea furtim ad radicem fortissimae turris, quae est sita in capite pontis contra Sanctum Servandum. Media autem nocte, Sarraceni coeperunt mittere fortissimum ignem de alcadran in lignis cum ballistis et cum sagittis, ut cremarent turrem; sed christiani qui in turre erant verterunt multum acetum vini super ligna et mortuus est ignis. Erant autem simul cum domno Alvaro in civitate magna turba senum magni consilii et multa futura praevidentes, quos ibi reliquerat rex ex suo semine, qui eam liberaret a bello Sarracenorum.

(99) Hoc videns rex Ali, magna ira accensus est et in sequenti die, summo mane, iussit principibus militiae suae statuere magnas acies de azequtis peditibus cum omnibus ingeniis, et deinde alias Agarenorum, et post ipsas alias Moabitarum et Arabum deducentes ingenia ad radicem muros civitatis per opportuna loca. Statueruntque ad illam portam de Almaquara et ubique multas ballistas et machinas et ignis iacula, et tormenta ad lapides iactandos, et spicula, et scorpios ad mittendas sagittas, et fundibularias, vineas et arietes cum quibus suffoderent muros civitatis et scalas, quas ponerent super turres.

(100) Fecerunt autem christiani machinas adversus machinas eorum et pugnaverunt per dies septem, nichil civitati nocentes. Septimo vero die audacter viri bellatores christiani eruperunt de civitate per portas ad occasum solis et, fugientibus azequtis et Agarenis, miserunt ignem in omnibus machinis, quas fugientes reliquerant, et in omnibus ingeniis cum quibus rex Ali et principes sui cogitabant suffodere muros civitatis. Civitas autem, Dei adiutorio, remansit illaesa.

(101) Dum ista bella geruntur, archiepiscopus domnus Bernardus, Toletanae ecclesiae, cum clericis et monachis et senibus et mulieribus et pauperibus, postrati in terra in ecclesia Sanctae Mariae, unanimiter rogabant Dominum Deum et Sanctam Mariam ut peccata regum ne reminiscerentur et populorum, ne ipsi darentur in captivitatem et gladium, et mulieres in derisionem, et infantes eorum in praedam, et civitas eorum in exterminium, et sancta lex Dei in opprobium et in pollutionem et conculcationem. Sed Dominus Deus excelsus exaudivit orationes eorum et misertus est populo suo, et misit Michaelem archangelum qui custodiret civitatem Toletanam et firmaret muros eius ne rumperentur, et confortaret animos virorum

foot—soldiers and sturdy young men, who, stationed on the tops of the walls and towers and gates, resisted the Saracens valiantly, and thousands of Saracens were laid low there; forced back by the bravery of the Christians to a good distance from the towers of the city, they were no longer able to harm any part of it nor those atop the walls.

(98) Seeing this, King Ali ordered his infantrymen to bring up quantities of wood from the vineyards and woodlands, and to place this secretly by night against the base of an exceptionally strong tower situated at the head of the bridge opposite San Servando. Then at midnight the Saracens began to set fire to the wood with tar—laden catapult shots and arrows, hoping to burn the tower down; but the Christians inside it poured a great quantity of vinegar onto the wood and the fire went out. There were also inside Toledo with Don Alvar a good number of old men wise in counsel and able to advise about what was likely to happen, men whom King Alfonso had left there to guard the city until there should arise a king from his own seed who should finally free the place from the threat of Saracen attack.

(99) On realizing that this attack had failed King Ali, greatly enraged, very early the next day ordered his army commanders to form up great lines of infantrymen from their own praetorian troops with all their engines, and behind them others of the Spanish Moors, and behind them others again of the Almoravids and Arabs with their engines in strategic places aimed at the base of the city walls. Against the Almaquara gate and at other points they set up many catapults and engines, flame—throwers, machines for hurling stones, engines for projecting bolts and darts and sling—shots, mantelets, and battering—rams with which to undermine the walls of the city, together with ladders to set against the towers.

(100) Then the Christians set up their own engines to combat those of the enemy, and they fought for seven days. Nothing in the city suffered any damage. On the seventh day the warlike Christians burst out of the city through the gates towards the west, and, having put the praetorian troops and the Spanish Moors to flight, set fire to all their engines, which those fleeing had abandoned, together with all the machines with which King Ali and his commanders had hoped to sap the walls of the place. And the city, with God's help, remained untouched.

(101) While this fighting was going on, Bernard, Archbishop of Toledo, together with the clergy and monks and old men and women and the poor, all prostrated in the church of St Mary, with one voice prayed to God and the Virgin that the sins of the rulers and the people should be set aside, that they themselves should not be handed over into captivity or put to the sword, the women outraged and the children reckoned among the booty, their city laid waste and the holy law of God cast into shame and befouled and trampled underfoot. But the Lord God on high heard their prayers and took pity on His people, and sent the Archangel Michael to guard Toledo and to strengthen its walls that they should not be broken, and to comfort

bellatorum et defenderet corpora christianorum, quod fieri non poterat nisi Dominus eos custodiret, sicut David ait: 'Nisi Dominus custodierit civitatem, in vanum vigilant qui custodiunt eam.'

the spirit of the fighting men and defend the lives of the Christians; and this could not have happened had not God protected them, for as David says: 'Except the Lord keep the city, the watchman waketh but in vain'.

## 29.  The Pisans attack the Balearics (1114–15)

*The Balearics were the last of the* taifa *kingdoms to remain free of Almoravid domination (after Saragossa succumbed to them in 1110), and were an important base for piracy.  It was also said, doubtless with much exaggeration, that they held some 30,000 Christian captives in cruel conditions.  To protect their trade the Pisans, with Genoese collaboration, organized a naval expedition in 1113.  Their fleet arrived — accidentally, it seems — on the coast of Catalonia, and the Pisans gladly accepted the alliance of Ramón Berenguer III, Count of Barcelona, making him commander of the expedition.  The allies took Ibiza in June 1114, and soon after, Majorca.  A garrison was installed, but after a short time the islands were again lost to an Almoravid attack.  Ramón Berenguer went to Pisa, Genoa, and Rome in the hope of organizing another expedition, but the Almoravids were at the height of their power, and the Count found it necessary to defend his homeland.  The islands were not taken by the Christians until 1229–35.*

     Quem colit interea tellus Balearica Regem,
     Haerare Declus Burabe, perterritus istis,
     contususque, in coetum [...] convocat omnes,
     causas majores per quos tractare solebat.
5    Consilium quorum plano sermone requirit,
     sive moabitis optarent tradere terram,
     an cum Pisanis aliquod conjungere foedus.
     Respondere viri soliti majora referre,
     et qui noscuntur aliis praecedere sensu:
10      'Turba sumus, famulique tui, quodcumque videtur
     in ratione tibi constantius eximiumque,
     nos sine lite sequi confestim disce paratos.
     Respice nulla minus populum quod bella volentem;
     sedula velle suo tua gens in pace maneret,
15   haec nam culpa gravis dedit horrida scandala nobis.
     Undique gauderent Baleari subdita regno,
     si cum Pisanis nos foedus habere daretur.
     Inque moabitas nobis fiducia clara
     non bona sperat: tantum convicia prosunt,
20   quae tolerare gemunt Hispanae gaudia terrae.
      'Respice Dertosae quid agant, quantaque Dianam
     clade premant: nostras miseratus mente querelas
     accipe, captivos omnes perquirere, serva,
     et melius tracta, quia pax, et vita per illos,
25   ac regnum pariter tibi concedetur, honorque.
     Actis non habitis nunquam se dabitur hostis;
     christicolis quoniam, qui pro pietate laborant,

*The Pisan expedition of 1113—15 was the subject of a lengthy and in places spirited poem in strongly classicizing style by Lorenzo of Verona, a deacon of Pisa, who wrote about 1135. It is titled* De bello Balearico *and consists of seven books. A principal personage in it is Peter, Bishop of Pisa, who took the Cross and secured the papal blessing for all participants; the idea of Crusade is thus strongly present.*

*The extract is from the start of Book III. Naturally the poet was not privy to discussions held by the Muslim ruler, but the gist of them may have been reported by someone later taken prisoner; in any case, they reveal a real enough dilemma. The Christian allies did not accept the offer of the Balearic ruler to release his captives, pay expenses, and enter into a treaty: they immediately began the attack on Ibiza.*

*The text is published by Juan Dameto and others,* Historia general del Reino de Mallorca *(2nd ed., Palma, 1841, 2 vols), II, pp. 1142—1301. It is also in* Patrologia Latina, *vol. 163, cols 513—76.*

Meanwhile he to whom the Balearic kingdom owes allegiance as ruler, Mubashir Nasr al—Dawla, filled with fear and distressed by these events, called together all those with whom he was accustomed to discuss weighty matters. He asked them to tell him frankly what their advice was, whether they should hand over the land to the Moabites, or try to secure some agreement with the Pisans. The men accustomed to give opinions about grave issues, and who in good sense take precedence over others, answered him:

'We are your people and your servants, and we are forthwith prepared to carry out willingly whatever seems to you to be reasonable. You can see that your people want nothing less than war; but they would really prefer in their careful way to remain at peace, for this grave crime [of piracy?] has brought desperate problems for us. On all sides the subjects of the Balearic kingdom would rejoice if we could achieve a treaty with the Pisans. With the Moabites a clear bond of faith awaits us, but not a good one; the lands of Spain groan to support such joys, and for us produce only abuse.

'Consider what they are doing in Tortosa, and with what slaughter they are oppressing Denia. Receive our requests with pity in your mind, have the captives sought out and treat them better; for by so doing peace and life may be granted to you, and your kingdom and honour guaranteed. If this is not done, the enemy will never be placated; for the Christians, who

chara magis essent captorum corpora fratrum,
quam videatur eis regnorum copia centum.'
30    His habitis verbis, regis praecordia diri
contremuere metu: captivos protinus omnes
praecipit inquiri sparsim, veteresque, novosque.
Tunc de bona rate quos sors, ventus et unda
vexerat invitos, curat tractare decenter.
35    Pisanis etiam chartam pro tempore scripsit,
in qua Pontificem, patres, populumque salutat.
Qui quamvis prorsus diversum mente retractet,
ditia verba tamen mittens, nil supplicat hostis,
neque constantem sine proditione fatetur.
40    Ampuriae Comitem testem narrantibus addit,
Jerusalem, dicens, peregrino dum petit actu,
conspicuae famae natus Comes Ampuriensis,
illius illaesam servavit foedere terram:
nullum quippe virum bello seu pace fefellit.
45    'Si Pisana manus mecum vult pacis habere
foedera, continuo captivos reddo, measque
dono paratus opes; linquat mea regna, suasque
impensas reddam pariter, pretiumque laboris.
At si forte suis armis contendere mavult,
50    bellandoque meam putat armis vincere gentem,
ubi communi cum se defendat ab hoste
urbs, nihilum faciunt ejus mea regna labores.'
His intellectis, chartam Pisana recepit,
et respondetur brevibus sermonibus illis,
55    qui tales apices, et talia scripta tulerunt:
'Nil tolerare mali portantes nuntia lex est
communis viris, debemus moribus uti.
Non possunt jungi cum vestro foedera rege,
nec fas est nobis ullam sibi reddere pacem,
60    ni prius in vestras conduxerit agmina terras.
Rex qui cuncta videns Judex cognoscitur aequus,
illuc decernat Judex pius, ille patenter
inter nos cunctos hominum qui judicat actus.'

strive in the name of religion, would sooner recover the dear persons of their brethren held captive than have possession of a hundred kingdoms.'

After these words, the King's heart trembled with great fear. He ordered the scattered captives, both old and new, to be sought out. Then he saw to it that those whom fate, storm, and sea had outraged should be decently treated. At that time he wrote a letter to the Pisans, sending greetings to the Pope, the leaders, and the people. He might in his heart have been intending something else, but still he sent these helpful words, and said that he was not asking for anything as an enemy, and was speaking sincerely without any deceit.

He added as a witness to this, for the benefit of the emissaries, the Count of Ampurias, saying that when the Count — known for his outstanding reputation — went off on the pilgrimage to Jerusalem, he [the King] had by treaty respected his [the Count's] land; he had never deceived anybody either in peace or in war. 'If the Pisan people wishes to have a peace treaty with me, I will at once hand over the prisoners, and I am disposed to make a grant of money; if they stop attacking my kingdom, I will pay their costs and the expenses of the expedition. But if the Pisans prefer to fight, and think they can overcome my men in war, provided the city can defend itself against the common enemy, their efforts shall achieve nothing against my realms.'

Having heard this, the Pisans received the letter and made a brief reply to those who had brought the message and the document: 'It is a law common to all men that no harm should be done to those bearing an embassy, and we must follow this custom. We cannot make a treaty with your King, nor is it right for us to grant you peace until we have led our forces into your territory. Let the King [i.e., God] who sees all things and is recognized as a fair judge, and who clearly judges all that men do, decide the matter there as a merciful arbiter.'

## 30. St James cures a Muslim ambassador (1121)

*The following is from the* Historia Compostellana *(II.50), whose parts, completed in about 1140, are credited to five authors under the direction of Diego Gelmírez (see text 16). The work is of value as a history of the reigns during which it was composed; it is also a work of propaganda for St James and his cult, and a justification for the actions of Gelmírez. For St James, see texts 7, 8, 13, 16, 17, and 27. The extract*

[...] Sarracenorum rex Ali nomine, qui et citra mare et trans mare Hiberiae sceptrum habet in Agarenos, miserat Ismaelitas nuntios, viros discretos atque illustres, ad reginam Urracam eiusque filium legationis gratia. Qui cum iter carperent ad occidentem, audito quod regina cum filio suo in Gallaeciae moraretur finibus, vident peregrinos christicolas quam plures ad B. Iacobum orationis causa euntes et redeuntes: et admirantes sciscitantur centurionem Petrum nomine, quem christianum praeducem et manutentorem inter christianos habebant, qui et eorum lingua satis peritus erat. 'Quisnam', inquiunt, 'iste est quem christianorum multitudo tanta frequentat devotione? Quis iste tantus et talis, quem innumeri christicolae transpyrenaei et citra repetunt orationis gratia? Tanta est euntium ad eum et redeuntium multitudo, ut vix pateat nobis liber callis ad occidentem.' Respondetur illis, hunc esse B. Iacobum Domini et Salvatoris nostri apostolum, Ioannis apostoli et evangelistae fratrem, et utrumque Zebedaei filium, cuius corpus in Gallaeciae finibus habetur humatum, quem Gallia, Anglia, Latium, Alemania, omnesque christicolarum provinciae, et praecipue Hispania veneratur, utpote patronum et protutorem suum. Discit insuper stirps Ismaelitica, quod idem Jacobus Hierosolymis sub Herode passus, et Gallaeciam fuerat advectus.

Cum autem ventum fuisset Compostellam, qui prius super auditis mirabantur, apostolicam conspicientes baselicam magno percutiuntur stupore. 'Pappae', inquiunt, 'quam nobile, quamque gloriosum Jacobi vestri praecellit aedificium! Infra et citra nostrum mare non vidimus huic comparandum. Per Mafomet, magna ei gloria collata est, si tantum pollet in superis, quam praeclarum eum habetis in terris! Quid igitur patrocinii, quid auxilii colentibus se et venerantibus impartitur?' Ad haec centurio lingua Ismaelitica: 'Tantam', inquit, 'a Domino nostro Iesu−Christo meritis et intercessionibus suis consequitur gratiam, quod per Dei misericordiam caecis visum, claudis gressum, laeprosis aliisque diversorum morborum generibus compeditis, salutem largitur. Subvenit atque opitulatur omnibus se devote deposcentibus, et trans Pyrenem et citra innumeris miraculis pollet. Hos enim compeditos, et carceri mancipatos liberavit, alios diuturno languore detentos sanavit: illis in difficilimis opem praestitit: ubique terrarum omnipotens Deus meritis et intercessionibus beati Iacobi miracula sua ostendit. Ob hoc corpus eius tanta frequentat multitudo, ob hoc innumeri

*is taken from* España Sagrada, *XX, pp. 350—55. The text continues beyond the end of this extract, the Muslims praising the Apostle and promising to tell of his glory in their own land. They are not, however, converted.*

*'King Alí' at the start of the passage is Ali ibn Yusuf, as in text 28. Urraca ruled León and such parts of Castile as could be freed from the domination of her estranged husband Alfonso I of Aragón, from 1109 to 1126; her son ruled after her as Alfonso VII (see the next extract). The text is also in Vázquez de Parga, pp. 141—47.*

[...] King Ali of the Saracens, who rules the Agarenes [Almoravids] on both sides of the Mediterranean, sent Ishmaelite ambassadors, wise and noble men, on a mission to Queen Urraca and her son. As they were travelling westward, having heard that the Queen and her son were residing in Galicia, they observed very many Christian pilgrims coming to the shrine of St James and going home from there; and marvelling at this, they asked a certain officer, Peter by name, who was evidently a kind of leader among the Christians and who spoke Arabic tolerably well, what was the reason for it. 'Who', they asked, is this man whom the mass of Christians honours with so much devotion? Who is so important and of such qualities that uncounted Christians from this country and from beyond the Pyrenees come to pray at his shrine? So great is the press of people going to and fro that we can hardly make our way along the road to the west.' Peter answered them that the man in question was the Apostle St James, brother of John the Evangelist and Apostle, both sons of Zebedee, whose body is buried in Galicia, venerated in France, England, Italy, and Germany, indeed in all Christian lands, and especially in Spain as is natural as her patron and protector. The Ishmaelites were also told how James was martyred in Jerusalem under Herod and translated to Galicia.

When they arrived at Compostela, still marvelling at all they had heard, they were struck by amazement as they gazed upon the cathedral. 'How nobly and gloriously the church of your James rises up!', they exclaimed. 'We have seen nothing comparable on either side of our sea. By Muhammad! his name is to be glorified. If he has such power in heaven, no wonder he is so famous on earth! What benefits are there in protection and aid for those who worship him?' Peter answered these questions in Arabic: 'By his merits and intercession he obtains the grace of our Lord Jesus Christ, so that through the mercy of God sight is restored to the blind, movement to the lame, and health to lepers and to others suffering from divers kinds of disease. He helps all those who pray devoutly to him, and shows his power by innumerable miracles here and beyond the Pyrenees. He has freed people from their fetters and from prison, and cured others who suffered long illnesses. To others he has given aid in their troubles. Almighty God has worked His miracles in all lands by the merits and intercessions of St James. That is why so many

opem eius indubitanter exposcunt.' Ad haec stupent atque mirantur Ismaelitae, et nihil aiunt; suum scilicet Mafomet, nil tale posse fatentur. Centurio quidem utpote vir eloquentissimus atque prudentissimus, gentilium assidue confundebat incredulitatem, et christianorum fidem laudibus et veritatis assertione extollebat, verissimis atque evidentissimis argumentis adstruebat gentiles ignorantiae nube caecatos varioque delussos errore. Contra hoc Ismaelitae nullatenus praesumebant repugnare, cum et prae oculis veritatis haberent indicia, et tanta beati Iacobi obtupescerent gloria. [...]

Post haec eisdem Ismaelitis Compostellae diutius morae indulgentibus in cuiusdam eorum cervice apostema exortum contumuit, quod insanabile atque mortiferum penitus videbatur: huiusmodi enim solet vitae aditus praecludere. Eamdem autem domum in qua et ipsi hospitabantur, quaedam frequentabat vidua, quae cereis et oblationibus apostolica quotidie visitabat limina, et orationibus insistens saepius ibidem pernoctabat. Quod Ismaelitae conspicientes sciscitantur quo et quare vidua illa tanta solicitudine defferret supradicta? Responsum est eis quod beati Jacobi apostoli clementiam pro remedio animae suae, et parentum suorum, ceterorumque fidelium, his atque aliis exoraret. Forsitan et gentilium perfidia huiusmodi improperare atque deridere auderet hostias, nisi evidentissimum apostolicae virtutis miraculum in praedicta archiepiscopi et legati deliberatione vidissent. Iam vero nec miraculo derogare, nec apostoli gloriam minuere praesumebant; at ille in cuius cervice apostema extumescebat, 'Obsecro', inquit, 'intercede pro me ad apostolum vestrum, cuius patrocinia petentibus praesto esse videmus; precare ut et mihi dignetur esse propitius, quandoquidem potens est per Dei misericordiam. Fer quoque ad eius altare pro me hunc cereum (et dedit) et supplica et ut ab huius apostematis tubertate me reddat incolumem.' Ad hoc vidua prae gaudio subridens, ait: 'Gratias ago Deo et beato Jacobo, qui vobis suae virtutis patefecit mirabilia, et veritatis lumen; non tamen adhuc ad plenum vobis ostendit.' Et accipiens cereum, cum eodem cereo illius apostema tetigit facto desuper signo crucis; deinde abiit ad ecclesiam, et more solito obtulit oblationes, orationem fecit; expleta oratione cereum quem acceperat ab Ismaelita obtulit, orationibus orationem addidit, supplicans beato Iacobo ut praedictum Ismaelitam incolumitati restituat, eumque per Dei misericordiam ab apostematis peste mortifera liberum reddat. Vix peracta oratione apostematis conglutinatio exinanitur. Ismaelita incolumitati restituitur. Remanet tamen cicatrix, signum videlicet exinanitae pestis. Magna et ineffabilis Dei misericordia quae per crucis signum, quod gentilibus

people come to his shrine, and why so many freely beg for his help.' The Ishmaelites were struck with amazement at all this, and said nothing; they knew in their hearts that their Muhammad could do nothing like this. Peter — an exceptionally eloquent and judicious man — went on to condemn the unbelief of the infidels, praising and asserting the truth of the Christian faith; with just and proper arguments he showed how the infidels were blinded by the fog of their ignorance and duped by divers errors. The Ishmaelites did not venture to make any rejoinder to this: they had indications of the truth before their very eyes, and were overwhelmed by the glory of St James. [...]

After the Ishmaelites had been in Compostela some time, one of them developed an abscess on his neck, which seemed to be incurable and likely to lead to his death: this kind of complaint does indeed seem to be fatal. But in the house where they were lodging, there lived a widow who daily visited the Apostle's shrine with candles and offerings, and often stayed the night there at prayer. On seeing this the Ishmaelites asked why the widow was showing such devotion. They were told that she prayed that St James would have mercy on her soul, and the souls of her parents and ancestors, and the souls of all the faithful. The unbelievers in their perfidy might have been tempted to attack and deride such offerings, but they were aware of the very obvious miracle worked by the power of the Apostle in the earlier freeing of Diego Gelmírez, Archbishop and Papal Legate [Gelmírez, Archbishop of Compostela from 1120, was imprisoned by Queen Urraca in 1121 and released when the clergy and people of the city rose in his support]. Hence they did not dare to belittle the miracle nor to diminish the Apostle's glory. Instead, the man who had the abscess on his neck cried: 'I beg you, intercede for me with your Apostle, whose help we see is available to those who seek it. Pray that he may deign to favour me, for through God's mercy he has great power. Take this candle for me to his altar' (he handed her a candle) 'and pray that he may free me from the swelling of this abscess.' At this the widow, smiling in her joy, said: 'Thanks be to God and St James, for He has shown you how wonderful is His power, and the light of truth; but as yet He has not shown these to you in their full extent.' Taking the candle, she touched the abscess with it and made the sign of the Cross over it. Then she went to the cathedral, and in her usual way made her offerings and said her prayers; having done this, she offered the candle which she had taken from the Ishmaelite, and added a new prayer to the others, asking St James to restore the Ishmaelite to health and, through God's mercy, to free him from the deadly threat of the abscess. Scarcely had she ended her prayer when the mass of liquid drained away from the abscess. The Ishmaelite was restored to full health. A scar remained as a sign of the complaint now cured. God's mercy is indescribably great, since by the sign of the Cross, which according to the Apostle is held by the infidels to be a foolish act, He is not unwilling to grant remedies making for good health to those same people. Great also is

secundum Apostolum est stultitia, salutis remedia ipsis etiam gentilibus conferre non refutat. Magna quoque beati Iacobi apostoli clementia, qui pro quibuscumque opem sibi deposcentibus Dominum suum exorare eisque salutis gratia subvenire non destitit.

Postquam Ismaelita praesensit beati Iacobi patrocinia et mortiferi apostematis pestem exinanitam, ipse et complices sui prae nimietate gaudii obstupefacti laetantur, tantique miraculi virtutem admirantur. Ostendunt centurioni ceterisque christicolis quid qualiterve acciderit, et Apostoli virtutem medicinae suffragium praevenisse conclamant. Quid plura? Collaudatur atque magnificatur a fidelibus et ab infidelibus beatus Iacobus apostolus ...

[...]

the mercy of St James the Apostle, who does not refuse to help whomsoever begs his aid for the sake of their health by praying to the Lord.

As soon as the Ishmaelite became aware of St James's favour and felt the deadly threat of the abscess depart, he and his colleagues were overjoyed and marvelled at the power of the miracle. They explained to Peter and other Christians all that had happened, and proclaimed the power of the Apostle's medicine obtained by prayer. What more can one say? The Apostle St James was praised and extolled by the faithful and the infidels ... [...]

## 31. Alfonso VII's first Andalusian campaign (1133)

*Alfonso VII was obliged to spend the first years of his reign from 1126 establishing his authority after much civil turmoil, and recovering Castilian towns and castles occupied by the Aragonese. By 1133, after several years of skirmishing round Toledo and expeditions by Christian nobles into al–Andalus to take booty, Alfonso felt himself strong enough to undertake the major and, in its outcome, extraordinarily successful campaign described in the text which follows. We can here see that the old relative tolerance and unwritten 'rules of warfare' between Christian and Moor have given way before a new ferocity: the Islamic fundamentalism of the Almoravids was opposed by the fervour of the Cluniacs who came from France to occupy important positions in the Spanish Church, and all were aware of the scale and nature of the*

(33) Anno septimo regni Adefonsi regis Hispaniarum, filii Raymundi comitis et serenissimae reginae dominae Urracae, discurrente Era CLXXI post millesimam, rex praefatus, consilio accepto cum rege Zafadola, convocavit omnes comites suos et maiores regni sui et duces, et habuit cum eis misterium consilii sui, dixitque omnem intentionem suam in eo esse ut iret in terram Sarracenorum ad debellandum eos et accipere sibi vindictam de rege Texufino et de caeteris regibus Moabitarum, qui venerant in terram Toleti et occiderant multos duces christianorum et destruxerant castellum quod dicitur Acecha usque ad fundamentum, et omnes christianos quos ibi invenerant, perdiderant gladio. Sed Tellus Fernandi, dux eorum, cum aliis captivis christianis, captivus missus est trans mare. Quod dictum, placuit omnibus.

(34) Et omnis exercitus universi regni sui congregatus est in Toleto et fixere tentoria iuxta fluvium Tagi, et profectus est ipse rex, et Zafadola cum suis militibus cum eo, et divisit castra in duas manus, quia non sufficiebat eis aqua ad bibendum nec herba bestiis ad pascendum. Ipse autem rex cum suo exercitu intravit per Portum Regem in terram Moabitarum, et alius exercitus cum comite Roderico Gunzalvi intravit per Portum de Muradal; et ambulaverunt quindecim diebus per eremum, et uterque exercitus coadunatus est iuxta castellum Sarracenorum quod dicitur Gallello, et ex illa die acceperunt sibi herbas bestiis et frumenta abundanter, et erat innumerabilis turba militum et peditum et sagittariorum, qui operuerunt faciem terrae sicut locustae.

(35) Et inde rex movit castra et coepit ire per campaniam Cordubae, a dextris et a sinistris praedando, et occupavit totam illam terram et praedavit eam, et misit post se ignem et fecit magnam captivationem et pervenit ad fluvium qui dicitur Goadalquivir, quo transfretato, ex altera parte dimiserunt Cordubam et Carmonam a sinistra, Sibiliam vero, quam antiqui vocabant

*conflict in Palestine during and following the First Crusade. Alfonso himself was half French, the son of Count Raymond of Burgundy, whose family had strong Cluniac ties.*

*The extract is from the* Chronica Adefonsi Imperatoris, *for which see text 28. Throughout it, the biblical echoes are a fundamental feature not merely of the writing but of the whole concept, for Alfonso is depicted as a modern Israelite prince who fights God's battles against the heathen. Thus, for example, part of section 35 is modelled on Judith 2.17–18.*

*In section 33, 'King' Sayf al–Dawla was the son of the last* taifa *ruler of Saragossa before it was taken over by the Almoravids in 1110, and became an ally of Alfonso VII against them. 'King' Tashufin was the son of the Almoravid ruler Ali ibn Yusuf, and governed al–Andalus on his father's behalf in the period 1128–38. Tello Fernández died a prisoner in Marrakesh.*

(33) In the seventh year of the reign of Alfonso [VII], son of Count Raymond and the most noble Queen Urraca, that is in Era 1171 [= AD 1133], the King, acting on the advice of King Sayf al–Dawla, called together all the counts and principal men and commanders of his realm, and held a council with them. He said that his mind was wholly fixed upon the following: that he should invade the lands of the Saracens in order to defeat them and to avenge himself on King Tashufin and other emirs of the Moabites [Almoravids] who had invaded the lands of Toledo and had killed many leaders of the Christians and had torn down the castle of Aceca [east of Toledo] to its very foundations, putting the Christians they found inside it to the sword. Moreover Tello Fernández, their commander, together with other Christian captives, had been taken beyond the sea. Everybody agreed with this pronouncement.

(34) The army, gathered from all parts of the realm, assembled at Toledo and pitched camp beside the Tagus. Thence the King, together with Sayf al–Dawla and his men, set out. They divided their forces into two, since there would not be sufficient water for all to drink together, nor grass enough for the horses to eat. The King and his army went through Portus Regis [not certainly identified] into the land of the Moabites, and the other army under Count Rodrigo González went through the pass of Muradal [Despeñaperros]. For two weeks they traversed the wasteland, and the two armies met up near the Saracen castle of Gallello [unidentified: near Santa Elena, province of Cordova], finding from that day onward an abundance of feed for the horses and of grain for themselves. The massed force of horsemen and foot–soldiers and archers was uncountable, and they covered the face of the earth like locusts.

(35) Then the King struck camp and began to cross the plain of Cordova, raiding to left and right, occupying all that land and taking booty from it, burning as he went and taking many captives. Arriving at the Guadalquivir, he crossed it, leaving Cordova and Carmona on his left and

Hispalim, relinquentes a dextera. Eratque in diebus messis et succendit omnia sata, et omnes vineas et oliveta et ficulnea fecit incidi; et cecedit timor illius super omnes habitantes in terra Moabitarum et Agarenorum, sed et ipsi Moabitae et Agareni, praeoccupati timore magno, reliquerunt civitates et castella minora et miserunt se in castellis fortissimis et in civitatibus munitis; in montibus et in speluncis montium et in cavernis petrarum, et in insulis maris absconderunt se.

(36) Sed et omnis exercitus castramentatus est in terra Sibiliae et quotidie exibant de castris magnae turbae militum, quod nostra lingua dicitur *algaras*, et ibant a dextris et a sinistris et praedaverunt totam terram Sibiliae et Cordubae et Carmonae et miserunt ignem in totam illam terram et in civitates et in castellis, quarum multa inveniebant absque viris; omnes enim fugerant. Et captivationis quam fecerunt virorum et mulierum non erat numerus, et praedationis equorum et equarum, camellorum et asinorum, boum quoque et ovium et caprarum non erat numerus. Frumenti, vini et olei abundantiam in castra miserunt. Sed et omnes synagogae eorum, quas inveniebant, destructae sunt; sacerdotes vero et legis suae doctores, quoscumque inveniebant, gladio trucidabant. Sed et libri legis suae in synagogis igne combusti sunt. Praedantes vero milites a castris regis octo dietas progrediebantur diebus octo cum praeda revertentes ad castra.

(37) Deinde, praedis iam in circuitu deficientibus, rex movit castra et pervenit ad quandam civitatem opulentissimam, quam antiqui dicebant Tuccis, nostra lingua Xerex; praedavitque eam et fregit et destructa est. Deinde ipse rex movit castra praedando in circuitu, et pervenit ad illam turrem quae dicitur Gallice, quae est iuxta ripam maris.

(38) Quidam vero milites insensati, filii comitum et ducum, et alii multi, quorum mens non erat sana nec ambulabant secundum consilium regis, audierunt quod quaedam insula vicina erat plena equis et bobus et erant in illa opes magnae, et transfretaverunt pergentes illuc cupide: sed obviaverunt eis paratae acies Moabitarum et Agarenorum et comiserunt bellum cum eis. Sed, peccatis exigentibus, victi sunt christiani, et filii comitum et ducum et alii multi, gladio perierunt. Alii autem fugientes reversi sunt in castra et narraverunt exercitui omnia quae illis acciderant. Tunc demum, omnis exercitus coepit timere regem et obedire ei et ex illa die nullus ex militibus ausus est exire de tentoriis suis sine imperio regis.

(39) Fuit autem ibi rex per multos dies et reversae sunt universae praedatoriae cohortes cum magnis victoriis, portantes secum multa milia Sarracenorum captivorum et maximam multitudinem camelorum, equorum et equarum, boum et vaccarum, arietum et ovium, hircorum et caprarum, quae erant regum et reginarum, et alias opes plurimas.

Seville — known to the ancients as Hispalis — on his right. This was at harvest—time, so he burned all the crops and had all the vineyards and olive—groves and fig—gardens cut down. Terror took hold of the inhabitants of the land of the Moabites [Almoravids] and the Agarenes [Spanish Muslims], so that these peoples in the grip of great fear abandoned their towns and lesser forts and shut themselves up in their strongest fortresses and defended cities; they hid themselves in the mountains and in caves among the hills and caverns among the rocks, and in the islands of the sea.

(36) When the whole army had set up camp near Seville, there went out from it each day strong companies of horsemen, of the kind that in our tongue are called *algaras* [raiding—parties], which went in all directions taking booty from all the lands of Seville and Cordova and Carmona, burning the whole area together with towns and forts, many of which they found devoid of inhabitants, for all had fled. One could not count the number of captives they took, both men and women, nor reckon up the quantities of horses and mares, camels and donkeys, cattle and sheep and goats which they took as booty. They brought back to camp huge quantities of grain, wine, and oil. Those mosques that they came upon they completely destroyed, and when they found holy men and doctors of their law they killed them. Also, they burned the books of their faith which they found in the mosques. After being away from the King's camp for a week, these raiding—parties returned to it.

(37) Then, since there were no further opportunities for taking booty in the surrounding areas, the King struck camp and advanced to a certain extraordinarily rich city which the ancients called Tuccis, Jerez in our language; this the King plundered and then destroyed. After that the King moved on and plundered the lands round about, advancing thence to the fortress called Cadiz, which is on the coast.

(38) Certain rash men, sons of counts and commanders, and many others, lacking all sense and refusing to behave according to the royal orders, heard that a certain island nearby was full of horses and cattle and other kinds of wealth, and they crossed over to it in greedy fashion; but they found in their path lines of Moabites and Agarenes drawn up, and these began to attack them. The judgement upon their sins was such that our men were defeated, and the sons of counts and commanders and many others perished by the sword. Others managed to escape, returned to the camp, and recounted to the army all that had happened to them. Finally, then, the whole army began to fear the King, and to obey him, and thenceforth no soldier dared to go out from among the tents without the royal command.

(39) The King stayed there many days, till all the raiding—parties had returned in great triumph, bringing with them many thousands of Saracen prisoners together with vast numbers of camels, horses, cattle, sheep, and goats, of prime quality, and many other kinds of booty.

(40) Deinde rex movit castra et direxit faciem suam et venit in Sibiliam, transivitque flumen quod dicitur Goadalquivir. Sed magna multitudo Moabitarum et Agarenorum, quae ibi erat congregata, paratis aciebus circa muros civitatis, festinanter inclusi sunt a paucis christianis armatis; depredata est autem tota illa terra in circuitu Sibiliae, et miserunt ignem in messes et in domibus eorum et destruxerunt vineas et ficulnea et oliveta; et multas almuneas regum, quae erant ex utraque parte fluminis, fecerunt incidi. Et omnes Moabites neminem captivabant, sed capti eorum capitalem accipiebant sententiam.

(41) Hoc videntes principes Agarenorum, secrete mittebant nuntios regi Zafadolae dicentes: 'Loquere cum rege christianorum et cum eo libera nos de manibus Moabitarum, et dabimus regi Legionensi tributa regalia amplius quam patres nostri dederunt patribus suis, et tecum secure serviemus illi, et tu regnavis super nos, et filii tui.' Hoc audito, rex Zafadola, consilio acepto cum rege et cum fidelibus consiliariis suis, respondit nuntiis: 'Ite, dicite fratribus meis principibus Agarenorum: capite vobis aliqua fortissima castella et aliquas fortissimas turres civitatum et movete in omni loco bellum et ego et rex Legionensis succurremus vobis velociter.'

(42) Deinde rex movit castra et transivit illum Portum de Amarela et exivit in civitatem suam, quae dicitur Talavera, et his peractis reversi sunt unusquisque in sua cum magno gaudio et triumpho, laudantes et benedicentes Deum, qui regi et illis dederat vindictam et ultionem de Tello Fernandi et de suis sociis, qui perierunt in Acecha, et de Guterrio Hermegildo, alcayde Toletano, et de caeteris ducibus, quos Moabites occiderant cum aliis militibus christianis in terra Toleti.

(40) Then the King struck camp and turned his face towards Seville, crossing the Guadalquivir. A great mass of Moabites and Agarenes which had gathered there and was drawn up close to the city walls was speedily cut off by a few armed Christians. Then all the lands around Seville were raided, crops and houses were destroyed by fire, and vineyards and fig—gardens and olive—groves were cut down; and many farms belonging to. the royal estates, on both sides of the river, were destroyed. The Moabites captured none of our men, but those we took prisoner from them suffered the extreme penalty.

(41) When the leaders of the Agarenes saw this, they sent messengers secretly to King Sayf al—Dawla to say: 'Speak to the King of the Christians and, with his aid, free us from the hands of the Moabites; we will give the King of León royal tributes greater than those which our forefathers gave to his, and together with you we will be firm in our service to him, and you and then your sons shall reign over us.' On hearing this, King Sayf al—Dawla, having taken counsel with the King and with his loyal advisers, replied to the messengers: 'Go, and tell my brethren the leaders of the Agarenes: they should occupy certain strong fortresses and equally strong positions within the cities, stir up war in all parts, and the King of León and I will speedily come to your aid.'

(42) Then the King struck camp and traversed the pass of Amarela [unidentified] and came to Talavera in his own kingdom, and, these operations being concluded, each one returned to his home with great joy and in triumph, praising God and blessing His name, since He had given the King and his men revenge for Tello Fernández and his comrades, who died at Aceca; and for Gutierre Hermegildo, governor of Toledo, and for other chief men, whom the Moabites had killed together with other Christian soldiers in the region of Toledo.

## 32. A sense of chivalry? (1139)

*In 1139 Alfonso VII raised a new army and besieged Oreja (Aurelia), a major Almoravid fortress on the Tagus east of Toledo (now in ruins, but with its name preserved by the nearby village of Colmenar de Oreja). The governors of several cities of al—Andalus rushed to its defence, and as a diversionary measure attacked Toledo itself. Whatever their real motive for withdrawing from that city, the Muslims are here credited with feeling 'shame' at so insulting the Empress who was in command; or perhaps, if any such motive was indeed in play, they could not be seen to discredit*

(150) Deinde coeperunt destruere vineas et arbusta, sed in civitate erat imperatrix domna Berengaria cum magna turba militum et ballistorum et peditum, qui sedebant super portas et super turres et super muros civitatis et custodiebant eam. Hoc videns imperatrix, misit nuntios regibus Moabitarum, qui dixerunt eis: 'Hoc dicit vobis imperatrix, uxor imperatoris: nonne videtis quia contra me pugnatis, quae foemina sum, et non est vobis in honorem? Sed si vultis pugnare ite in Aureliam et pugnate cum imperatore, qui cum armatis et paratis aciebus vos expectat.' Hoc audientes reges et principes et duces et omnis exercitus, levaverunt occulos suos et viderunt imperatricem sedentem in solio regali et in convenienti loco super excelsam turrem quae lingua nostra dicitur *alcazar*, ornatam tamquam uxorem imperatoris; et in circuitu eius magna turba honestarum mulierum cantantes in tympanis et citharis et cimbalis et psalteriis. Sed reges et principes et duces et omnis exercitus, postquam eam viderunt, mirati sunt et nimium verecundati, et humiliaverunt capita sua ante faciem imperatricis et abierunt retro, et deinde nullam causam laeserunt et reversi sunt in terram suam, collectis a se suis insidiis, sine honore et victoria.

*themselves by such an easy conquest of a weak woman. In a strange way the equation of a city with the feminine personality who is its ruler or its representation announces the theme of part of the fine* Abenámar *ballad ('Casada so, el Rey Don Juan') (62 in Roger Wright's collection). Berengaria (Berenguela) was the daughter of the Count of Barcelona, Ramón Berenguer III. The Emperor's forces received the surrender of Oreja in October 1139.*

*The text is from the* Chronica Adefonsi Imperatoris, *for which see text 28.*

(150) Then the Moors began to destroy vineyards and plantations, but in the city there was the Empress Doña Berengaria with a great number of knights and *ballista* men and foot−soldiers, who stationed themselves on the gates and towers and walls of the city and defended it. On seeing this the Empress sent messengers to the Moorish commanders to say: 'This the Empress says to you: cannot you see that you are attacking me, a woman, and that this is dishonourable for you? If you want to fight, go to Oreja and fight the Emperor, who with his battle−lines all ready is awaiting you.' When the emirs and chiefs and leading men and the whole Moorish army heard this, they raised their eyes and beheld the Empress seated on her throne in a commanding position on top of a very tall tower which in our language is called an *alcázar* [i.e. the principal tower of the citadel], dressed as befitted the Emperor's wife; while round her was a great crowd of noble women singing to small drums and lyres and cymbals and psalteries. When the Moors saw this, they were astounded and overcome by shame; they hung their heads before the Empress's face and went away, and thenceforth caused no trouble. They withdrew the ambushes they had prepared and went home bereft of honour and victory.

162

## 33. Spain as crusading territory (about 1140)

*The* Historia Turpini *(see text 8) has as one of its appendices the following letter spuriously credited to Pope Calixtus (compare text 15) as author. It was modelled on two principal authentic sources, and since the second of these originated in Compostela and was unlikely to have been known outside that city, the assumption can be made that the present letter was produced there, probably at a rather late stage in the confection of the whole* Codex Calixtinus. *Certainly the concept of 'crusade' continued in full vigour, and it may have been that in about 1140 the project for what was to become the Second Crusade to the Holy Land (1147) was already envisaged. Its direct application to Spain in respect of any particular campaign was quite another matter (see text 17) in view of the authority which the Pope might assume over the rulers and lands of the Peninsula.*

Calixtus episcopus seruus seruorum Dei, dilectis in Christo fratribus episcopis ceterisque sancte ecclesie personis, omnibusque Christianis tam presentibus quam futuris uniuersaliter salutem et apostolicam benedictionem. Crebo dilectissimi quanta mala quantasque calamitates et angustias Sarraceni in Yspania fratribus nostris Christianis inferre usi sunt audistis. Quot ecclesias, quot castra et hora deuastauerunt, quotque Christianos, scilicet monacos, clericos et laicos, aut gladio perimerunt, aut in horis barbaris et longinquis sub captiuitatis dominio uendiderunt, aut diuersis catenis ligatos tenuerunt, aut uariis tormentis angustiauerunt, nullus est qui enarrare queat. Quot sanctorum martirum, episcoporum scilicet abbatum et sacerdotum ceterorumque Christianorum, corpora iuxta urbem Osquam, et in campo laudabile, et in campo letorie, ceterisque mediis finibus Christianorum Sarracenorumque ubi bella fuere inhumata requiescunt, nullo sermone fas est explicari. Milia super milia iacent. Idcirco dilectio uestra, filioli mei, queso intelligat quanta auctoritas sit ire ad Yspanias causa expugnandi Sarracenos, quantaque mercede qui illuc libenter perrexerint remunerabuntur. Fertur namque quod Karolus magnus Galliorum rex famosissimus, magis pre ceteris regibus, itinera Yspanica innumeris laboribus gentes perfidas expugnando disposuit, et beatus Turpinus archiepiscopus Remensis, consocius eius, coadunato tocius Gallie et Lotharingie omnium episcoporum concilio apud Remis urbem Galliorum, a uinculis omnium peccatorum suorum cunctos qui in Yspania ad expugnandum gentem perfidam et ad augmentandum Christianitatem, captiuosque Christianos ad liberandum, et ad accipiendum ibi pro diuino amore martirium tunc ierunt et post ituri erant, ut in gestis eius scribitur, diuina auctoritate corroboratus relaxauit. Hoc idem omnes apostolici qui postea usque ad nostrum tempus fuere corroborauerunt, testante beato Urbano papa, illustri uiro, qui in concilio Claromontis regionis Gallie, adstantibus circiter centum episcopis, hoc idem asseruit, quando ytinera Iherosolimitana disposuit, ut codex Iherosolimitane ystorie refert. Hoc idem et nos corroboramus et affirmamus, ut omnes qui aut in Yspania aut in

*However, it clearly did no harm to equate the centuries—old war in Spain with the much more glamorous expeditions to the Holy Land, and the Spanish rulers occasionally had to prevent their subjects from going off to the East when there was so much to do at home. In this sense a spurious document is just as illustrative and full of motivation as an authentic one.*

*It is not clear why Huesca in Aragón is specially mentioned, but it had been the object of a famous siege from 1094 until its surrender in November 1096, and several French bishops and commanders took part in the operations; also, the Cathedral of Compostela held substantial properties in the city by a royal gift of 1098, and among the Spanish towns listed in chapter 3 of the* Historia Turpini *one finds, exceptionally, 'Osqua in qua nonaginta turres numero esse solent'.*

*The text is taken from the source used for text 8, pp. 347—48.*

Bishop Calixtus, servant of the servants of God, to his beloved brethren in Christ the bishops and other members of Holy Church, and to all Christians now living and to come: to all, greetings and my apostolic blessing. Often, dearly beloved, you have heard how many evils and calamities and sufferings the Saracens in Spain have inflicted upon our Christian brethren. How many churches, how many towns and regions they have devastated, how many Christians — monks, clergy, laymen — have either perished by the sword, or have been sold into captivity in barbarous and remote regions, or have been kept in chains, or have been made to suffer diverse tortures, nobody is able to tell. How many bodies of holy martyrs — bishops, abbots, priests, and other Christians — lie in honoured cemeteries at Huesca, or lie unburied in other Christian or Saracen lands where there were battles, nobody can properly tell. Thousands upon thousands lie there. Therefore, my children, I want your loving minds to understand how strong is the reason for you to go to Spain in order to attack the Saracens, and how great will be the favour with which those who freely go there will be rewarded. It is said that Charlemagne, the famous King of the Franks, more renowned than any other monarch, undertook his Spanish expedition and after innumerable hardships defeated the infidels; and the blessed Turpin, Archbishop of Rheims, comrade of Charles, having assembled at Rheims a council of all the bishops of Gaul and Lotharingia, supported by divine authority, freed from the bonds of their sins all those who were then going or would later go to Spain in order to attack the Saracens and sustain Christianity, to free Christian captives, and to suffer martyrdom for the love of God, as is written in the account of his deeds. This all the Popes from that time up to the present have supported: witness blessed Pope Urban [II, 1088—99], an illustrious man, who at the Council of Clermont [1095], in the presence of some hundred bishops, confirmed this when he ordained the expedition to Jerusalem [the First Crusade], as the manuscript of the history of this campaign tells. This then we again affirm: that all who either in Spain or in Palestine go to attack the infidels as said

Iherosolimitanis horis ad expugnandum gentem perfidam ut superius diximus, eleuato signo dominice crucis in humeris perrexerint, ex parte Dei et sanctorum apostolorum Petri et Pauli et Iacobi, omniumque sanctorum et nostra benedictione apostolica, ab omnibus peccatis de quibus sacerdotibus suis confessi et penitentes fuerint absoluantur et benedicantur, et in celestibus regnis una cum sanctis martiribus qui ab inicio Christianitatis usque ad finem seculi martirii palmam ibi acceperunt uel accepturi sunt coronari mereantur. Numquam profecto fuit tanta necessitas olim illuc ire, sicuti est hodie. Quapropter rogantes uniuersaliter precipimus, ut omnes episcopi et prelati in sinodis et conciliis suis et ecclesiarum dedicacionibus hoc super cetera apostolica mandata precipue annunciare non desinant, presbiteris suis etiam exortantes, ut in ecclesiis suis gentibus laicis renuncient. Quod si libenter fecerint, mercede parili pergencium illuc remunerentur in celis. Et quicumque hanc epistolam transcriptam de loco ad locum, uel de ecclesia ad ecclesiam perlatauerit, omnibusque palam precidauerit, perhenni gloria remuneretur. [...]

above, bearing the sign of the Cross on their backs, for God and the
Apostles Saints Peter and Paul and James and for all the saints, and with
our apostolic blessing, should be absolved of all their sins when they have
confessed them and done penance and should be blessed by their priests,
and in the heavenly realm together with the holy martyrs who from the
origins of Christianity until the end of time received or will receive the
crown of martyrdom should themselves deserve to be crowned.    For
undoubtedly at no time in the past has there ever been so much need to go
as there is today.    For this reason we command, in this message to all,
that all the bishops and prelates in their synods and councils and dedications
of churches, should not cease to publicize this more than any other papal
order, urging their parish priests also to make this known to lay people in
their churches.    If they freely do this, may they be rewarded by a like
mercy when they reach Heaven.    And whosoever helps this letter to be
copied from place to place, or from church to church, and preaches its
contents openly to all, shall be rewarded with everlasting glory. [...]

### 34. Peter the Venerable has the Koran translated (1142)

*Peter the Venerable was Abbot of the great abbey of Cluny from 1122 to 1156. In 1142 he went to Spain in order to inspect the houses of the Cluniac Order in the province, and for a time accompanied Alfonso VII at Salamanca, Carrión, and Burgos, as the court travelled about, for the Cluniacs had enjoyed the strong support of the rulers of León—Castile for some generations. One of Peter's main reasons for going to Spain must have been to find Christian intellectuals who would undertake, on behalf of Christendom as a whole, a task hitherto oddly neglected: the translation into Latin of the holy Koran. The motive was naturally not that of any genuine interest in Islam or any concern for its spiritual and intellectual achievements (the latter at the time far superior to anything existing in Christian lands), but simply the need to 'know thy enemy' in order that by preaching and pressures the infidel might be converted. As a parallel and in order to show that conversion of a whole people was not a mere dream, Peter wrote a long section about the conversion of the English to Christianity, largely drawn from Bede, with mention of the part played by Pope Gregory and Augustine's arrival in the heathen kingdom of Kent (597), concluding that for the Muslims 'Decet vos hoc idem facere' ('It behoves you to do the same'). It is curious to note that Peter's work, entitled in one version* Adversus nefandam sectam sarracenorum, *is in another version more specifically* Liber contra sectam sive haeresim Sarracenorum *('A book against the sect or heresy of the Saracens'): if Islam were no more than a 'heresy' of Christianity, the conversion of Muslims to orthodox Catholic belief was a reasonably practical task.*

*Among the Christians who translated the Koran, the Englishman Robert of Ketton or of Chester seems to have played a principal part. He is*

Contuli ergo me ad peritos linguae Arabicae, ex qua procedens mortiferum virus orbem plusquam dimidium infecit, eis ad transferendum de lingua Arabica in Latinam perditi hominis originem, vitam, doctrinam, legemque ipsum quae Alchoran vocatur, tam prece quam pretio, persuasi. Et ut translationi fides plenissima non deesset, nec quidquam fraude aliqua nostrorum notitiae subtrahi posset, Christianis interpretibus etiam Sarracenum adjunxi. Christianorum interpretum nomina: Robertus Kecenensis, Armannus Dalmata, Petrus Toletanus; Sarraceni Mahumeth nomen erat. Qui intima ipsa barbarae gentis armaria perscrutantes, volumen non parvum ex praedicta materia Latinis lectoribus ediderunt. Hoc anno illo factum est quo Hispanias adii, et cum domino Aldefonso, victorioso Hispaniarum imperatore, colloquium habui, qui annus fuit ab Incarnatione Domini 1141.

*recorded as going to Barcelona in about 1140 to learn Arabic so that he could translate scientific works, and he remained in Spain until at least 1147. In a preface to the version of the Koran he says that he had to take time off work on astronomy and geometry, but was glad to do so because he found contemporaries too tolerant towards Islam, the translation being needed to correct this. A number of MSS of the translation are known, including one at Corpus Christi, Oxford (MS 184), and the work was printed at Basle in 1550. 'Armannus Dalmata' is better known as Hermann of Carinthia, recorded in Spain between 1138 and 1142; he worked on other translations also. Peter of Toledo is little known; it was said of him that his Arabic was better than his Latin; he also translated the* Risalah *which was to be important in anti—Islamic polemics. The 'Muhammad' in question presumably spoke Arabic and a Spanish vernacular but could hardly have had any Latin. At all events the collaboration between these very diverse men was extraordinary enough. Their products and others formed what Norman Daniel calls the 'Toletano—Cluniac corpus' of twelve items concerning Islam; Daniel's book* Islam *and the* West *(Edinburgh, 1958) deals with them at length* passim, *with references to special studies by d'Alverney in 1948, etc., and is of great interest for all these matters. In 1209 Marcos de Toledo, a doctor and canon of the cathedral, again translated the Koran into Latin, and composed other works on the theme (listed by Daniel, p. 403). Don Juan Manuel recorded that his uncle Alfonso X (1252—84) 'fizo trasladar toda la secta de los moros', presumably the Koran and presumably into Castilian, but this is lost and nothing further is known of it.*

*The extract is section 15 of Peter the Venerable's prologue to his* Liber, *from Patrologia Latina, vol. 189, col. 671. See further J. Kritzeck,* Peter the Venerable and Islam *(Princeton, 1964), and Kedar, pp. 99—103.*

I therefore approached specialists in the Arabic language, from which proceeds the deadly poison which has infected more than half the world, and I persuaded them — by entreaties and also by offering payment — to translate from Arabic into Latin the origin, life, teaching, and laws of that damned soul [Muhammad] which is called the Koran. In order that the translation should be completely accurate, and in order that no element should escape our notice by any deceit, I added a Saracen to the team of Christian translators. The names of the Christians were Robert of Ketton, Hermann of Carinthia, Peter of Toledo; and the name of the Saracen was Muhammad. These, looking closely into the contents of the secret bookshelves of the infidels, have produced from the aforementioned material a far from small volume for Latin readers. This was done in the year I went to Spain and held conversations with Don Alfonso, the victorious Emperor of Spain, which was AD 1141 [really 1142].

### 35. Preparations for the Almería campaign (1147)

*For the background to this, see the next text.* The Poema de Almeria *is a part of, and in its present state the final section of, the* Chronica Adefonsi Imperatoris *(see text 28): the author explains that at this point the events he is to recount require the grandeur of verse. If much of his prose had had biblical echoes, the tone here is that of Virgil and of heroic verse in medieval Latin, as befitted the noble theme. The verse—form is that of the hexameter, but as adapted in medieval Spain and elsewhere this had evolved far from its classical exemplar: any analysis in terms of vowel quantity shows up great irregularities, and it best to regard the line as having a rhythmic basis with prominent stresses. Many lines are also*

(1)      Rex pie, rex fortis, cui sors manet ultima mortis:
da nobis pacem linguam praebeque loquacem,
ut tua facunde miranda canens et abunde
inclyta istorum describam bella virorum.

(2)      Doctores veteres scripserunt proelia regum,
scribere nos nostri debemus et imperatoris
proelia famosa, quoniam non sunt taediosa.
Optima scriptori, si complacet imperatori,
reddantur iura, quod scribat bella futura.

(3)      Dextra laborantis sperat pia dona Tonantis
et bellatoris donum petit omnibus horis.
Ergo quod elegi describam, bella sub Urgi
facta, paganorum, quia tunc gens victa virorum.

(4)      Convenere duces Hispani Francigenaeque:
per mare per terras Maurorum bella requirunt.
Dux fuit Imperii cunctorum rex Toletani.
Hic Adefonsus erat, nomen tenet imperatoris,

(5)      facta sequens Caroli, cui competit aequiparari.
Gente fuere pares, armorum vi coaequales.
Gloria bellorum gestorum par fuit horum.
Extitit et testis Maurorum pessima pestis,
quos maris aut aestus non protegit, aut sua tellus.

(6)      Nec possunt visum mergi vel ad aethera sursum
suspendi: vita scelerata fuit, quia victa.
Non cognovere Dominum, merito periere.
Ista creatura merito fuerat peritura.
Cum colunt Baalim, Baalim non liberat illos.
[...]

(29)      Post hos Castellae procedunt spicula mille,
famosi cives per saecula longa potentes.
Illorum castra fulgent coeli velut astra;
auro fulgebant, argentea vasa ferebant,

*'leonine', that is, internally rhymed both with assonance of one or more vowels and with full consonantal rhyme; and they are of course grouped in stanzas. There is a fine analysis of the poem in all its aspects by Salvador Martínez, El 'Poema de Almería' y la épica románica (Madrid, 1975).*

*In the first extract, stanzas 1–6, the apocalyptic tone and the comparison of the Emperor Alfonso VII with Charlemagne are to be especially noted (and in stanzas 47–49 recent Spanish heroes, Alvar Fáñez and the Cid, are compared with Roland and Oliver). In the second extract, stanzas 29–33, the Castilian contingent gathers for the campaign; the Leonese have preceded them, and after come descriptions of contingents from the other regions, including the seaborne Catalans.*

(1) Merciful and powerful King, with whom resides the final decision about death: give us peace and provide a fluent style, so that I may sing eloquently and copiously of thy wondrous deeds, and may describe the famous battles of these men.

(2) The sages of ancient times wrote the wars of their kings, and we must also write the famous battles of our Emperor, for they are anything but wearisome. If it please the Emperor, let the writer be given the greatest facilities so that he can recount campaigns to come.

(3) The right hand of the labourer awaits the merciful gifts of the Thunderer, and at all times the right hand of the warrior seeks a reward. So I announce the theme I have chosen: the campaign undertaken against Almería in which the tribe of pagan people was defeated.

(4) The leaders of the Hispanic and Frankish peoples came together; by land and sea they make war on the Moors. The commander of all was the ruler of the Toledan Empire, Alfonso, who holds the title of Emperor,

(5) continuing the deeds of Charlemagne, to whom he is justly compared. They were equal in their peoples and in the strength of their weapons. There was an equal glory in the campaigns which they undertook. There stood forth as witness the evil pestilence of the Moors, whom neither their land nor the ebb and flow of the sea protected.

(6) They cannot hide themselves from sight nor escape upwards into the air; their life was sinful, and so they were defeated. They did not know the Lord, and rightly perished. This people was rightly doomed: they worship Baal, but Baal does not set them free.

[...]

(29) After these there come a thousand spears of Castile, famous and powerful men through long centuries. Their camps shine like the stars in the sky, and blaze with gold; they use silver vessels; no poverty, only great wealth, exists among them.

non est paupertas in eis, sed magna facultas.
(30)       Nullus mendicus, neque debilis aut male tardus,
sunt fortes cuncti, sunt in certamine tuti,
carnes et vina sunt in castris inopina,
copia frumenti datur omni sponte petenti.
Armorum tanta stellarum lumina quanta,
(31)       sunt et equi multi ferro seu panno suffulti.
Illorum lingua resonat quasi tympano tuba.
Sunt nimis elati, sunt divitiis dilatati.
Castellae vires per saecula fuere rebelles.
Inclyta Castella ciens saevissima bella
(32)       vix cuiquam regum voluit submittere collum:
indomite vixit, coeli lux quando luxit,
hanc cunctis horis domuit sors imperatoris.
Solus Castellam domitavit sicut assellam
ponens indomito legis nova foedera collo.
(33)       In virtute sua durans tamen inviolata,
fortis Castella procedit ad intima bella,
velis extensis; pavor oritur Ismaelitis,
quos, velut evenit, rex postea mucrone peremit. [...]

(30) There is no beggar, weakling, or laggard among them; all are strong and firm in battle; there is an abundance of meat and wine in their camps, and a generous supply of corn is freely given to him who asks for it. Their weapons are as many as the stars,

(31) and their many horses are protected by metal or cloths. Their speech sounds out like a trumpet accompanied by a drum. They are very proud and exceptionally wealthy. The men of Castile were resistant to authority down the ages. Noble Castile, stirring up savage conflicts,

(32) could scarcely bring herself to bow her neck to any ruler; she lived untamed, while the light of heaven shone [on her?]; but now the good fortune of the Emperor has permanently tamed her. He alone has tamed Castile like a she—donkey, placing upon her indomitable neck the new covenant of the law.

(33) But continuing inviolate in her strength, mighty Castile marches on deeply penetrating campaigns, with banners flying; terror arises in the Ishmaelites, and the King was — as it turned out — to destroy them with the sword. [...]

## 36. The Genoese expedition to Almería (1147)

*The Almoravid empire collapsed after its ruler died in Morocco in March 1145, under the attacks of the Almohads; and at this time Alfonso VII successfully stimulated a rebellion by the Moslems of al—Andalus against their Almoravid masters. Al—Andalus was again about to fragment into a collection of* taifa *states. In late May 1146 Alfonso, exploiting this situation, advanced to take Cordova, the former capital of the Caliphs.*

*While at Cordova, the Emperor received an embassy from Genoa and Pisa which proposed a joint operation to take the important port of Almería and put an end to the widespread piracy which was based there. He agreed, and sent his own ambassadors to seek Peninsular allies, and to Montpellier. Although no formal crusade was preached, there seems to have been a stronger than usual religious inspiration behind the enterprise, no doubt an echo of the preaching of the Second Crusade to the Holy Land by St Bernard and others in France. It is to be noted that according to Caffaro in the text which follows, the Italian cities had been prompted by the Pope. The attack on Almería was set for the summer of 1147; preparations are described in a section of the texts which follow.*

*The Emperor's forces concentrated at Toledo in late May 1147, and moved by way of Calatrava to the banks of the Guadalquivir in mid—July. Assisted by his Moorish ally Ibn Ghaniya whom the Emperor had installed in Cordova, they went on to Baeza where in mid—August news reached the Emperor that the Genoese and Aragonese fleets were already off Almería. After taking Baeza, Alfonso seems to have allowed a substantial portion of his forces to go home; one may suspect that some companies were content with booty already acquired, or felt a need to attend to the harvest, as had often happened in earlier campaigns, but the Genoese clearly found the fact incomprehensible and gravely prejudicial when the chief objective —*

Patet fere uniuerso orbi, quoniam olim per multa tempora christiani a sarracenis Almarie longe lateque mari et terra per multas regiones capiebantur, alii interficiebantur, et multi in carcere ponebantur et diuersis martiriis et penis cruciabantur; de quibus multi legem Dei, pro timore cruciatus, relinquebant et nomen diabolicum Machometi inuocabant. Quapropter tandem tanti sanguinis effusionis uindictam inde Deus facere non dimisit.

Ianuenses namque, per apostolicam sedem a Deo moniti et uocati, exercitum supra sarracenos Almarie iurare fecerunt, et parlamentum, in quo consules sex pro communi de melioribus et quattuor placitis ciuitatis electi fuerunt, quorum sensu et ducatu ciuitas et exercitus eo tempore regerentur. [...]
        Predicti uero consules post eorum electionem parlamentum statim fecerunt, in quo omnibus discordantibus pacem iurare preceperunt. Illico sancto Spiritu superueniente, omnes qui guerram habebant in uoluntatem

*Almería — was still to be attained. When the Emperor with his small remaining force did reach Almería, the Genoese attack on it was already well under way.*

*What happened next cannot be precisely determined, though one suspects that Caffaro's account is closest to the truth. The Emperor and his immediate Peninsular allies did a deal with the Moors besieged inside Almería — to put it bluntly, they were bought off — and took no further part in the action. The Genoese perservered and eventually took the city, installing one of their number as its governor; but Spanish sources say that Alfonso installed his man Ponce de Cabrera as governor, when in December 1147 he left for Toledo. The annals of the Peninsula differ amusingly in their attribution of credit for the victory: the Catalans and Aragonese put it down to their Count Ramón Berenguer IV alone, the Leonese to their Emperor alone, the Toledans (generously) to the Emperor and the Count, while in another version recording only that 'Prisieron christianos Genueses Almería en el mes de octubre, era M.C.LXXXV' ('the Genoese took Almería in October of AD 1147'). Presumably the piratical menace was for a time reduced, but no source mentions this; in 1157 Almería returned to Muslim rule, and it had clearly never been the intention of any party among the Christians to hold it permanently.*

*Caffaro lived from about 1080 to 1166 and was a soldier, diplomat, and writer, author of several works of which the most important was* Annales Ianuenses. *He was in Catalonia in 1127, and in 1146 commanded the Genoese expedition which attacked Minorca and Almería; it was during a truce in this that the Genoese sent their embassy to Alfonso VII. His account of the 1147 expedition is entitled* De captione Almerie et Tortuose *and was written before 1154. The extract is taken from the edition by Antonio Ubieto Arteta (Valencia, 1973), pp. 21—30.*

It is plain to almost the whole world that for a long time past Christians have been captured, and others killed, in many regions far and wide by sea and by land by the Saracens of Almería, and that many have been imprisoned and tormented with divers kinds of martyrdom and sufferings. Many of them, from fear of torture, have abandoned the true faith and have invoked the devilish name of Muhammad. On this account God cannot at last fail to exact vengeance for so much outpouring of blood. The Geneose therefore, inspired and called by God through the Holy See, had their forces sworn in for an expedition against the Saracens of Almería, and held a council in which six consuls for the body of chief citizens, and four by the votes of the city, were elected, according to whose decisions and leadership the city and its forces should for that period be governed. [...]

After their election, the aforementioned consuls at once held a council, at which they ordered that peaceful settlements should be sworn to all disputes. Then, with the Holy Ghost guiding them, all those who intended

consulum et archiepiscopi pacem firmauerunt, et ad inuicem osculati fuerunt. Unde mulieres et uiri ualde letabuntur, ita ut stipendium exercitus consules acciperent unanimiter ortabantur.

Consules uero, amonitione Dei audita et populi uoluntate cognita, omnibus hominibus Ianuensis districtus sub debito sacramento preceperunt, ut unusquisque quae in oste sunt necessaria festinanter haberet: cibum multum competens sine penuria, arma multa et onesta tentoria, et uexilla pulcra et honesta ualde, et omnia que ad tale opus sunt necessaria, uti castella et machina et omne opus instrumentorum capiendi ciuitatem.

Postquam enim bellatores ciuitatis precepta consulum audierunt, ita se de armis et tentoriis et de omnibus rebus necessariis ornauerunt, quod a mille annis in sursum tan pulcra et honesta et tanta in una oste uisa nec audita fuerunt.

Postquam uero, ut diximus, omnia parata fuerunt, taliter ire inceperunt cum galeis LXIII et cum aliis nauibus CLXIII. Et sic omnia parata et iter inceptum infra quinque menses fuit.

Et postquam ad Portum Magnum uenerunt, Baldoinus consul inde cum galeis XV iuit pro guardia in antea ad Almariam, donec exercitus insimul ueniret.

Et postquam uenit ad caput Cate, Ianuenses, non inuenientes Imperatorem, per mensem ibi steterunt cum timore magno, quoniam extra portum erant, et miserunt legatum Otonem de Bonouillano ad Imperatorem, qui erat aput Bagenciam et dederat licenciam recedendi exercitui suo, et non habebat secum ultra CCCC milites et pedites mille. Et cum audiuit quod stolus Ianuensis uenerat, fuit mestus de hoc quod licenciam milititibus dederat, et uenire dixit, sed moram fecit.

Interim uero sarraceni Almariae letantes et sepe extra ciuitatem exeuntes, pro bello incitando cum galeis XV. Tunc Baldoinus consul, qui cum galeis erat in guardia, mandauit ad socios, scilicet Oberto Turri et Phylippo et Ansaldo de Auria, ut uenirent ad bellum faciendum Almarie. Quod non placuit sociis, donec milites haberent. Interim comes Barchilonensis cum tanto nauigio uenit, quod duxit secum milites cum equitibus LIII. Ilico mandauerunt Baldoino, ut ipse summo mane cum galeis ueniret ad muschetam ostendendo quod uellet facere bellum, ad hoc ut sarraceni extra exirent, quia comes cum militibus summo mane erit ad flumen per terram et galee XV post Lenam, et galea una stabit in capite Lene; et postquam sarraceni exierunt ad bellandum, illico galea faciat signum militibus et galeis XXV et ita factum est.

Sarraceni postquam uiderunt XV galearum homines terram ascendentes et quasi bellum facere uolentes, timuerunt ne aliquid clam lateret. Ideo

to go off to war confirmed the peace of the consuls and the archbishop, and in their turn received the kiss of peace. Men and women rejoiced greatly, and unanimously urged the consuls to take money with which to pay the army.

The consuls, aware of God's will and knowing the wish of the people, ordered all the men of the region of Genoa, under an appropriate oath, to bring, each one with all due speed, such things as are necessary for an army: an abundance of food supplies (without creating want at home), many weapons and goodly tents, handsome and honourable banners, and all things that are needful for such an enterprise, such as towers and engines and all kinds of machines for capturing a city.

When the soldiers heard the orders of the consuls of the city, they equipped themselves with weapons and tents and all things needful, so that for a thousand years past such splendid and goodly and numerous things had not been seen or heard of in one army.

Then after everything had been prepared as we have said, they set sail in 63 galleys and with 163 other vessels. This was all made ready, and the voyage begun, in five months.

After they reached Barcelona, Baldwin the consul went on from there with 15 galleys to Almería as an advance party, until the main body of the force should join him.

After he reached the Gata headland the Genoese, not finding the Emperor [Alfonso VII] there, stayed a month in great fear, since they were outside the harbour. They sent Otto de Bonovillano as emissary to the Emperor, who was at Baeza, and who had given leave to his army, having with him no more than 400 horsemen and 1000 foot−soldiers. When he learned that the Genoese fleet had arrived, he regretted that he had given his troops leave, and he said he would come, but then he delayed.

Meanwhile the Saracens of Almería were in good spirits and sallied forth frequently from the city, trying to get the 15 galleys to engage in battle. Then Baldwin the consul, who was keeping watch with the galleys, sent a message to his colleagues, that is to Oberto Turris and Philip and Ansaldo de Auria, telling them to join him for the attack on Almería. This the colleagues were not prepared to do until they had their troops with them. Meanwhile, the Count of Barcelona arrived with a large fleet, bringing with him soldiers and knights to the number of 53. Then they ordered Baldwin to approach the mosque early in the morning with his galleys, acting as though he were about to launch an attack, so that when the Saracens came out, the Count and his men would at first light be at Lena, on land close to the river, with 15 galleys beyond Lena, and one galley at the Lena headland; after the Saracens came out to fight, that galley would send a signal to the soldiers and the 25 galleys; and so it was done.

The Saracens, when they saw the men from the 15 galleys coming up the beach as though about to launch an attack, suspected that something

miserunt duos milites, unum album et alium nigrum, qui tumulum quendam ascendentes et circa prospicientes, et non uidentes milites qui latebant, fecerunt signum cum uexillis, ut sarraceni de ciuitate exirent et ad bella uenirent. Statim milia quadraginta armati extra uenerunt, et cum hominibus XV galearum bellum inceperunt. Et sic Ianuenses galeas ascendentes VIII de suis interfecti fuerunt et tenuerunt. Interim Ansaldus de Auria, consul, cum galea una de guardia fecit signum, quamuis non tempestiue. Galeae uero XXV et milites una motum fecerunt, et iste galee inuenientes alias recolligentes steterunt secum. Et infra hoc consules Obertus Turris et Phylippus, qui erant ad caput Cate, moti cum toto stolo, et isti consules cum duodecim galeis in antea pergentes per mare, et milites per terram, et iste duodecim galee transeuntes ad alias que erant ad muschetam, perrexerunt usque ad darsanam. Milites uero obuiantes sarracenis qui de ciuitate exierant, diuino auxilio existente, contra sarracenos uiriliter ire ceperunt; et sarraceni uolentes terga pre timore galearum, contra ciuitatem fugere inceperunt. Milites uero secuti fuerunt eos. Inter quos quidam miles Ianuensis, Guilielmus Pellis nomine qui erat, et sine licentia comitis ceteris cicius precucurrit, et prima fronte sarracenum unum prius lancea interfecit, postea uero sicuti leo inter bestias corpora umgulis scindens, sic iste capita sarracenorum ense truncando in litore Almarie multos ultra ceteros interfecit. Et statim predicte consules cum hominibus de una galea terram crebo contra sarracenos descenderunt, et homines qui erant in galeis de muscheta terram descendentes, insimul cum militibus sarracenos ultra quinque milia interfecerunt, et iusta litus mortuos dimiserunt. Et galee qui in mari erant bellum recuperantes, et sarracenos in mari fugientes interfecerunt.

Et ibi garbino facto, consules preceperunt ut homines cum galeis et milites irent ad portum Lene; et sic fecerunt, et tentoria in terra posuerunt. Et ibi facto parlamento, reddiderunt gratias Deo de tanta uictoria data. Et facto consilio, placuit consulibus ut galee in plagia traherentur. Et facto hoc, machina scilicet et castella et gattas ordinare preceperunt. Et hoc incipiendo sarraceni extra exierunt usque prope galeas, et sic per tres uices facientes, uicti et pars eorum interfecti, ciuitatem fugerunt.

Et factis manganis et castellis et gatis, infra hoc imperator uenit cum militibus quadringentis et pedibus mille. Et statim duximus castellum et mangana iusta ciuitatem ad belliora loca et competentia. Sarraceni uero uictos per multas uices impetum facientes, die et nocte cum igne et armis et manganis contra castella nostra repugnantes. Ianuenses autem inde solliciti, contra sarracenos bellando et multis de eis interficiendo semper eos in ciuitate introducebant. Castra uero Ianuensium duas turres ceperunt, et decem et octo passus muri destruxerunt.

Infra hoc sarraceni, de hoc ualde territi, consilium clam ceperunt cum

further was being planned. Accordingly they sent out two soldiers, one white and one black, who climbed a hillock and looked around. Since they could not see any troops in hiding, they made a signal with their flags, to tell the Saracens to come out of the city and start the battle. Immediately, 1040 rushed out fully armed, and began to attack the men from the 15 galleys. In this way the Genoese from the galleys drawn up to the beach lost eight of their men killed. Meanwhile Ansaldo de Auria the consul, from the single galley left on watch, sent a signal, not a moment too soon. The 25 galleys and their men began to move, and these galleys meeting others, all stayed together. The consuls Oberto Turris and Philip, who were at the Gata headland, having advanced with the whole fleet, and those consuls who had earlier arrived by sea with 12 galleys, and the soldiers on land, and the 12 galleys joining the others which were at the mosque, all went forward to the docks. Our soldiers blocked the way of the Saracens emerging from the city and, with God's help, bravely began to attack them; and the Saracens, from fear of the galleys, began to flee towards the city, with our men after them. Among the latter one of the Genoese, by name William Pellis, without waiting for his commander's order, rushed ahead of the others, and first killed one Saracen in the front line with his lance, then, like a lion among cattle that tears at their bodies with his claws, killed many others on Almería beach by cutting off their heads with his sword. At once the consuls with the men from one galley landed to attack the Saracens, and together with the men from the galleys at the mosque who also landed, killed 5,000 Saracens, strewing the shore with corpses. The galleys still at sea joined in the battle, killing the Saracens who tried to escape by water.

Since a strong wind was getting up, the consuls ordered the men in the ships and the soldiers to go to Lena harbour; this they did, and pitched camp on the shore. There they held a council, and gave thanks to God for their great victory. When the council was concluded, the consuls ordered the galleys to be drawn up to the beach of Almería. Then they ordered the engines and siege–towers and catapults to be drawn up. While they were doing this, the Saracens emerged and came towards the galleys, three times, but they were beaten back and some of them were killed, the rest fleeing back into the city.

After they had set up the mangonels and siege–towers and catapults, the Emperor arrived with 400 horsemen and 1,000 foot–soldiers. At once we drew a siege–tower and battering–rams up to the city wall and positioned them in strategic places. The Saracens, many times beaten back as they rushed out at us, attacked our siege–towers with fire and weapons and mangonels by day and night. But the Genoese persevered, fighting off the Saracens, killing many of them, and always forcing them back into the city. With their siege–towers the Genoese captured two towers and destroyed eighteen yards of the wall.

Meanwhile the Saracens, now really terrified, held a secret parley with

legatis imperatoris, scilicet cum comite de Orcegi et cum Garsia rege, et debebant eis dare miliaria marabotinorum centum et auxies exinde dederant. Et propter hoc imperator debebat inde receaere et Ianuenses relinquere. Consules Ianuensium, hoc audito, consilium fecerunt ut cito sine mora, Deo auxiliante, alio die summo mane sunt consiliati facere bellum introeundi ciuitatem. Mane ueniente, in uigilia sancti Luce, festinanter parlamentum fecerunt, et ordinauerunt compagnas XII cum uexillis XII et in unaquaque compagna mille uiri armati erant; et consules preceperunt qualiter incedere debebant. Et consules per multas uices ad imperatorem et ad comitem Barchilonie perrexerunt, deprecando eos ut suos homines armare preciperent et ad bellum uenirent pro capienda ciuitate. Imperator, hoc audito, uix uenit et compagnias Ianuensium in campo armatas inuenit.

Consules namque preceperant bellatoribus, ut cum sonitum tubarum audirent, sine uociferatione cum silentio ciuitatem preliando introirent. Et sic fecerunt, et milites secuti sunt eos; et paruo tempore, infra tres horas diei, Deo auxiliante et fauente, cum ensibus Ianuensium sarracenorum sanguine multo effuso, ciuitas tota capta est usque ad subdam. Et illo die de sarracenis uiginti milia interfecti fuerunt, et ab una parte ciuitas scilicet deripata X milia fuerunt, et in sudam XX milia; et inter mulieres et pueros decem milia Ianuam adduxerunt. Sarraceni uero infra quattuor dies sudam et personas reddiderunt et miliaria marabotinorum triginta milia dederunt, ut personas euaderent. Consules quidem de peccunia capta pro communi utilitate ualens LX miliaria marabotinorum tenuerunt, et soluerunt debitum quod communis erat, scilicet ualens librarum miliaria XVII. Aliam uero peccuniam per galeras et alias naues diuidere fecerunt.

Et ciuitatem in guardia Otonis de Bonouillano cum mille uiris dimiserunt. Et parlamento facto, preceperunt ut omnes cum galeis et nauibus a ciuitate recederent, et ita factum est. Et cum gloria et triumpho incolumes usque Barchinoniam deuenerunt; ibique galeas et naues in terra posuerunt, et consulatum nouum fecerunt.

the representatives of the Emperor, Armengol of Urgel and King García Ramírez [of Navarre], agreeing to pay them 100,000 *maravedís* and more beyond that.   In exchange for this, the Emperor should withdraw and abandon the Genoese.   When the consuls heard this, they called a council as quickly as possible.   With God's aid, their decision was to attack and *enter the city early next day.   When morning came, on the day before St Luke's Day [18 October], they immediately held a council of war, and formed up in twelve companies each with a banner, each company consisting of 1,000 armed men;* and the consuls gave orders about the plan of attack. The consuls went many times to the Emperor and the Count of Barcelona, urging them to order their men to arm and join in the attack to capture the city; but the Emperor came only reluctantly, and when he did, found the Genoese companies already armed in the field.

The consuls ordered their men to begin the attack on the city in silence, without battle—cries, as soon as they should hear the sound of the trumpets.   This they did, and the horsemen followed them.   After a short time, in less than three hours, with God's help, and after a great deal of Saracen blood had been shed, the whole city was taken right up to the citadel.   On that day 20,000 Saracens were killed, and in one part of the city alone 10,000 were cut down, and near the citadel 20,000.   Our men took 10,000 women and children back to Genoa.   Within four days the Saracens surrendered the citadel and their persons and handed over 30 million *maravedís* in order that their lives should be spared.   The consuls kept 60,000 *maravedís* of the money that was taken for the common good, and they paid off the debt of the community to the extent of 17,000 pounds.   Then they divided up the rest of the money among the galleys and other ships.

To garrison the city they left Otto de Bonovillano with 1,000 men. After holding a council, they ordered everybody to withdraw from the city with their galleys and vessels, and so it was done.   They then returned in triumph safely to Barcelona, put the galleys and ships into port, and elected new consuls.

Printed and bound by CPI Group (UK) Ltd, Croydon, CR0 4YY

13/04/2025

14656566-0003